A JOURNEY INTO DARKNESS?

We first detected the *Parchments* on the back of a Tinker's cart in the middle of the Gobi Desert, among a stack of foul smelling crubeens. How they got there from a builder's skip outside the Savoy I wouldn't really like to speculate. They were hidden inside a camel's hump and could easily have been lost forever. I had to exchange a few gold bars and seven photos of Marilyn Monroe for the pleasure of holding them. They appeared to be of great age, but then so does Hayley Mills. Most of them were in perfect condition except for a few wine stains round the edges. We travelled home by way of the Nile and arrived back in the UK in a state of great confusion. Were the pages, as some experts suggested, a battle between the traditional polar opposites of 'good' and 'evil,' or were they simply the utterings of a mad-man who became possessed as a result of contact with demonic forces? A collection of the original work was known to be squirrelled away in the Vatican vaults but we were too scared to ask Pope Benedict XVI to see them in case he had a complete nervous breakdown. Copies were placed inside the porch of every church in the country in 1996 but many were taken by *little green men* or ravaged by dogs. Some were believed to be sold on the black-market. An advertisement asking for their return brought little response. The parchments do appear to contradict the early teachings of the church yet they begin with a very traditional view of right and wrong. A few damaged pages were discovered among the Archbishop's artefacts just after he collapsed doing press-ups on his house-keeper.

PARCHMENTS FOUND ON HILL

What do we discover in these sheets of misery, if not compassion and an insight into the mind of a socio-path? People who can't or don't want to spend time understanding someone will often label them or put them in a box...

At Ragnarok Loki will help to destroy the Aesir. Civilizations must come and go. Loki is certainly the rightful son of Woden. In ancient times the Sun was thought to die at night and to travel through the underworld, only to be reborn the next day. Perhaps this tale of woe will one day bring light back to those who live in shadows...

To my little sister,

who no longer speaks:

In memory of 'Gregor Samsa'

INIMICUS HUMANAE NATURAE

So you think that I am mentally deranged,
and all my scattered verbiage to decay,
that all my valiant efforts were in vain,
to see beneath your skin of meretricious lies.

For mind is grizzled with a sea of pearls,
exploding variables of living fire,
among these gems of Universe I hiss,
the staff of life into a Spoiler's breath.

Under the morning cloud I hold my knife,
a rampant wolf with teeth of grinding ice,
my furious longing twisted into rope,
with which to hang me from Horizon's eyes.

By your decay does my abundance grow,
beneath the vibrant whirring of the glows,
dividing flame I clap and raise my arms,
and bring this tearful conflict to a final close.

A flood will I become and rivers wild,
burning fields of pestilence and plague,
the landbound comet into your lap,
submerge the features of this loving world.

FOREWARNED

quem tu qua lubet, ut lubet, moueto
quantum vis, ubi erit foris paratum:

Catullus c.50 B.C.

How to correctly insult a *Milesian woman*

This book is a statement on the demise of
innocence, and a swipe at the bog-trotter's two-
faced palter of lies, where vengeful Eros
degenerated into vice.

The truth should, forgive the expression, 'all
hang out,' as an enchiridion of contemporary
Scylla and internecine conflict, where 'to censor
nothing is an act of love'...

'This' deviant desire, which turns to bastard
beauty, invokes the *Judas kiss of morality* above
the jesuitry of 'human rights,' inherited from
discredited ideals, to energize the pioneer spirit
in our flying-man to higher and greater 'deeds of
disorder;' to 'baldly Odyssey where no bird has
flown before,' emplaned by the sudra's lust for
punishment, whose inner chord recalls *its* wayward
beast, and then feasts on the carrion. For even
fickle Ge must teen, that 'moil' within the human
mollusc will lead to 'strife' outside the home.

But this sucked orange caste which shanghai's
an increasingly powerful sex drive cannot invoke
at any particular whim in time, by the 'divine
right of government,' through its mutant benchmen
and *Daanite* President, proclaiming as a pit of
abiding folly the childlike error of 'free' will,
the double-headed Cyclops of crime and punishment.

The Swarm's hierarchy of industrious establishment
puppets, who are the *actual* foul Scythians in all
of this; looting like leeches on the active
artery; the parasite 'equality;' a strangulating
hernia raping the function of emuete, whose whore
surgeons of the retrospect distil sentences
pathetically from one to another, as their
contrivance interferes with an absolute necessity;
will provoke them to passion.

Didn't an old world prophet once Rq that; 'he
who is without guilt let him cast the first
stone?' Or as the North American Indians used to
account 'do not judge a man until you have walked
a mile in his moccassins,' and since 'no rat
crosses the same river twice...'

Yet at the moment of impact we *l'*agents de
provocateur, painting with the brushstrokes of our
words, are under attack from tellurian hellcats
and crusading Amazons, who would castrate us in a
jar of moralic acid, if fortune favoured them.

If we are indeed *to judge a goat by its coat,*
then I can only urge the *Outlaws* to turn the board
and wreck the table.

If the Clansmen laud to the skies are a thorn
in your side, then be as a dart in their tribunal
gut; become what you are; burst the chains of your
imprisonment and play the starring role; as a
Battering Ram to wooden laws and castle gates.
Realize your fondest fain to fertilize our *horrida
bella* between the sky and the earth; and reassert
hyperion influence in the Universe. Overthrow the
widespread perjury of the masses who would steal
our assimilate thunder and rob us of the golden
dawn to come; learn *'how to correctly insult a
Milesian woman!'*

However, if you are of the people, run for the
larder, little spider, I am about to switch on the
light!

landru   Dublin: March 1989

FLIGHTS

TRANSMISSION ONE   Page

OO.   DANNY   1
1   PRETTY BABY   5
11   MAMMY'S BOY   15
III   CHRISTENED WITH TEARS .   23
IV   THE RING   36
V   IN THE CUPBOARD   43
VI   GREEN   48
VII   FOUR FEATHER FALLS   54
VIII   WAVING TO ME SADLY   63
IX   THE 'HOLY FAMILY'   73
X   THE STARS THAT PLAY WITH LAUGHING SAM'S DICE   80
XI   KOYANISQAATSI   86
XII   THE 'LEAVING PARTY'   93
XIII   MIDNIGHT PROWLER   101
XIV   THE 'WHITER SHADE OF PALE'   111
XV   GARBAGE   132
XVI   MOTLEY COLOURED CHOCOLATE BROW   144
XVII   THE 'IMPOSSIBLE DREAM'   153
XVIII   CHICAGO   160
XIX   MIGHTY JO YOUNG   164
XX   FART   172
XXI   BALD EAGLE   185
XXII   THE 'CARROT MUNCHERS'   193
XXIII   FALLEN IDOL   201
XXIV   FORBIDDEN PLANET   208
XXV   HEART OF GOLD   219
XXVI   THUNDERBOLT   226
XXVII   WICKER MAN   243

POEM   'All-the-World'

How now my *Diaeneces*! It's a fine April morning, don't
you agree? Why not remove your mantle and settle
with me for a while on this charming knap of rising
ground, as we glance through that sparkling partition
of leaves at the beginnings, among the synged wade of
once proud buckwheat where the yellow sun shines, and
beyond where the cottages are still smoking.
     Do you see him?...there!...there where the tall
Cathedral stares, under the sleeping shadow of the
Mountain's of Mourne. Like a carrier pigeon he floats
through the ramage as Dagda supines plucking on his harp.
     And now he's hopping over stepping-stones on the wind
tunnel from the barn. Swinging on the chute he's given
them the slip dearheart. In the Apple tree he climbs
filled with virgin blossom, and that infectious grin of
his. He's so full of mischievous laughter!
     Scattered like dust his procession of petals
embellish the emerald carpet below. Look at his bright
blue eyes as the nimbus clouds drift across the heavens.
     'Do you think he's over the moon?'
     'Now that the school inspectors have hauled down the
     flag!'
     'Do you think he'll ever learn?'
     'Perhaps that time will come!'
     'Maybe he'll return with the rain?'
     'Perhaps they don't give a dam.'
'Oh! Daniel Pierce, your mother's favourite child, why
are you always playing down on Brady's farm?'
Or submerged in the sike at Red-Dan's place of rest...

     'The ambience will invigorate him; he's *Swallowed the
Golden Sun!* Though the illness did him harm, they say
that now his head is cured.'
     'But doesn't he desire to lap by mammy's warm
fireside in the heimal after spring?'

'It's the savage beatings when he flits home every
night, to a hair's breadth of his life...he's not her
husband's son, he's not her husband's son!'

So at sixteen, and flushed with wanderlust, dharma's
lamb grew ready on the boat...to Albion, land of 'hope
and luck,' recovering fresh from war, Danny kissed the
ring-prowed ship. Rising on the surf the churning deep
corbeau reflected in Danny's boyish eyes the seagulled
sky of perse...

Nomarchy and toparchy, and occasionally shire took
him in, where yes, Eire's greenhorn youth sowed a few
wild oats on the foreign soil.

For seven long years while her sore vexed dial at
the window often prayed they never received a line.

Until the season when the 'Embassy' telegram
confirmed the seventh son had not foundered as they
feared.

Near the bank where the buckled river rushed, the
vital textile centre and *Hall of luddite fame*, where
Danny's dandy duds made him stand out in the crowd, at
the Mechanics Institute Ball.

In the dowdy shanks of threshold with his finger
in the pie...well, it must have come from somewhere,
and she hadn't been bathing in the spout before his
idle moment of pleasure.

Virgin birth, immaculate misconception! How, how
trust a heathen's word? But 'our' Danny's always
been a gentleman; he'll do the honourable thing.

Impregnated by a single drop and her hymen still
intact the daughter of Eva blushed with pride at
being married to 'the handsomest man in town!'

Immaculately dressed, the happy couple emerged
from their inaugural orifice to confetti in their
locks of wool. He weighed his oars. Shy little
mill girl. Trainee midwife. See how the land lies.

Didn't even know about the facts of life.
'Now that you've made your bed you can lie in it!'
Shall we remove the fig-leaf to make them conscious
of their nakedness?

*

The wretch in the wicker chair rocked like a peevish
bairn, unfurled himself from his familiar foetus
position, and rose with faltering steps to jolt
determinedly across the floor to the cupboard where
the cider was kept.

It was all that was left...
As his dithering hands, once so reliable, reached
insistently for the surreptitiously stolen booster
they shook uncontrollably as the bottle lip neared
his lip, and glazed blank eyes stared vacantly into
space, where the itinerant tripped once more in a
world we could not visit.

But F. didn't mind a jot; he was welcome to the
tipple...and anyway there'd be no remigrating the
squandered park of harvest.

He rubbed his chapped lips with the back
of his palm and gave a loud aaaah!...resuming that
mischievous grin, reminiscent of the old days,
trying to wink good humouredly and cod it was just
a passing foible.

On the fringe of his unsteady hammock the tatty
suitcase belched punts amid his riggings...as a
yawning belt strap fell unbuckled around the whole,
failing in its duty. He retched the phlegm from
his chest.

His thick and powerful hands with their
passionate greedy pads still gripped like visors,
flippers like shovels, the like of which you've
never seen before (his fingers were like floating
logs), and the strong and hirsute torso, still
proud, now stooped and limped along the way.

The sable of satisfaction which had rippled
and rolled like waves of the drink, still
conjured up Ireland's turlough bloom...but now so
hoary and so vague, fluttered like a deserted kite,
worn, like a grey winter's coat on the coast after
summer has reached journey's end.

His aquiline hook, with its noted 'knot' and
'split' at the bourne of the pier, still pressed
its adamant passage to the whirl...

But the old man's profile, once so handsome and
so honoured...grown so jaundiced and abused; had
changed beyond belief!

Gone, gone forever was all innocence, and old,
much older than before, was his frown, grown more
worried now of late.

A large scar desecrated the cerebrum from some
inebriate car accident, half remembered, and many
blood vessels had burst beneath his tegument. His
soul more dead than alive. The gold fillings had
long since bade farewell and his ears were cabbage
leafed.

His disenchanted hues still echoed salad days,
as he leaned forward to place his manly arm around
F.'s neck to grind his cutis with the rough and
spiked bristle, with its prevalent dimple chiselled
vertically in the middle, as he'd done when they
were still children and squirmed to escape because
it chaffed.

And hugged him in his way of veiled affection,
and would not let him go...would not let him go!

The careful mouth, now so lonely and so sad,
stumbled over unfathomable words, brought on by a
suspected blood clot in the brain, and strained to
utter syllables, as vermilion eyes spoke from the
white verdoyed roller, undiminished by tears, which
trickled down now gentle cheeks.

"I'm s,s,so, I'm s,s,s,so..." he stammered.
His head rolling from side to side. Was he striving
to tell F. something? But he'd forgiven him ages ago.

Perhaps, perhaps he was wrong after all...Daddy did
love him!

I
PRETTY BABY

Beneath Buckhurst hill, whose cobbled texture,
known by locals as the *Anaconda*, drawn like a
draughtsman's stroke from another place upon the
earthly gradient, wound its way down from
Rombald's summit, where a ghostly army sometimes
trod across the desolate moors in winter, passing
a primeval quarry of red brick along the route,
slithering between a series of undulating burial
mounds, and an old straight track leading to a
hive of dilapidated buildings over-grown with an
orgy of blackberry thickets, until the Incalike
scales, shining with an ochreous skin, petered-out
in the lower reaches, at the second row of quaint
stone cottages above the farmhouse.

A trail of snuff dribbled from one of those
monstrous chimney stacks over the ancient valley
to Riddlesden. The spandrel finally crept by
Walls Shipping, where the reptile secreted its
sebaceous fluid, overlooking the nearby coal yard,
and Ramsden lymph towers beyond the croft, before
laying its gleaming fangs in the line of sullen
tinker trucks at the bottom: constantly being
harassed to move on.

The snake, like a prowling *cthonian* spirit
lying in wait for the tribe of young innocents,
who pranced across the big green field in summer,
carrying their jam-jars of newts and tadpoles,
from the small pond perched in the dip, below the
third wooden copse in the hill's mist.

Like a plethora of tiny unleavened copings with
their diary of woollen weeds vermiculating their
crammed cracks, which suddenly awoke erect to the
piercing scream of a woman's fraught voice, just
as the streak steamed under the railway bridge at
the nadir of the knife edge.

"Von't somebody help me please?" she pleaded, as
her waters burst, and she sunk into
unconciousness...

She was haemorraging profusely on the bare
floorboards close to death now, which spread
around her like a crimson lake, as Danny, propping
up the bar in bad company, boasted of his manly
prowess before the gruff of his gamesome cronies.
Her Silver cross pram conducted its lonely vigil
by her side.

Only the auricular organ of the eavesdropper
gleaned her empty echo, as the piebald munching
grass at the paddy-wagon in the maize above her,
jerked his decaying mane, and snorted in annoyance
at the raven.

The *byleg of revelation* ringed to the ankle of
Apollo caught fire as he sneezed through a chink
in the sublunary sphere.

"Is he dead? Is my baby behind the veil?"
asked the wearied young host recovering from her
toxaemic coma, as they brought the fruit of her
womb bound in the layette already tarred in his
own vintage. The vulsella had gashed a furrow in
his nut as a welcome to this doltish cabaret.

After her caesarian section the sickly young
child with the face of an angel hung on
desperately for life.

Clinging to her solitary finger he fastened
rarely to the maternal blocks of light.

His luxurient shades fluttered like a Spanish
parasol.

"But Mary," sighed Mrs. Ramsbottom, as the
widow pryed through the ward.

"He's a bonnie wee laddie! What a pretty
baby...surely he must be a little girl? He's
certainly got his father's good looks. He's the
spitting image of Danny."

Before long Mathew was accompanied by another
little visitor. A third child, Michael, was
offered a 'dud' lottery ticket, only survived for
an hour before being buried in an unmarked grave
in the bliss of *Buckfast* cemetery...due to a
'punch in her abdomen after another supersonic
spermatozoa infiltration.'

Esmerelda arrived to pay her respects. She was
so enamoured by her younger sister's exploits that
she went straight out 'to capture a man'
herself...

"I'll tell you what we'll do as a special
treat", said Danny to the infant. "We'll go for a
game of football down on the croft, you'll like
that won't you?"

There's still time enough to play, even though
it's nearly sunset.

The pretty baby eagerly agreed, and
enthusiastically followed his father down the
sinews of the muck cinder patch. Danny could kick
the leather so high that the ball came down soaked
in sap. But each occasion he ran over the rough
uneven surface, with 'increasing strength' a stout
push would send the toddler careering backwards,
as Danny's powerful forearms did their work.

In the uncanny atmosphere of the planet,
beneath the moribund star, each shove was more
brutal than the last, ending with a final
clout...which sent the changeling spinning into
the undergrowth. A broken bottle on edge in the
acid green spell where he fell, stabbed his hand
so deeply that a scarlet fountain spurted into the
air...he let out a little cry, but was too shocked
to speak.

"It must have pierced an artery?" sniffed
whitewashed Esmerelda. "What on earth were you
thinking of?" Mary was due back from the spinning
looms at any moment.

She washed his hand under the cold water tap
overlooking the road through the rear window.
Stigmata? The mark of respect was 'V' shaped.

When the dregs of the kindred brood faded with the
sunlight down the blackening inches of the reptile
Danny rubbed his palms with glee. Now he was left
alone the real fun could begin.

As he stood him nude in the kitchen basin for
everyone to see he splashed the child with stone
cold slabber...just to have a dekko how high he
would jump.

He grinned and ushered them into position for
the Game of *general knowledge*.

Sitting in his place further away on the couch
Mathew stared at the letter '7' disfigured on the
sulphur-coloured ceramic of the hearth.

How often did he contemplate the blue flame
burning among the coals, brought on by the draught
blowing down the flue in silver thaw, imagining a
myriad of images in their kaleidescope of dancers
the form of things to come...

Danny always enjoyed the croquet lawn so why
was Mathew too dull to comprehend? All you had to
do was wait until he gave the signal!

The first child to pronounce their surname
correctly was to 'dash to daddy,' flinging their
arms around his neck, where he rocked on the
silver chair to the right of the snub. With,
quite naturally, a display of affection to show
how much you loved him.

But no matter how hard he tried each time that
Mathew correctly articulated the address, and
trotted innocently forward to embrace the hoodlum,
a nasty jolt would knock him into kingdom come,
and Gretel would push him aside to claim the rich
reward.

Perhaps he was just a 'sore loser?'
"Who are you?" slavered the sly dictator.

"Get away from me ya' scrawny little bleeder,"
he yelled.

Mathew was puzzled. He didn't understand the
riddle of the Sphinx. Had there been a subtle
flaw in his accent?

Gretel hissed out-loud with the sinuous tongue
emerging from her mouth. She weaved her fingers
in a circular motion over the thinning patch of
higher ground on Danny's scalp.

"Your bald patch is getting bigger!"
That was before he carried her up to bed...

When he returned Danny pointed into the
fireplace at the descending order of *blacktotems*
queuing on the strand of the hob.

"Would you like to try some boy, that'll make a
man of you," he said, "that'll make you slumber!"
Opening a bottle with his boot, and testing the
red hot poker in the forge to observe if the blade
was ready.

Lifting the glowing iron from the flowers of
culm he pressed it into the perspiring tankard,
whose lather whistled like a gang of dying
lobsters.

The liquid fizzed and spluttered its rising
gold-white plume, which bubbled over the brim of
the kerb to drift to a ring mark on the outline.

He magnanimously handed him the draught to
gulp.

"I'll give you a shilling if you can drink it
down in one. But you'd better finish it soon
before the bitch gets back!"

A miscellany of intonation entering the dry
stone yard threw Danny into a panic; he sincerely
urged him to dispatch his second before they came
in through the door.

Father Murphy, on one of his parochial visits,
greeted Danny like a long lost brother; with a
handshake and a hug.

Danny responded with a grin and a wink, and the
return of that instant cupboard love. The usual
pleasantries were exchanged and garnered before
the priest stole away to further his ambitions.

The 'Pipe smoker,' who had married Mary's best school friend, pushed up the rims of his spectacles to verify his own eyes, and held the stick animatedly in his grip, as the child careered helter-skelter round the room clattering his head against the trimmings.

As the shy little boy took his potty round the back of the sofa they retrieved his pjamas from under the stove and undressed him in front of the blow lamp...

The childless couple turned away to save his embarrassment and went to prepare for the outing.

His mother did glance gingerly at his poorly hand but relapsed into silence. No stitches?

Only wishing to be proud Mathew moved his tiny penis without the use of his hands, and his mother gandered at his guiltless antics.

"Just look at his *little tinkler*," she chuckled to her husband.

"Don't encourage him!" blared Danny... He walked over to his son to *fart* furtively in his face. It was a frequent shenanigan of his which made him quite ebullient. The shaft of his hind-end smelt like a poxy drain.

"Better out than in!" he chuckled.

Mathew craned his neck at the window of their bedroom which peered onto the fulgurate wedge of the eminence, wantonly removing the wings from *Archamara's*, and pondering on the sea of storms, supposedly made of cheese.

"I'm going to be an astronaut when I grow up!" he pledged.

"I'm going to be the first man on the moon." With the *Great Obscurity* leaning behind a cloud he knelt beside their single bed, and imagined a wicked presence in the darkness.

The realization made him jolt back from his incantation, shaking with fear at the haunting which had frightened him.

10

"Do you think he'll come in tonight?" he asked. "I don't know," shivered Gretel. "They should be here soon though."

She began to sob with alarm underneath the sheets as she sucked her thumb against the lemon frayed blanket...Uncle Stan sucked his until he was twelve. By then it had withered away. It was just beginning to spit against the glass.

The rain started to lance more saliently, when they noticed the spooks clambering slowly up the pass. The Big-people were arguing about a man who had looked at her in the Shoulder. A car headlights dazzling the pattern hurried him back in the refuge.

Almost immediately he came creeping up the stairs, grinning wildly, with Mary snapping like empty thunder.

Her body bounced like a golf ball as it ricocheted down the steps to every steady thump of their heart.

"The 'Bogeymans' gonna getchya! The 'Bogeymans' coming up to getchya!" Danny jibed as he came staggering into their room clothed in ebony, and swiftly cracked on the switch.

The terrified beings vellicating in the swaddling pretended to be hard on.

Like a *private detective* he carefully inspected the bedroom carpet, feeling over the course woollen matress on his hands and knees with the expertise of a craftsman. Danny was up to his armpits in nicotine. The man in the moon had a gleam, and should have been fast asleep...

"Have you been out of bed, have you?" he screamed. "What did I tell you would happen if you ever disobeyed me again?" he stormed. "If you'd given them your tit he wouldn't suck his fucking thumb."

Danny reached instinctively for the hard metal strap with its axel of steel studs from the hook...and then he noticed the striking likeness

11

made with grease chips on the **wallpaper above** her
headboard...and went over **the top!**

It had been chucking it down at Buckhurst Airport
as they consulted pillows. The cabin crew
sprawled around the gaming table drinking, smoking
and *getting warm*, expecting the afternoon flight
to arrive dead on schedule.

Shy reticent 'Uncle' John; with his cardinal
and flocculent glove, a candid smile and hearty
laugh, who, with his flame of broken water and
fresh complexion had sometimes been caricatured as
a 'man of the cloth.' He had been dating Mary's
younger sister at the fair one sweltering weekend.

Seamus; a sharp, callous, and vindictive man,
tall and muscular, a former masked wrestler,
arrogant and full of himself. A confident lady's
man...and Danny somewhere between them both,
showing signs of their opposite natures.

In the recess of the refectory lounge
travellers mangled their noses to the condensated
board as the conversation revolved around John,
who had already been crying once between the
bludgeons of muzzle.

"Nay! he'd run a mile if a woman dropped her
drawers in front of him," sneered Seamus.

Danny dispatched his jocund stunt with the
cigarette smoke; inhaling and making it come out
of his ears.

Seamus nodded invidiously at the four year old
boy curiously examining the cigarette lighter
stretched out near the ashtray, before conspiring
with his closest of kins.

On the cover pirouetted a dancing girl lifting
up her skirt. It was pigmented in scarlet and
white enamel and studded with jewels at the four
points of the compass.

They whipped the silver machine between them
like *pass-the-parcel* before slapping the unit
smartly in the centre of the slippery arena.

Danny winked as he cottoned on to the slop and the
far far too innocent fiddled steadily with the
catch.

He was hypnotised by the miraculous bullet of
fire which periodically issued from the bonnet as
it was handed round the smouldering circle of the
cutting crew.

"Why don't you show him how?" smirked Seamus.
Danny leered over the child with open mouth and
pedantically instructed him in the use of fire
arms, while craftily adjusting up the gas.

His infant son gaped over the tunnel hole to
view the gem hidden inside the cabin hold, and
wondered why he held his hair so tightly.

"Hold him right down!" barked Seamus. "Don't
let the brat get away. Now you see it, now you
don't. Ya silly little limey sod."

When Danny executed the downward trend an
enormous jet of heat shot upwards into Mathew's
astonished face, which convulsed
backwards...Pretty Baby!

There was a flash and the flair of burnt budge.
His follicles were frizzled to a stump...along the
plane of the ecliptic.

Seamus sniggered outrageously, and began to
declare 'blue' jokes. So *then* Danny decided to
part·company, injured by their innocuousness!

Jilted John stared shamefully into space as the
Air Lingus Jet positioned itself on the edge of
the fizzle. There were no aeroplanes flying that
day.

"The poor little divil..."
They rode home on his 'new' second hand Norton
motorbike.

Danny was in a brazen mood so there was no need
for a helmet.

As the pillion passenger plummetted down the
melting vision he attached the umbilical chord to
his father's waist.

Danny assured him that it would be better along
the chevron by the cherry orchard. The wind
blasted through the roots of his hair and made his
cheeks go cold. The iron horse brayed with a
shovel-full of sparks.

A lorry reversing blindly into the main road
from the knacker's yard knocked them clean-off
their pedestal. The bike slid onwards across the
tarmac and connected with a lamp-post...

"I'm terribly sorry," admitted the chap. "It
was all my fault!"

He was a bag of nerves and was full of remorse,
but who would volunteer the compensation?

"Accidents will happen," said Danny grimacing.
He stubbornly remounted his motorcycle with a deep
gash gushing its gravy down his leg...Mathew's
wound was insignificant in comparison. But still
they didn't need an operating theatre.

The Ulsterman adamantly refused to charge for
any treatment.

II
MAMMY'S BOY

'Sleep oh babe for....hums...the silent twilight falls,
....from the cradle comes to rock the world in throng,
Oh....my child, my joy, my love, my hearts desire, the
cricket sing you lullaby, beside the dying fire......'

They tuned in the stained knob of the·tan-brown Pye
wireless set on the side of the dining room table to
'Listen with mother' while she cleaned the sleep from
his pretty blue eyes with a sponge dipped in the white
tin bowl filled with warm water, and he sucked his
thumb contentedly in her arms.

"Is it the Sandman mammy", he whimpered. "When is
he coming back?" She touched her glasses.

"Oops! Watch my diddies," she said. "You are getting
a big boy. Don't press too hard my dear."

So he gently moved his head to a more comfortable
spot, hugging her voluptuous form to him, as she
lovingly squeezed him in to her neck.

"Ying tong ying tong yiddle-ah hoo"! she sang,
mimicking the 'Chipmunks' song,' prancing her heels
like a pianist, as 'Michael row the boat ashore' came
playing over the air waves.

Mary.giggled as she dandled her infant son in her
safe-keeping; her pride and joy; the one precious
thing truly her own that she had ever had in her
entire life, and cuddled him fondly with complete
attention.

"Down at the bottom of the deep blue sea,
catching fishes with a one, two, three, and u.u.up you
come!" as she hawsered him sharply by his wrist and
he chuckled merrily, making his heart beat faster...
leaving his tummy behind.

Never were mother and son ever so close. She made
him the centre of the entire universe. Mary had a
natural affinity for the nursery and rubbing noses.
She hummed the 'Garten mother's lullaby.' Never was a
'hand-me-down.' No need for a Comforter?

"This little piggy went to market, this little
piggy stayed at home, this little piggy had roast beef,
this little piggy had none...and this little piggy ran
all the way home," she clapped, tickling him nimbly
under his arms.

Those were the *happy days*; smothered with affection
romping in her dalliance...

"Listen quietly," she whispered, "can you hear a
pin drop?"

Mathew harkened silently...his hair was as neat as
a pin.

"I heard it Mammy, I heard it crash on the tiles!"
he bleated excitedly...but Gretel *never* noticed a tinkle.
"Stroke my head," he begged her. So she did. "Oh, you
are a big softy," she teased. "What am I going to do
with you?"

"Who's Mammy's little boy then?" toyed Mary as she
fondly caressed his curls..."And how much do you love
me?"

"I love you Mammy, more than anything in the whole
world," simpered Mathew sincerely.

"What, more than all the tea in China?" she asked...
"Of course more than that!" he insisted seriously.
"That isn't very much at all."

"Now I'm going to put you down," she said. "You
know what Daddy says about you sitting up on my knee,
and you really mustn't be such a big baby any more.
You're nearly five years old."

He protested desperately; "You don't love me
anymore," he wailed, but to no avail.

"Eat your chucky eggs, Mathew, Clara's watching you!"
she said.

He fluttered sweetly at the *predella* with the tea
cosey that Mary had knitted inverted on his mount,
and squinted through the glass leaded window. The
dazzling sunshine devaricated where a small dark
object darted in between the crenellate of the
verdigrised brick, temporarilly blotting out the
luminary.

'Binkie' the tabby cat stirred sleepily above the
grate as she warmed herself in its rays on the ledge
...meow!

"There she is look!" exulted his mother alertly,
pointing in an arc. A rustle. Legs of spindle-
shanked tubsy clawed in the shrubbery.

"She's making sure that you eat up all the rich
brown eggs which she has made for you, or you'll
never get hairs on your chest."

An old red hen pecking at some seed on the edge
made his eyes open wide in wonder. Pearly whites
and peggies. Playing the field, jumbo-sized.

"Where's Clara, where's Clara?" he murmurred loudly.
"There she is! I've seen her!" He dipped his husk in
the yellow yoke. "Is this Clara's egg I'm eating
Mammy? I'm not eating anyone else's you know!"

A musket shot! The haunch-tubbed Brobdingnagian
thundered down the track...

Charging forth onto the spiney cartilage of the
'Snakeback' he could see some of the local kids
speeding from their warrens on a lookout for Orlando's
ice-cream van.

With a mien of certain fury he called his sister to
sandblast or she would miss the amusing spectacle.

He squinnied at a familiar deity bumping towards
them over the brow of the hill. The figure appeared
from *Aliunde* motioning mechanically over the hazardous
scales as regular as clockwork.

He earnestly screamed for the others...
"Look Mammy. It's that funny man from up the road
again," he laughed. He dashed into the middle of the
twist so he couldn't be avoided by the stranger.

"Don't look at him," warned Mary. She even took in
her washing. The band teapoyed solemnly as he swore an
oath over the ramp.

The '*Fantastic tumbledown man*' perambulated alongside
the slivering pair perched astutely at the brink of
their bay...everything was bigger in those days, even
'tumbledown' men! His sleeves did not match his boney
wrists, and the turn-ups on his ashen suit exposed his
rickety ankles...

All his buttons were absent. Did the phantom walk
on stilts? Nothing seemed to explain his drop from the
clouds. Were his collars laced with starch?

As Mathew focused intently the jerk toppled over just
as he was winding near them.

With a face like chewed-up toffee Gretel purposefully
threw the handful of muddy stones that had been grinding
in her grubby paw, wiping her mit on the front of her
snow white frock.

Mr. 'Tumbledown' *always* came a cropper when you
stared at him!

The odd phenomena struggled self-consciously to his
feet, dusted his coat...and immediately collapsed on the
gravel again. He dabbed his forehead with a damp
sweat-rag. A precipitation of rust even besmirched his
doyley.

He could not spot you directly in the optic; his
favour was blank and his eye sockets stuffed with *balls
of wool.*

It was rumoured that he may have flown from
Outer Space but there were no skid marks from his
Flying Saucer in the track. He hit the deck in a
rhyme of recurring decibels.

Tumbledown persevered on the one in two gradient
deep into the horizon and round the bend where he
promptly shot from view.

"Don't laugh at him," remarked Jeanie. "You
might be like that yourself one day."

As her discarded trinkets lay untended around the
cabinet floor Gretel explored the outer hemisphere
teeming with a legionary of blue-bells.

Gripping her butterfly net she was attempting to
snare the abundant *Red Admirals* that swooned the air in
those days. Two flew over the cuckoo's nest.

She poked around in the gestating foliage with the
bamboo stick sending a shower of sycamore spiralling
to the earth beneath her feet, until Acky hollered her
up to his pen...

He had something to show her down on the pig-run.
She was always stuffing her mouth with grubs so no
wonder she was consistently riddled with worms.

Mathew collected all of them together, and began
their mid-day *banquet.*

His mother felt cause for concern, but decided not
to say anything since he was managing so peacfully.

Annabelle, Golliwog, Jemima, Raggy-doll, and Teddy
bear were each lovingly fed *cream and honey* by the
sensitive young lad.

He lifted them soberly from the cardboard budgerow
he had fashioned, and circumstantially attended their
apparel in a manner which was totally blameless.

Browsing on the bristle doormat he tenderly brushed
their unkempt filaments, administering to their every
need and packing them neat in the box.

As the lemon flare sparkled serenely through the
fecund hatchery, touching the brass plateframe, he
smoothly cradled his special resolve swaying in his
arms, before laying her down along the rail.

Mary froze in the threshold with the remains of
the baking bowl oscillating in her fingers.

Suddenly, as if from nowhere, a black figure stood
in the doorway, blocking the sunlight from his vision.

'He hadn't heard anyone clambering over the leather!'
Danny's towering shape burgeoned on the step with
his brawny nippers resting against the door reveal,
the stink of the 'Shoulder of Mutton' still reeking
on his breath...as Mathew, looking up, raised his hand
instinctively to cover his face from the glare, and
the man fired on him with spiteful venom.

Binkie had parted company long since! He stabbed
the Woodbine on his shield. No chance licking the
bowl out now! The clown had another think coming.

"What's this little *bastard* doing in *my house*?" he
cried, swaggering to sequest his wife with mock
astonishment. Then his pique settled on the comic
muse caught napping.

Grabbing a teetotum roughly from his son's embrace,
he sneered, and threw it contemptuously on the flames,
lashing out brutally with his leg at the light-minded
young child.

"I told you what I'd do if I caught your son
playing with dolls again," he jeered menacingly.
"How many times have I told him...he'll turn out rum
when he grows up!"

"The little 'nancy boy,'" leered his father
mockingly in an extended mellifluous tone, rocking
his head from side to side, and posing in an
effeminate stance with a hand upon his hip.

"Go on, get out of here ya 'sissy git,'" he
bellowed. "Get out of here where you don't belong,
and find somewhere else to kip!"

Mathew began to sob as he cowered trembling in the
nook of the crevice. So Danny grudged the tray
bearing the fruit of his carefully prepared
stodge, and slammed it violently across the
lounge.

"I'm not scoffing any of that shite" he scorned, as
the dinner clawed over the drapes.

"Stop crying, or I'll hit you!" he threatened,
as his wife scurried to the defence of her son, who
reached tentatively for her support...but she was too
late; a kick from his father in his testicles sent
Mathew spinning towards the archway, which he sought
desperately in an endeavour to escape.

Grinning now, Danny crudely tried to push his hand
up her skirt. "No, not in front of the children," she
squealed, just like her mother. A common course of
conduct...*diddi meo!*

As the woman stumbled over the cinders helped by a
sturdy crack from the pretender, knocking over the
fender, he chased his son away from the entrance...
"G.o.o.o on," he roared. "Piss off ya dirty scum!" he
hissed.

Nowhere to go, nowhere to run, nowhere to hide,
Mathew peeped first in the direction of 'Aahboo's'
cottage...then elected to steer for the open scat.

He stopped to rub his eye around the corner, before
sneaking back to shelter in the dry and dusty
recesses of the dustbin plot on the perimeter.

For what seemed like eons he stooped in the cool
dimlit welkin, gazing at the frame to bring it closer.

Discarding the lid he climbed inside, where a
gossamer thread blew serenely in the wind, and
observing the far rampart, as the ebbing pollen of the
fluctuating sunlight contrasted with the rising gloom
in the dip, hardly aware of the odious rank from the
tubs decreed alongside him...in a state of consummate
catalepsy.

Mathew removed the thumb from his mouth, just as a
miniscule red money spider ran across his hand (they
were supposed to be lucky), and realized that though
his face was covered in grime he had finally finished
blubbing.

Applying the match to a train he rose to depart the
Augean stable, pressing down the hook and eye of the
obscure maw he closed the arch fastidiously in front of
him.

If you'd bamboozled in the vestibule you might just
have perlustrated the bobble of his black woolly *hat*
passing clearly across the sill of the ventanna as he
galloped salvably forward on the stiff wooden horse
which had been slung in a carrier bag.

"Come on, giddy up Neddy!" he sniffed, slapping the
pole with his palm and frantically clicking his tongue.

Since there was no reply when he tapped meekly on
the latch he reached up for the handle, and shyly
pushed the door open.

The 'outsider' auditioned nervously...and imagined
he caught his mother's voice mewling in the kitchen.
Perhaps daddy had finally retired to the bed chamber to
redress his recreation?

Banking on meeting his mother he careened headlong
over the pillory hoping to catch her unawares, and
popped his head around the niche of the opening...all
he could do was gape!

The woman, who appeared to be half crippled, and
aching to catch fire, though tolerantly indulging her
conjugal duties, was copulating tumultuously with
Danny on the fallow surface of the squalid ground.
Greasy knifes and forks rattled rhythmically on the
draining board overhead to each steady thump of her
head against the base. The spectacle-glass lay strewn
across the oil-cloth.
A pile of veg hung over the wash-tub next to the
cabbage-patch shrimp. Pots and pans still festered
with a harridan of slops.
His father veered with a bestial expression on his
torrid countenance, as the woman groaned in ecstasy,
and Mathew indexed his cornea in a false position...
before he could even scramble a discordant "Boo!"
"Are you still here ya little runt?" he coursely
snapped. "Get out a here before I get me belt off to
'yuss!" The momma nearly split her side in glee.
Mathew urinated in his short pants, and swerving
from the scene bolted across the room. Then he
scarpered as fast as he could through the unclenched
access.

III
CHRISTENED WITH TEARS

When his mother Mary dropped him at the school gates
there was a desperate struggle to free his grasp from
her fingers as he protested vehemently at having to
wear his sister's duffle coat. Always a parting in the
hair-line young sir!
She said it would all be alright and that he was
'just being silly little fuss-pot.' How could she
betray him like this? Mathew worried that she would
never be returning until the gegenschein turned purple.
The headmistress and the caretaker led him away
handcuffed by their hands to the infant class.
Thunderstruck with grief he glanced back to where she
stood below the church railings in the sharp autumnal
spectrum. Harking back I re-open these old wounds...
It was Tuesday, and the 'carol singing' had already
begun as he entered upon the varnished yellow floor of
the Academy (where he would one day strike down seven
in one blow!) You twisted old grouch!
The animated hands of the piano teacher hovered high
above their keys as she looked up to see who had been
lagging outdoors.
A nativity scene rotted in the grotto.
"Mathew Moonighan come over here and sit down at once!"
she screamed (the class were going to grow accustomed
to 'that' name being called out!)...so he slinked over
the ice-rink. "Let me make this abundantly clear...get
in your place you little twit!"
"Everyone look at titch!" foared the fat boy loudly.
"Why, he's even wearing red socks!"
Mathew stared down through the holes in his sneakers
below his short tweed trousers and his face lit up the
colour of a ruby. Gretel had buckles on 'her' shoes.
Who was the tender bud who did not laugh along with
all the crowd, but turned and smiled unobtrusively
across the open space? "Lydia, Lydia, Lydia..."

He sought a place in the cluster not far behind her and sat down uncomfortably on the boards wincing as he did so, as she whispered and told him her name.

"Aren't you shy?" giggled the girl with melancholy eyes...but he denied it vigorously of course.

Sitting meekly on the hard polished beam Mathew was forever smitten and loved her in an instant.

"She loves you, yea, yea, yea!" someone sang, imitating a current 'chart-topper' at number one.

It was widely acknowledged in the infant class that Ringo Star was the ugliest member of that famous quartet...'Sticks and stones will break my bones!'

Then the sea of swaying flowers broke into a penultimate peal of 'the first day of Christmas,' and the music teacher, Miss Lennon, closed her pianoforte lid with 'my true love said to me,' nearing the end of the session.

She listened for the children to answer in a collection of mellifluous singing voices... "and a partridge in a pear tree!"

"Thankyou Miss Lennon," chortled the class in unison as they noisily clapped and retired to their form room.

They gathered their pencils and crayons for the dawn of the 'drawing' lesson. Blinker still carried his musical triangle...

Sister Gabriel, her feminine body carefully hidden and disguised, ushered on her bustling compatriot as she held the handle for the 'Visitation.'

Her 'veluti in speculum' suddenly sped in like a wind blown leaf to greet them with a 'halo round her smile,' hesitating briefly at the portal like the greater and lesser seraphim.

There was an effigy of the light of the world crushing the viper under foot near the ventanna.

The pious Gaelic sister ran briskly forward with her arms outstretched to the front of the class as Mathew sprang from his wooden stool on the right. He dashed across the distance with his arms thrown wide to fling around his surrogate mother's tiny waistline.

She lifted him gaily into the air, and swung him round her like a paper windmill; the panacea of all his woes.

Sister 'Marry,' 'Reparatrice,' had just flown down, like a chirpy seasonal sparrow, from the 'Convent of the Sacred Heart,' up Spring Gardens lane, to amuse the cacophany of children whom she adored. A splinter group of the original order whose vows dedicated them to a life of abject poverty.

This petite 'bird of peace' with fine attractive features; dark eyebrows, and an olive coloured skin, glanced towards the auxiliary for her observations. Far too pretty for a nun they agreed.

Her darling boy buried his head unconsciously in her black gown, restricted by the nipples of the amber rosary beads which caravanned down her breasts.

"A whee bit more penitent today, Sister 'Marry,'" she scoffed. "I think he's starting to settle down at last."

"Here is something he's written in a rush," presenting the single sheet of runic script.

"While the other pupils work contentedly at their sums he refuses to obey our foremost rules!"

She examined the short story through her gold-rimmed spectacles, which really wasn't very much at all, as he follied in the folds of her habit.

He'd soon past by the *Janet and John* to imbibe the vernacular of *the Blue Fairy Book*.

The beguinage grinned bemusedly. Miss Lennon flew in rage.

"Can't you write anything else besides these stupid made-up stories?" she fumed.

"From now on you'll definitely tow the line during painting."

"Moonighan still believes in fairies!" was the chorus...

The schoolteacher turned her mind to the blooming best as Sister 'Marry' bent down to show him how to do his shoelaces properly; they had come undone in his dart for her affection.

"Always remember Mathew my love," confided the bride of Christ. 'No matter who you are, everyone has a special Guardian Angel who watches over us, and who protects us from any harm.'

"Even when we are tempted to stray from the Roman road the 'holy spirit' leads us back onto the path of righteousness."

She started to examine his face under the rainbow. Had he been stung by a B.? Ariel fell to earth.

"For better or for worse; tell the truth and you will never have anything to fear. Honesty is the best policy! Never be cruel and always be kind."

"Don't worry, my child," she said. "I'll return to see you later. Size isn't everything."

"We're all god's children, and we all have wings."

Nothing seemed to be plain sailing.

When Miss Lennon said it was time for games Mathew had spun around in state of nervous panic.

He had been dreading that moment since dark...and in the confusion he flung off his braces.

"He's taking down his trousers! Isn't he a case?" grinned the buck-toothed red-head near the playing sand.

All the class tittered with beer and skittles. "Only your shoes and vest," hissed the teacher expressly.

What a to-do there was! Swore he belonged on the funny-farm.

Petra Lazzarone threw up his hand longer than a shoplifter's pocket.

Pulling the braces back over his shoulders he tampered self-consciously with the buttons and hung his head in shame.

He trembled as she studied him correctly to see if he would remain upright. Only the best things come in small packages.

The teacher approached to investigate the complaint...

"Your shirt Moonighan, why haven't you removed your shirt?" she snapped. He was really getting on her nerves that humid afternoon. Point him to the nearest leper colony?

Mathew blushed, and struggled hyper-actively with the hem, while Fatso mimed his attempts to conceal the cynosure of the 'train;' pushing up his bottom lip and nibbling at his gum.

"Titch won't take off his shirt!" he shouted boldly. "Titch won't even take off his shirt Miss!"

"There's no need to be so embarrassed," said Miss Lennon calmly. "All the boys have to...!"

Later in the Orange Canon Holdright came blustering into the stockade wringing his hands zealously in the tinsel centre stage to lobby his prevalent clamour from the cardinal prodigies.

"Good afternoon Canon!" cheered the multitude...he'd already been on the milk round once that tide but he just couldn't stay off the menu.

Beneath the snow white hair his town-crier tongue screed enthusiastically 'twenty to the dozen.' The forthcoming trip to Lourdes. Their imminent First Confession, Holy Communion, and the saving of 'Grace.'

The celibate prattled the parable of the 'Good Samaritan' standing proudly at the vertex of the classroom.

Festering down the front of his dog-collar like a statue of Baal he demanded their undivided attention.

His pock-marked clock converted to the intensity of a volcanic eruption when he described how adeptly the Redeemer had transferred the demon into swine, witnessed, of course, by the blessed Virgin.

"We live in the best country in the world!" he stated robustly, "but even Catholics can sometimes sin," he lashed.

"I love the little children best of all!" he effused. "Why do they ever have to change into those loathsome adults?"

It was true that some of them would never question the compulsory daily worship.

And naturally assumed that one set of values were *the good* and any other belief *contrary to the good*.

The 'non-believer' would burn for *ever and ever and ever* he assured them. Grinding his teeth unmercifully he shaped his clasp into a steeple and evangelized *glad tidings* of Tartarus.

'Inside each and every one of us we have a glowing white orb which is called the soul, whose original sin is washed away by the sacrament of Holy Baptism, and whose only stains are caused by the committing of venial, or Mortal sin, this latter Mortal sin being the cleft palate of evil corruption.'

That there were strict codes of moral discipline and social behaviour they should follow pedantically, but that it didn't really matter being ignorant of the complex ideas involved (in the faith of transubstantiation;) to enter through the propylon of Heaven all individuals must, of necessity, become as a 'child in heart,' it transpired. The number of Commandments were ten. 'Honour thy father and mother' et cetera, et cetera.

To christen his crowning glory only the most exemplary of the little girls were allowed to dust his dorp at lunch-time, and administrate a few extra chores that needed straightening round his private area. Gretel was one of the 'chosen few;' for which a bag of jelly-babies seemed suitable reward for her services. He had a housekeeper suffering from *elephantisis* who stuck her bowl at the Dog and gun - conveniently it transpired.

The corpulent Canon in his black lead smock continued with his sermon at the top of his iron throat. As he enthused about the 'immaculate conception' he reached a fever pitch of ecstasy, his synchronizing blob coloured sharply in alternate hues of 'fire and brimstone' boiled over with images of Satan carnal. How the Senate lay back on scented couches until they spewed their guts up...

He sizzled like a firecracker hypnotizing the herd with his market banter.

(What's mine is yours, and mines me own - Red stormy-petrel.)

The children fiddled with their pencils; they were still not old enough for pens, churning them in the wrinkled pits on the desk face as they fidgeted underneath the table.

On the wallchart his cannibal had only reached the second step to celestial bliss...although he'd been tossed someone's tatty monochrome from Biafra.

The Canon cordially smacked his palms and scouted the congregation for signs of 'espionage;' bringing the throng smartly to his bidding.

"Hands up those who attended mass on Sunday," he smiled.

Fatso's hand bolted straight up...well after all he was a choirboy.

"And hands up those who didn't!" he grimaced sternly.

One or two solitary hands fleeted back and forth, and Mathews was one of them...trust him to be a moonraker.

He fuddled in the gaping breeze of their synthetic indignation no more than knee high to a grasshopper.

"Dear God," he cried in disgust. "I can't believe my eyes. Oh, for the little children."

He sneered at the guttersnipe as if he had crept up from the limerick...it was something of an anti-climax compared with the previous ebullient lambastering.

"That's a horrible black Mortal sin blotching out your perfect snow-white soul," he instructed, arguing through the fence of suspicious conduct.

Canon turned his barrel in an alternative direction and began to announce the winning tickets of the St. Sebastian school raffle. Well, batter him over the head with a rolling pin.

Clawing with his fingers he mimicked their rise towards the grate. It wasn't the winning it was the taking part you could be sure of that!

'What I would do if I was prime minister.'
That the farmer's boy was the salt of the earth.

The teacher praised him gratefully, and the children copied her like clockwork, as the beaming Canon straightened his sweat-soaked circus white collar, and bade a reluctant farewell after his long drawn-out intrusion.

Boggie was the strongest boy in school!

He could whack the rounder's ball clean out of the big yard and over the top of the pavilion for a six in one easy swipe every time they played! One of each colour they said.

He could even hit the Protestant school on the alternative side of the terrace with a brick as they waited for the bus at hometime. But girls were always first in with Mr. Herdlay.

It was uncanny how his boot always skimmed over the *hardened loaf of bread* leaving an enormous bruise on the shin. His fist consistently followed his foot in quick succession.

They'd once tied him to the drainpipe with a skipping rope just for fun, and he'd snapped the sinews in half with his bare hands as if it was made of butter. His biceps grew like a bunch of grapes. When he ran, the thickness of his thighs seemed to interfere with the energy being released to propel him in leaps and bounds.

Only the tiddler had been willing to challenge the king of the castle; resulting in a bloody nose on three separate occassions.

As they returned through the catacombs they noticed 'Furry' Harry peering from the summit of the high stone wall.

His coagulate spectacles glimmered like empty milk bottles. That particular piece of the bluff surveyed the boy's toilets stinking down below.

He was often seen dressed in his old Afghan coat staring lewdly from the street gallery as the children cavorted in the playground sunshine.

The rays never seemed to penetrate the 'icelandic' shadowland where he took root.

"Fuck off you pervert!" spouted Boggie. He stuck two fingers in the air. "We don't want you round here!" yelled the cock-of-the-school.

The girls hissed and snarled, hurling a range of foul-mouthed abuse in *double-dutch* up the plastered precipice towards the hawker. How they despised his rank pervasion. Only the boys liked Napoleon Solo.

Then they began to screech and scram, causing the swarthy simpleton to freeze and vanish. As Mighty Mouse whizzed around the playground righting wrongs and settling old grievances...

Darka bucked them up with a rendition of her only psalter.

'*Frere Jacques, frere Jacques, dormez-vous? dormez-vous?*
Sonnez les matines, sonnez les matines, ding ding dong,
ding ding dong...'

The teacher approached the gang of five and paused when she spotted the multitude of matches resting scattered on the ground.

"Own up at once. Who's matches are these lying on the floor. Which one of you is the guilty culprit?"

The teacher's pet flickered his eyes as if he had a fly in their ointment. He was rapidly approaching a galvanic outburst but was unwilling to be martyred above the table.

'Blinker! Blinker!' chorused the mob. "Blinker asn't got no Pa-Pa!" Destined for the A-stream.

"Bre' Blinker," asked the assiduous academic. "Why is it that your eyes always pop when ever anyone talks to you...?"

Mathew stood shivering beside the empty Ritz in his woolly balaklava after sunset. His feet were like blocks of ice and slush was forming in the hammering sleet.

His discalced legs were turning pink and his hands had
pins and needles.

"Are you sure she's coming, where could she be
tonight?" asked Darka fretfully. 'My ma-ma will be
wondering if there's been a great big flood.'

Where could his mother be...had she indeed deserted
him?

"Will you be alright?" she asked...but waited
another half an hour longer just in case...

Mary came dragging Gretel along after a diptheria
swab at Doctor Ruths' where it was discovered she was a
'carrier.' So far he had escaped capture on four
separate occasions.

There was no point conveying her to the pendulum;
she couldn't even tell the big-hand from the little-
hand.

There was bound to be trouble at the ramshackle
roost if his gruel was not laid out on the plank.
Three into two wouldn't go!

"Are you certain you want to go to the flicks this
evening? I don't really feel much like socializing.
Though it will be nice to get out of buggerlug's track
for a while."

When the three dregs arrived at the hovel Danny
would not remove his Trilby despite her many pleas. He
just sat in his chair grinning for ages.

"Aren't you going to take off your Trilby darling?"
she asked. "I hope you haven't done anything stupid
again. Don't forget your cuff-links..."

The shrimp sipped his tea without a squeak but
despite his many efforts it was never quiet enough for
him. It almost seemed as if he were crouched on a
barrel of gunpowder.

Danny lifted his arm as if to strike, but instead
swiftly stroked behind his ear without making contact,
startling Mathew over sticks. Only three red stars on
'his' homework book!

He moved his tiny plate to the edge of the sugar
basin and timidly chewed his meal in order not to
offend him.

Mathew gazed timorously at the milk carton and pledged
to keep a good look-out from the corner of his eye.

Then suddenly from the unguarded side Danny's fleshy
'paw' connected with the bookworm...just when he wasn't
concentrating properly. The false note reverberated on
the side of his skull. Always the head; it was better
that way. The organ of Corti jangled its chords.

His father began *whinnying like pony.*
"What was that for?" whimpered Mathew repentantly. "I
didn't do anything wrong, did I?"

"That's in case you do do anything wrong," grinned
Danny with a sly wink and a nod, cuddling his daughter
lovingly on his lap.

There it was again...!
He gulped, and began to convulse, his eyes as Danny
desired them commencing to vellicate.

A hiccup. The plash of overloaded ducts from the
cistern. A distant rumble.

Any movement whatsoever seemed to drive him up the
wall. No matter how virtuously Mathew essayed to eat
it was too loud by half. Thud! O little star of
Bethlehem.

"You opened your mouth too wide! Try it again you
silly little twat!" he fulsomed.

"You'll never be like your sister. Why do you
always sound like a rabbit when you are munching?"

Bugsy attempted to redress the error of his ways.
Then he had a curious feeling as he steered out of the
leaded window. It was as if he was the burbler in an
aberration of light.

"Haven't you taken your hat off? Don't you know
it's bad manners, and supposed to bring us downhill?"

She placed his hot mug on the pot-mark.
The shaveling crumpled his scalene and lifted his brim.
Hey Presto! Bald as a coot.

"What do you think of this then?" he smirked.
"Now try rubbing your hand around my bald patch," Danny
chuckled to his Queen of hearts. And what did you
learn at school today?

He flicked his ear again,..."Buckshot!" he cried.

Suddenly he erupted, exploding to his full height,
pulling an odd kind of expression as if he'd swallowed
something rank.

He immediately threw the contents of the jar over
his nearby son who instantly shrieked with shock. Then
he accused Mary of attempting to poison him with the
filth in their culvert.

"And don't look at 'me' like that!" he threatened,
calling his wife a dirty scumbag, "or I'll give you
what for! What do you think I am?" he blared. "Who do
you think I fucking well am?"

It was cold and damp outside the hearth as they made
their journey into the dim recess of the cinema, but
the bulk of bodies soon warmed up the ice-chamber.

A youth who was listening to 'Wonderful land' on his
transistor radio was immediately ordered to cool it.

Mathew was looking forward to his first visit to the
movies. He ensconced himself in the flea pit next to
his mother...

Dumbo had been sent on general release, soon to be
followed by 'the kid of wood.'

The *freak* with sad blue eyes who 'didn't have a
friend in the world,' travelled on the train to town
after the Big Top fell down. So they made the
scapegoat into another clown to make a laughing stock
out of him.

"I'd just like to spank the living daylights out of
him!" bawled the prude, as they chained poor Dumbo's
mother in a trailer with iron bars;

DANGER; MAD ELEPHANT!

All the bulbs brightened as the team of clowns
encouraged their young prodigy to jump from the topmost
platform into a peripheral tub of water at the bottom
of the ladder. The jeering rabble taunted his
unassuming reluctance.

"Elephants don't have feelings!" teased the crupper
from the middle of the circus ring.

34

"They're made of *rubber*!" And everyone
laughed...except the little mouse!

Pink Elephants (Pachyderms) Elephants on parade!
"When I see an elephant fly!" sang Mathew along with
the tune, as he burst into tears...just as the blare of
the fire engine jingled toward Buckwell Institute.

He awoke in a dreadful chute with the jarring
disonance of his mother's painful sobbing throbbing in
his garret.

A shower of sparks rose high above the fabric as her
silhouette wavered miserably across the open archway.

The monotonous moaning of the ancient night liturgy
completely bewildered him. The 'sextet' and 'semi-
tone' of her protests tolled like a bell from their
room.

He opened his mouth and tried to catch the moon.

35

IV
THE RING

They were approaching the mid-day sun when Jeannie led the tribe down the hillside and along the Railroad track from 'Tyre-no-hog.' The rundle of Oaks had been the home to their naive rituals of initiation, as the 'sidhe' glared intensely from the surrounding grassland. Sleepers on the fishplate. Apple raiding. Setting fire to all the dead-wood.

Their jam-jars teeming preternaturally with luminescent beings they hurried by the tumulus, as Tarka darned his glass lens into the ruby-red eye socket watering from the heavy cloud of tear-gas.

He elected for a dreg of his 'dandelion and burdock' in a cranny of the nearby reptile; but the 'Tuatha' couldn't have given a monkeys; he was only their 'courier;' and always on the outskirts...

The Springald group congregated at the batch of dense shrubbery on the *holy* 'Croft,' having dragged their prog on the home-made bogie.

They loitered in the moss of the wind-shield embraced along its whole length by a hive of rhododendron.

Pieces of iron protruded from the soil like a poker across the table, which lay there, deep, resembling a black excrement of bile, suppurating like an old Wellington boot, as they gained admittance to the hiding place (especially when it pissed down!) and Brigitte complained of blisters on her aching feet.

In the clear ethereal sphere *Unidentified flying objects* fleeted like flashes of diamond above the electricity pylons blooming on the shelf. On the swing from the rowan the followers could touch the sky. Geronimo! Piggie in the middle. Shove half-penny...

The flock of five rested before trammelling the labial slit which diverted to the inner circle *making catapaults* and all that.

36

Near the standing stones of the cinder's coin the group laked in the blaze of a wide skimmed yellow.

Still clinging possessively to his arm Roxanne peeled open her new packet of 'love-hearts,' and after sifting through the entire bunch offered him a token of her esteem...

It said 'Hello handsome' in raised pink capitals. She leaned over and kissed him sloppily on his cheek.

Roxanne said that he was not like any of the boys at her school but she was still not his precious *Brown-eyes*.

She had a spell in her finger which could only be removed by a needle.

"I'd do anything for you my Mathew," she purred, with besotted pie in her sky.

Ever since the moment Mathew had been made *Vice-Admiral* he had become Roxanne's heroic idol tiresome though it was.

From the bunch of Dandelions spreading in the turf she plucked a hollow stalk with a 'Pop!' Making a clock she blew gently into her cup and offered him the proposal among the everglades.

Mathew expanded his lungs and blew fiercely toward the nucleus of frosty lights sending a flurry of crystals glistening into ballad. Some of the particles nestled in her darling hair.

'She loves you!...she loves you not!...she loves you...she loves you...'

He returned the rose until only a single hope was left. 'Fairies!' cried the host. 'Fairies on the breeze.' Songs of innocence and redemption.

A pulpit stem was always reputed to reveal the correct time if the memory fixed with cotton.

'We're going to guest with *Llude Llaw Ere 'aint!'* hailed the harbinger on his fob-watch.

She placed a daisy chain around his neckline and held the buttercup under his chin.

"Do you like butter?" she giggled. "Yes, you do!" By Jove.

Jeannie gave the signal and parted the malachite crevice with her hands.

37

They crawled in one by one through the hirsute portal
of the giant Spider's tabernacle like a slowly lapping
stream. Angus always wore his white collar.

The innocents of the *golden age* squirmed along the
vaginal passage-way rampant with earwigs and centipedes
picking gooseberries as they ramaged. Reeds, ferns,
and bulrushes. But no Moses...

When the mass of children arrived in the middle of
the *Ring* they squatted down on the ample structure of
their simple toe-stools.

According to tradition they swore their *oath of
fealty* to the Queen and prepared for the sacrament of
celebration.

Their white eyes glowed in the half-light at the
heart of malkin faces as they spawned the grains of
flour to dip in the *pool* of druid's tar.

With Jeannie elevated at their head twisting a
finger in the curls of her balding crown and sucking
her thumb like a peace-pipe they grinned at each other
across the earthen tablet.

She sanctioned the beginning of their rights with
the chiming of percussion. Each member of the cult
exposed their private parts in turn before the feeling
and touching games could be properly inaugurated.

Kneeling prostrate before Queen Bumble every
individual imbibed the drops of frogspawn issued
magnanimously from the urn of 'Precious Undry.'

Only Roxanne protested against the mature convention
held deep down in dingly dell.

Once again her brother Angus became over-
intoxicated!

The *aboriginal* chased Gretel around the
circumference with his antler hanging over the top of
his dungarees.

In those days Mathew played as one of them, fascinated
by the leader's budding breasts and advancing cycle,
though a number of *pollard* phases and she would have to
be *disassociating*...

With Roxanne departed he would be able to have a
gander.

Janet spun the bottle and another couple docked at the
equator. Jeannie blew smoke rings and soothed their
skin with dock leaves.

It seemed perfectly natural for them to leave traces
of corpuscle upon the perfumed leafage and braille upon
the bark.

At eleven Jeannie was the eldest of her kind. Her
cousin Moira soon became swift in the power of healing.

As the latest exiles gyrated to the gong of 'Ring-a-
ring-a-roses' she hissed for them all to hush.

"Atishoo! Atishoo! We all fall down!" they faded.
The sound of the 'look-out' galloping jerkily over the
track on his metal caliphers caused them to hasten
towards the bottlenecked exit. Hearts in mouth. It
was even rumoured that the gypsies kidnapped little
children to roast on a spit.

With skins of lily-white they scrambled desperately
to escape before Gilbert caught them with their pants
down and *Rudeyard Kipping* whistled.

As the *Children of Danu* quickly scattered into ether
the youth crawled quickly in through the gap to catch
whoever was eligible.

Shimmying from side to side over the rotten
vegetation and dragging his useless legs behind him he
emerged into the recess like *Uitzilopochtli*. Then he
froze like petrified wood...

"Have you thought some more about those games I
showed you?" he chattered verbosely.

Gilbert *Van der Swinehund* crept over to his stray
along the outer fringes of the ark, and crouched over
him like a black Medusa, exactly as he'd planned.

"Show you mine if you show me yours!" he snorted.
The older boy unveiled his glans and began to
masturbate on the damp grey sludge.

His trunk stretched to over thirteen inches.
Mathew stared down at his own shrivelled cock, which
paled to insignificance beside the buster's enormous
phallic.

"Why is yours so much bigger than mine?" he vexed.

The scheming rogue gleaned a strand of straw lying on the floor and shoved one end roughly into his socket...

On the winding shaft of the contour where the chuff-chuff clinked beside the trunk for a breather the two members skipped merrily to their favourite tune in the sunshine.

It was holiday-time and the girls were best of friends...*the Blinkered Brit* came down the bank.

"Ten green bottles hanging on a wall...and if one green bottle should accidentally fall..there'd be nine green bottles..."

'Who was the king of the sand-devils?'
They charged around calling like red Indians; their string was made of catgut and the tool of knotted beech. Made ready their stockade.

Wow, wow, wow, wow, wow!
Suddenly they noticed two strangers mildewing along the court from 'Little Hampton.'

She summoned the reserves to overlook the sleeve. As *Boggie* glimmered closer Jeannie fastened instinctively on the intruder with her once animal stare and tore the strands from her head.

He tried to sneak surreptitiously past in silence as they regally reclined above him on the bank top. His bravery and 'knuckle-dusters' had disappeared on vacation.

"Come ye here!" she commanded, sitting in judgement like a mabbish Shah.

Boggie motioned meekly across the gradient and whimpered contritely that he'd misinterpreted the *demarcation line.*

She challenged him directly to a contest and quickly defeated him on the *Great Bluff.* He was hurled against a pillar. Blood and guts all over.

Though full of bitter anguish and remorse they still took him prisoner. Marching Boggie to the *pike* she held him in the middle of an encircling band of pearl.

After releasing his associate they tortured him for hours under the ward of the stile.

40

He was required to accomplish nine extreme labours.
They stood him on the ashes of the bonfire and made him grip the bar of molten pumice while throwing sparklers in his face. Then each member had a leg on his.
When he finally snapped the tribe burnt all his pile...make him walk the plank. Kneel before the god.

Where the tongue of land leapt onto the spiral Danny hovered for him trotting reluctantly down the rawhide.

His fleece was ruddy from the argon in the Lion's den. How he despised being sent down to the Strid when tea was ready.

The half-caste oscillated fearfully to the opposite stretch of the lane where a trickle of water gurgled undaunted down the murky iron grating.

"Do as you're told!" he threatened. As usual his speech was slurred and his actions vicious.

"How many more times?" he screeched sarcastically. "Go home and wash the muck from your ugly mug!"

"You dirty git!" he bellowed. "You're face is black! Don't you ever get a bath in your house? What are you...a fucking chimney sweep?"

The *Outcast* stammered an apology and made another earnest plea.

The Springald was cajoled into fighting with the coollie.

"But I don't want to fight him daddy," he said. "This boy has never done me any harm."

"Tsch'...you bloody little yella' belly," his father scoffed with shame. His bangle glittered with a hazy whiff of carats...

When Mathew hinted about the beagling the natives played around the fort he reacted with a typical snarl.

"If ever I hear that 'you' did anything like that then you know what I'd do with you, don't you?" He frowned and pointed to the furthest peak on the distant horizon.

"After I'd taken me strap off to yuss," he vowed. "I'd run you over to yonder spot and dump you there forever."

41

"Don't ever let me catch you doing anything below the
belt. Don't let me catch you doing anything not in the
game at all, at all!" Mathew promised he would behave
good as gold.

Danny presented him with *Mein Kampf* and laid the
teaspoon he had been stirring on the back of his hand.
Ooh! Daily News. Time for our read.

"Don't worry daddy. I'll make you proud of me one
day," said Mathew. "Just you wait and see." How about
that Eh!

While he stuck to the sentence on the page and gazed
through the rubric of the farthing candle Danny dug his
ear with a matchstick stalk from 'England's Glory.'

Words like stupration were blacked-out. DeValera.
Storm-out. Said his surname could be traced back to
the building of the brochs.

"The greatest man who ever lived," he larked. "If
America hadn't a stepped in he would have ruled the
world."

"The cream of that generation didn't forfeit their
lives only to be invaded by a *skulking nigger army*," he
debated, casting a superior logic over the excesses of
another.

As Mathew rendered the lecture his father
interpretated the gloss. But Danny became increasingly
agitated and dissatisfied.

He shot him with a jealous stare and threw down the
gauntlet. Danny glared just once more.

"She's just as good looking as the other bitches on
the block," he snarled.

So mad he could spit. He declared.
"Did you hear that?" Danny rancoured.

"This little English runt can read better than I
can...so why's he getting such bad reports from class?"

He gave his son a bullying clout and whispered faint
obscenities. Bring back the noose for wicked fell
walkers!

"What's the madder you?" laughed Danny grinning
caustically. "Didn't I swat you hard enough?"

As little children Mathew and Gretel would often visit
the childless couple who lived together in the L-shaped
cottage at the end, stamped with 'Slime-house.'

The woman was a jittery waif from the loom who
perambulated lower than the tin plate on the gas-lamp.

Although kind-hearted in her way she would often
frighten them with her frenzied outbursts.

Her husband was a tobacco chewing cataleptic who
stood no taller than four-foot six, a veritable dwarf
in human terms, with vulcan pointed ears.

His hands were filled with calluses and his voice
sounded like the ulterior giggling of a creek. She
often shadowed him through the tottery with a dustpan.

There was an atmosphere of sterility which hung
about that place which left an imprint in the backwash.

All their artifacts were smudged with deadleaf, from
the sombre wallpaper and the tea-stained lace over the
musty windows, right down to the furniture marked with
crow's feet...their crank, and the 'Capstan full
strength.'

In a tank of gall and wormwood he encouraged them to
climb up on his knee. Gretel in her nightdress and
Mathew in his shirt-sleeves. Mary never lifted a
finger.

During hot hours his hand would slide in a southerly
direction. Ever made a toad hop?

Startled from the kitchen 'Aahboo' would whirl into
their umbrageous billet to find the puck pawing them
ebulliently on his britches.

"For god's sake Pip!" she would wail. "How many
more times do I have to tell you?"

A great deal of shirt pulling would ensue. The
'Puck' would turn sheepishly away and whisper unwisely
under his breath.

A slap across his face was the usual conclusion to
their bickering although they'd been in partnership for
over half a century.

Yet when old *Slippershanks* pegged-out under a
running stream she remained very lonely deep in the
empty chamber.

Aahboo began to rely on the young family for company
whenever Danny remained conspicuous by his absence.

She was still in mourning when Mathew wandered
passively upstairs to the bathroom.

The coffin lay in the center of the crematory as
Mary held her hand.

Jumping up at the glass beyond the tulip vase he had
stretched his mouth and snickered. It was before the
lodger tossed down a Milky Way. That was the
Marshall...on probation.

Relying on the frigid bannister rail to guide his
direction he mounted the fuscous steps to shudder along
the archaic gallery, where the gnomon had stopped dead
in its tracks.

Pulling the chord of the *glow-worm* he ambled to the
limit of the corridoor and lifted the wooden pillory.

Standing at the crystal lavatory he attempted to let
nature take its course totally unaware of the bizarre
circumstances surrounding the widow's estrangement.

Within moments he felt a tingling down his spine.
It was as if an invisible force were dragging its
finger nails over his vertebrae. The heckles on his
neck sprang bolt upright as he became aware of a
presence looking over his shoulder and watching every
move he made.

With his hand frozen to his tiny stem he attempted
to take a peep towards the recording angel.

A cold uncaring void trapped him with its piquant
scowl and refused to capitulate to his tendons.

The little 'un thought that he heard a castrating
snigger...but perhaps it was just his imagination.

There was a bronchiatic cough and the frowst of
latrant farmyard. Had her bellyfull of worms alright.

As the touch-paper skated over his paper-thin skin he
began to holler at the top of his range. Never had he
been so scared in all his life. The chain croaked like
a bag of rusty spanners.

'Aahboo' and Mary came racing frantically up the
stairs just in time to witness his cheeks drain of
colour, and his lips bleach like blue asbestos.

He trembled as if he had been discovered out-of-
doors in the midst of a howling blizzard. The stink of
the Pigman followed him round like a dense reem of
smoke.

*Snip through their whities, or they'll bite through
her nipples...*

"What's the matter Mathew love?" she asked. "Has
something turned your blood to water?"

They both seemed unable to take his story seriously
although there was a sixth sense that he was not
telling porkies.

"There's nothing at all to be afraid of here!" she
cooed. "You must be very impressionable. My goodness
Mathew! You look as if you've just seen a ghost..."

It was many months later that Mary Atkinson came
flogging on their door at after midnight. She sounded
worried as hell.

It was almost a *full moon*, and below the porch her
hair sparkled like silver cobwebs. Had there been a
disturbance? Gretel's cot had been mysteriously
wrecked by something.

"What on earth do you want at this hour of the
night?" asked his mother anxiously. "Don't you realize
we're all in bed asleep and Danny's got to get up for
work at the foundry."

'Ever since the eighth of December I hear him
tapping on the timber. He pleads with me to open the
latch and let him in and kicks his cloggs against the
lath as usual.'

Mary gave her a piece of sound advice...
'Whatever you do, don't pull out a drawer or you'll
certainly crack at the seams.'

'No matter how much he begs do not fling wide the gates
or he will drive you up the wall for keeps...'

Years later when he was still only seven years old
Mathew returned to sojourn in the fog of the barren
brown study on the ground floor. Its garbled symbols
left him soaked in sweat and terrified out of his
mind...

His urchin voice sorned for someone to release the
catch...*in the cupboard* where he was crimped! Like a
sardine.

But the unflinching stickpin barred the passage of
his extraction. The runaway match endeavoured to save
his bacon.

Pressing mordantly between his buttocks was the
tense stalwart of a serpent trunk. He fought
desperately but the pervading darkness enveloped his
feeble efforts to avoid suffocation...

Concentrating hard to release himself from the
sickening odour and plunge back into everyday reality
he burst like a ruptured spleen from his shackles and
fell spluttering through the shattered sinew into the
hearth of the living room.

Following in his wake chased wave after wave of the
demon. Dozens and dozens of the prodding wires hunted
round him like a nest of heathen vipers. Even by
making himself float he was unable to cut the hord tied
to his ankle. He actually had a spell in his palm. A
fact which was no doubt crucial.

In the wisp of the *lightroom* the naked child was
entwined by their voracious zeal as they rammed their
cartilage up his *protesting anus.*

'*I am not the King! I am not the King! I am...*' the
funnel whistled. Nobody could hold him down in the
sheep-shearer's chair for more than two minutes!

Mathew awoke on hearing his mothers scream, and
listened to her sob, sob sobbing all night long.

Still lying on the morgue he held the fulvous
crucifix to the single xanthous beam which issued from
the skylight overhead and orated the 'Lord's Prayer,'

which was printed in miniature underneath the small
circular magnifying glass, from Ireland.

Mathew suddenly became aware of a pervasion in the
lumber which had been summoned by his constant
resolution.

"Who is it?" he asked, perspiring with anticipation.
"Get lost! or else...are you the *Dark Angel?*"

VI
GREEN

Blackie had been slugged for all of six months when they burnt a trail for Shannon Airport. She had shadowed her umpire everywhere until that fateful day in the field of long grass in search of the Fire door.

As the fond stray cat trustingly gazed from the grandstand he raised the heavy fallen Yew to over vertical weight. Its underbelly of schismatic worms writhed among the hanging floss invigorated by the dawdling sunlight.

Mesmerised by their swing of the pendulum he realized all too late that the peristaltic was backsliding towards them both.

As the jinx jumped gingerly clear devoted 'Blackie' was caught unwarily by the full impact of the bark crashing on her unpropitious pin. Pinned by the brick she mewled for the atramentous den.

'Poor Blackie'..."Crippled for good," she said. "She'll have to be put down. Do you know that's seven years bad luck?" Tread on a nick, you'll marry a brick, and a spider'll come to your wedding..!

Winnowing from the touchdown they journeyed north to the border at *Ballynasty.*

Snug as a bug in a rug of the stone-grey saloon they cuddled together like brother and sister sucking their thumbs contentedly, as the forty knots harped its way to Erin.

A stroboscope of colours flickered through the glaze wriggling out of wet trunks behind a blanket.

It was a timeless 'Fairyland' which they passed through in those days; brimming with swaying emerald fother and warm greetings from the charming coterie of thatched shebang.

As they progressed along the budding lanes kerry sprites keel-rowed towards the turloughs glittering beneath the lantern of Setanta's blushing skin. Youth who set the fires with flame start the clocks.

Mathew opened his latches to observe the most beautiful nacaret sunset you've ever seen stretching from the plain where they plattered to the far horizon where heaven pierced.

From the *bleeding heart* a river of pulsing veins rippled over the earth and flooded the family with a multitude of moving shapes. The plane fell in the air-pocket stomach gipping.

As they convalesced closer to the glaucous ark, and the atmosphere became steadily more brumal, he watched his father's face bloom more happily than the sun and pollinate with fishermen's yarns.

Mary did not seem to pay any special attention to the garden of green flower but simply saw the special adventure as one more extra chore. Gretel was good as gold...

Just as the chrysalis was growing longer in the tooth they bustled in through the plot of *fertile soil* for supper.

The 'evergreen' gentle batchelor reaped up both the children in his arms and stood them back to back to assess who was the tallest. Were they really twins? The green, green, grass of home...dear John.

It was half past nine as they entered the fray of burning logs arrayed with Lydian measures. The prodigal was welcomed according to ancient custom.

"Oh Danny Boy, Oh Danny Boy, the pipes...the pipes are ca-a-lling..." Thrummed the minstrel on her squeeze box.

Danny beamed handsomely as his old acquaintances shook his fiery hand in turn. Dressed in a suit on the never-never. Black as the ace of spades.

He plucked the *tympan* from Sister Carmel to toss a spritely jig arm in arm with the Sinn Fein clan of brothers.

Mary instantly made for the throneroom to plant the
smell of her animal femininity well and truly on the
alien soil. People with double chins always slept on
too many cushions!

Cousin Fergus emerged robustly from his pindown to
astrodome who had been sorely missed.

Mathew assertively followed his father's teachings
and immediately wrestled the older boy quickly to the
horsecloth. Three times he had him pinned in a
headlock for a submission. Oran was as bloody as a
bloodhound!

When Mary came to tuck them into bed he attempted to
confide his worries. Perhaps her clouds were oafish?

"It's horrible!" he shrieked. "Have you seen my
daddie's tinkler...it's got hairs all over...Uugh! It
was all black! I wouldn't go near him if I was you! I
never want a hairy tinkler like his!"

Mathew awoke with the cock crowing on the strath. He
helter-skeltered quietly down the stairs to see if the
saucer of bread and milk had been drunk by the grateful
leprechauns.

And there was no sign of the farmhouse hedgehog or
the tramline going past.

Riding buoyantly on his shoulders he gripped tightly
to the material of his fawn felt collar.

A shallow stream ran across the vly where the herd
of cattle had branded the mud with their cloven hooves
on their curve to four-o-clock milking at Domdaniel.

The chilled water trickled lightly over the stepping
stones acting as a sieve to the Wishing-well in the
distance. The path of the salubrious orb coruscated
clearly over the red brick cavalcading to the wellhead.

Steering nearer to his resonance Mathew could see an
array of lustrous Goldfish swimming in the tank. By
cupping his hands he could capture one or two of them.
Ten prime frogs marched in a line to the cowshed.

He suddenly swung to his right as an irate gander
jibbed him with its ochreous beak.

The bird made vicious lunges at his bare young leg to
protect her rushing brethren.

John hoisted the pails like a pair of uneven scales.
His Uncle chuckled with amusement as he halted at
regular intervals to gather garlands.

*The white bells of 'spergularia rubra' with their
silvery stipules of pretty red spurrey; 'lepidium
campestre' with its soft yellow anthers picked on the
dry banks of the deserted cottages; 'oxycoccus,' the
red fruit of the Cranberry; the lanceolate leaves of
the Cowbane, with its bracteoles and white flower
dotted with vermilion, plucked at the foot of the
marshes; the 'American speedwell' with its oval leaves
and flower of blue; the long hairy stalk of the 'Dog's
Mercury' with its haze of green clasped in the delve at
the rear-end of the Faywood; and the 'Sweet Flag'
filled with fragrant scent from its Primavera...he
abandoned the 'adder's tongue' to St. Patrick.*

On his final syncopation near the cow trough as they
approched the chapter lodge his Uncle curiously
pondered...a *seven-leafed shamrock*. They had scorned
its very existence!

He dashed urgently forward bearing the omen between
his restringent finger and thumb in transmuting
woolpack weld.

When he entered the potato patch Oran implied that
his father was catching *Ram raj* in the bougie stone
cold sober before the flurry.

Shooting like an arrow up the yard he ventured round
the edge of the haystack and ricocheted over the rundle
of ploughed turf. Their smooth shadow tip-toed
ulcerously against the sun. Maybe there had been a
break in the ozone layer?

As *Tenderfoot* appulsed the hairy torso of the proud
built man sprawling in the vertiginous haugh like a
Giant's causeway he held out his *posey of virtue* which
he'd carefully collected parietaling the hedgerows
flowing from the dixie.

When he gauged how contagious the lad had become
Danny grimaced at the impending close encounter.

Smiling innocently Mathew offered the libations
harvested especially across the open precinct in his
outstretched palm.
    Danny crashed them violently from his thread and
began to stamp his authority on the lot.
    "You little sissy git," he snapped. "Don't pester
me you irksome bloody stray."
    "I wish you'd go to fucking hell!" he screamed.

FATHER, WHY DO YOU BLEED

Where the land and the sky
    meet in harmony,
and the oceans and fleece touch the sand,
    where the yellow sun shines,
and the heavens in rhyme,
    Father, why do you bleed?

Where the birds cross the sky,
    you return the dark fields,
the horse, the plough, and the stars,
    in the hedgerow you roll,
your face in the stream,
    Father, why do you bleed?

Where you bathe the bright seed,
    in the west where you ride,
sunning the air which we need,
    too strong for my eyes,
you light up the earth,
    Father, why do you bleed?

On the heels of your soul,
    cross the skies where you fall,
the storm wind, the cloud, and the spring,
    in the sunset you weep,
reclined at your feet,
    Father, why do you bleed?

VII
FOUR FEATHER FALLS

After the blessed Sacrament of Confession, at the age
of seven, going on eight, came Holy Communion, quickly
followed by Confirmation as a 'soldier of God' into the
Catholic faith; and a vaticination that they would
remain so for the rest of their natural lives!

Treading on the heels of the bishop's benison and
the infallible edict from Rome the procession of meek
young children proceeded up the aisleway of Saint
Sebastians.

Mary watched suspiciously as the white-haired old
Canon nervously wrung his hands, highly aware of the
auspicious nature of the occasion. The priest smiled
like a rubicund 'Cheshire cat' and summoned on the
flock of 'in statu pupillari' with the unction of his
sweaty claque.

"The *Body of Christ!*" decreed the priest stoicly,
reaching to place the broken disc of unleavened bread
into the gaping apostle.

"The 'body of Christ,'" repeated the sorrowful
seraphim in 'parrot' fashion likewise. He casually
fingered her breast.

They suggested the host might gush with blood if you
didn't make your fasting last from the previous
evening. And no rashers of smokey bacon on Fridays...

By omitting austerities in the devout wooden booth
as a preliminary angels from heaven would fly down the
blue and silver chimney thrusting their swords of
torture in your eye.

Soon it was Mathew's turn to take his place in
single file as the prefect ushered them relentlessly
from the pew. The over-wrought nagging housewife
nudged him sternly from behind and compared his shabby
appearance beside Martin's neatly brushed and parted
livery.

One by one the children fell in with the wake of the
stream following as a shadow to the golden altar rail,
their rigid hands pressed devoutly together and pointed
religiously towards the firmament.

Whereupon they kneeled in loving admiration to kiss
the glistening pommelled surface of the Bishop's
bulbous ring; the symbol of his authority, the sealing
of the ceremony and their fate.

This august company in drag was conducted beneath
the shaded ceiling of an occult eclipse with the Canon
acting as chief conductor and the Bishop as 'Christ's
deputy.'

Except for a single band of magic yellow where an
altar boy had left the side door ajar, and where, as
each initiate passed the stained glass window in their
duds, a play of colours pencilled with a glowing shard
their favour and their sainthood.

Even Mathew wore an unsoiled white shirt as he
tottered along the marble surface of the void. Hair
combed in a quiff; Parrot's peak. Couldn't wear wool
next to his skin.

The intensity of light buckled the bridge of the
goblet.

"I hope you know that I'm only doing this for your
benefit. I'm not a Catholic!" she muttered
impatiently. "Although I think they sing the Ave Maria
superbly."

Once more officialdom scurried hastily through the
stocks to slam the barnyard orifice. He ordered the
ostentatious fanatic to quit her antics or he would
curtail the over-running of the fixed regime.

The lovesick child watched earnestly in wait as his
pretty sweetheart knelt before the proletarian drab.
He turned his head. Prostrate on the red velvet carpet
before the nuptial step Lydia kissed the celebrity's
jewel before he could say 'Jack Robinson...'

During dinner hour the *most mischievous boy in
school* dispensed with queuing at the canteen, and re-
entered the cool dark recesses of the muted dungeon,
with his libretto of pressed posy.

He paused for the group of jesters to conclude
smooching holy icons.

They rolled in stitches each time they genuflected
and made a sign of the cross from the baptismal font.
Boggle made obscene gestures in the direction of the
empty pulpit. Someone had wee'd in the basin.

The Canon appeared briefly at the vestry door, and
as he turned to pass the holy altar piously observed
protocol. He reverently inspected his iron grille
before locking the cell and propylon.

[*A manhunt had begun for a bogus priest, after he
had given two brownies holy orders in the
Confessional.*]

Mathew began to slowly passage forward, obeying the
'modus operandi' committed to his cataract.

A few scattered missals expended from earlier
benediction.

Parting company with the seven grey stations of the
cross, and passing to the left of the grotto dedicated
to dutiful Joseph the simple carpenter, he pattered
surreptitiously over the frigid ground of the
crepuscule before solemnly circumambulating the
baldachin.

The pavonian lily of 'Our lady the Virgin Mary'
shimmered beautifully on its pedestal in a separate
alcove above the purple...

"Bless me father, for I have sinned..."

"That will be one Hail Mary, one Our Father, and one
Glory be, for your penance against the lies you have
told. Make a sign of the Cross and an act of
'Contrition'!" reproved the Canon.

He rose to place his only sixpence in the coin box,
and reached blithely for a candle which he could now
mount in its rightful place, as the mild Madonna nodded
in the wings pursed in her tranquil hood.

There were already three candles burning in their
byre, but the magnificence of a fourth lit up the
darkened grotto with a further source of light, and the
golden summer rinsed Mathew's glowering face with a
ripple of childlike pleasure.

'Hail Mary, full of grace, blessed art thou among
women, and blessed is the fruit of thy womb Jesu...

The twerp begged her to grant his unpaired wish and
promised to remain forever virtuous. He swore to
protect her from all the dragons and sea-monsters in
the watery waste...and so on and so forth.

That night at the alternative concert hall many
children stood around in fancy dress waiting for their
chance to clamber up on the stage and take their bow.

Walter gave Mathew the present of a comic book and
invited him to his next birthday party.

The rivals had already staged a race to find the
fastest boy in prep, which Walter had won by the skin
of his teeth.

The book contained the biopic of his favourite super
hero; who could zip through time and space...and become
invisible.

The *Quicksilver* dart dressed in mercurial red and
gold was usually able to make an instant getaway from
any danger. He could sprint through matter faster than
the *speed of light*.

He laughed when Mathew bounced his silver spoon on
the surface of the jellydish. "Is it made of
'rubber?'" he joked. "I've never had any of this
before."

It greatly annoyed Mathew how some of the gang still
fished for Fatso. Wasn't he the only one who could do
one-arm pull-ups on the birch?

"Hurry along you miserable specimen!" postulated
Walter. "I'm going up, so why don't you come with me?"

"My cowboy suits no good," he squeaked. His uniform
was slightly less than perfect.

He glanced at Fatso's suit which was of a slightly
superior style and quality.

The bullets were missing from his belt and his
holster had been deleted. The feathers in his hat were
fake. Who ever heard of a rider without a buckskin?

"He's scared!" laughed one of the three Wise men.

"He's really scared to hop on the high seas!"

Mathew crimsoned and crept to hide behind his mother. The erstwhile ringleader tugged at her skirt in the dog-house.

"We can still see you!"
There was nothing any of them could do to placate or persuade him. They eventually abandoned the ditherer in disgust. What a silly nidget...with a football placed ahead of him he could bolt like grease lightning.

Fatso pushed himself assertively centre stage. M. watched in horror as his little sister understudied. With her arms around his blubber Fatso led the crew of pirates and milkmaids in a Conga grinning beneath the spotlight. Fatso was the biggest show-off around. St. Knickerless's sleigh was driven by Raindeer...to Billy J. Kramer and the Dakotas.

There was Fatso right at the front of the show in a new cowboy suit which was much finer than his own. He really loved himself...and eventually won first prize.

Mathew had been the only child in hospital 'not' to have 'ice-cream' on the morning they were to be sent home.

"I don't like vanilla sundae!" he repeated while the other patients tucked into their second helping. Thunderbirds and Fireball XL5 on T.V.

At two o'clock on Boxing day they all returned together in the mini-bus after having their tonsils removed in the theatre.

He peered joyfully through the back window as the driver reversed into their narrow courtyard in the middle of a desperate season.

The driver opened the slide door just as 'Fly' came bounding happily to greet him. He doffed his cap and scratched his head as the undernourished terrier left a spray of tiny droplets over every inch of space.

It was certainly a change from the small-holding where he had originally been fostered. *Brandy* had nearly made short work of him though.

'Fly' came to whimper softly at his hand because he thought that Mathew might be cross with him.

He was lucky if by four o'clock they had freed him from the bunker.

Poor old Fly! His temperament remained unaltered throughout his life of hardship...

'Rub their noses in it!' Couldn't be blamed if he...bit the hand that fed him?

Up in the bath-tub Danny was singing at the top of his voice, and had forgotten to bolt the cellar door properly...

'On top of old Smokey all covered with snow, I lost my poor lover, for courting too slow.'

The hound howled as Mary mopped the puke up at the side of their double.

"What ever do you mean?" she whimpered.
"I never even knew your brother Seamus until *after* we were married."

Danny spat a ball of mucus into the grate which boiled over the brim of the kiln. So mad he could gob out brads.

"Your brats arrived!" He gave a crafty wink, before pulling a straight face.

Then he suddenly noticed that Fly had escaped and was watering the geraniums to celebrate his new found franchise.

Cursing loudly Danny dashed limping into the stone clad priory.

As he trapped the pariah in a mossy corner of the ranch the trembling animal closed its eyes and turned over in an attitude of surrender.

Fly offered his belly in resignation.
But before Danny could fasten his rope around the black and tan the beast rattled along the gutter of the wall. His eye was hanging on by a wafer thin piece of skin.

Where a passing motorist knocked him down and he was *killed instantly...*

A burnt cork soup bubbled stinking from the sinking
neolithic hole of its abode, until its poisonous fork
stuck like a needle in the gullet of the chevron, and
licked its foul saliva over the barbed-iron primrose of
the tyrant.

Danny scaled the dustbin wall like an evil King Kong
in the eye of a thunderstorm, gripping the drainpipe as
the gurk showered down on his anger and his pointing.

He teetered on the edge of the grimalkin slate above
the thunderbox and nearly lost his balance as he peeped
in through their bedroom archive.

She'd warned him. If he came back drunk again she'd
turn the key. That was the depth of Mary's cure and
the treatment for his ailment.

"My rooftree!" he cussed. "My chimney corner!"
He dropped the draught to shatter way below on the
dissenting pavement before releasing his berserker rage
with the fury of a thunderbolt.

Mathew awoke with his heart pounding like a siren to
the sound of 'breaking glass' as he nevelled the
excelsior. 'Only ever after one thing!' she smiled...

With unremitting violence he pummelled the defences,
tearing aside the leaded window brace and flinging away
the jesse of Joseph's peacock bearing.

His brawny forearms finally forced a jagged entrance
and his legs plunged in and out swivelling like
pistons. He wobbled like a bog-eyed monster...

"What's he gonna do...what's he gonna do with us
tonight?" bleated the terrified children.

Mary came to hide with them and retreated under the
quivering bedclothes. Then she cowered behind the
household curtains. With a thunder-cry he attacked
anything he could lay his hands on...storm in a T-cup?

In an act of naked aggression he ripped the wardrobe
from its moorings and threw the jacket crashing to the
floor intent on smashing the remnants of impedimenta.
A chair was uprooted from the lounge and pulverized
through the casement. He even ignited his prize
possession with a can of petroleum. Nursing his
bleeding fist Danny left his wife lying in a pool of
blood and hunted the children with a bread-knife.

Panting his frightful odour from the brewery he kissed
his daughter's ruddy ecythmed face.

"If I leave for the mother toft will you take-off
with daddy?" he softly squalled.

Gretel eagerly agreed, but Mathew put his spoke in.
"But what about Mammy? Won't she be coming too?"

"Who's asking you ya little twat?" his father
hissed...

All the pupils felt fatigue creeping in at the 'ell' of
the next day but Mathew couldn't sit still on his bench
despite her calming presence.

By ten to four it appeared he'd last out the throng.
Then someone shouted out in class; "Hey look at
Moonighan everybody. He's got big red spots all over
his face!" That caused a great stir. Had he caught
the *Bubonic Plague*?

Lapin had long vied with him to be the focus of her
attention, and had recently conquered the much shorter
'Boggie' to be the new 'cock of the school' in the top
playground. He waited until hometime and caught up
with him beyond the salver. He was already a whole
foot taller than Mathew but there was no shock in that.

Lapin soon had him engaged in a headlock and
battered him to ignominious defeat amid the surrounding
chants. There had to be some 'bad hats' in every good
Western...

At Lapin's precise importuning other hopefuls
gleefully extended his ongoing trial. More 'brownie'
points! No winkle-pickers in school son!

The headmistress loomed from her office on the way
to her mobile. Mathew's consumptive legs were
vellicating like a timorous young Bambi's. His nose
had burst again. Trust him to get into trouble.

When Miss Jones heard that someone had been fighting
she stealthily approached the victim of their gossip.

The problem child turned sharply to a crack across
his skull.

"What have you been doing, you little twit?" she
roared. The schoolteacher shook him like venison in
her claws.

"You weren't listening again were you? Were you!" she
exasperatingly cried, and all the class fell about
laughing, followed by another prolonged silence.
The idiot's ears were still ringing when he
dismounted from the trolley-bus. He was surprised to
see his grandfather cooling his heels near the tavern.
He asked him what he was doing there but the fellow was
struck dumb.
With its flat cap daggling the fence the 'nicotine
pincer' reached distractedly for the tab-end perched
behind his tiller.
Had he forgotten how his brother had once died
playing with matches in the outside thunderbox?
With a stern expression the swarthy engineer scanned
the ambient helix before returning to scout the
homeward tract, where the heap of dozing caravans
loitered grimily at the basement.
Ogger tipped the scales at over five hundred tons.
He could hit the bulls-eye with every single shot.
Taller than a house the *Giant Copenhagen* droned but
never said goodbye...
Snorting like bison Ogger restored the smouldering
incense to its location; pillioned beside the 'Elijah's
mantle' of his ear lug, before attending to the shirt
sleeves rolled up to his biceps.
A wrinkled shadow ducked in against the wall and
shuffled silently out of range.

VIII
WAVING TO ME SADLY

Glued to the chair Mathew churned over the landmark
like a 'pig-in-a-poke' in his brain.
It was after ten o'clock when his mother rushed them
both from his bed, flinging a dressing gown round their
stem, and hurrying them down the stairs.
The heroic *man in black* had just returned from night
duty at H.Q. He marshalled at the exit to guard their
safe exodus through the hailstone.
In the large pier-glass distortion swaying on its
chain above the hearth Danny had brandished the poker
luridly above his head like Vlad the 'impaler.'
"Over my dead body you fucking wench," he'd fumed.
"I'll see that you live to regret this!"
"Oh, Mathew will be alright," she reasoned. "Big
boys don't cry, big boys don't cry."
It was one week after his eleventh birthday and his
cards were still scattered round the old familiar
crisis centre where he'd confounded expectations.
But a strange feeling dis-associated him from his
surroundings.
He sentinelled across the beachhead a miserable waif
whose *scarecrow* features resembled the *white cliffs of
Dover.*
Was it just a phantom...? Had he caught mumps?
Concentrating desperately once more he resisted the
tears prickling beyond his eyelids. But still he
couldn't remember why he was late for school that
morning.
Lead him by the scruff of his neck to sister!
Suddenly the classroom door swung open and young Mr.
Oates appeared to spot the suspect. That brought him
sharply to his senses.

He blushed to hear his name called out in class and rose to drift down below where his presence might steer the flowing tide.

As they entered the cyst pod the teacher eye-pointed towards the object of his dull concern.

Gretel was sitting with her head in her arms. She was flat at a desk by herself while all the other little girls made rude faces behind her bent over back and pulled on her pigtails. My dad's bigger than your dad! So what smartarse. Some held their noses.

"She's been like this all day," he said. "Is there anything you can do to calm her down? On Friday she ran away from school to search for your father (in the wilderness) but we've told her what will happen if she repeats this misdemeanor. I don't know what I'm going to do if this continues...expect a visit from the nit-nurse."

Mathew ran fondly forward to comfort his little sister but when she saw who had arrived it only seemed to make matters worse. He did put his arms around her to try to make the world seem a friendlier place. It was the closest they had been since the *iron age*.

"Now you're not to run away again!" he chided. Mathew looked round to acknowledge the teacher's sly approval. Very mistrustful of politicians?

"Do you remember the day when daddy parked all night outside the Sally Army Citadel!"

This incident recalled memories of that summer on the beach in Blackpool when they eventually traced her to the pen of 'Lost Children.'

Clutching a discarded stick of candy floss she had run towards them sobbing that they had abandoned her beside the pier on purpose...

The Mogadon-man in the Morris Minor talked with his hands and seemed about to push down the handle, but Mathew wasn't waiting around for him. He had already been reported once for kerb crawling.

Mathew immediately began speeding towards the Town Hall square scattering most of the change jangling in his pocket.

For a whole shilling they could share the public suds after very umble pot-walloper, with a bar of slimey soap like a dollop of cottage cheese from the marriage guidance bureau, where thieves in the night beshrewed through the peep-hole.

"It's all no good," she cried. "I haven't got anything left. What am I going to do to get out of this terrible mess?"

Below the unshaded 50-watt bulb and cobwebs Mathew wondered how long it would be until they were all gonners.

Something pittar-pattered beyond the jaundiced newspaper across the derelict windowpane.

The dreary walls, the *'post-mortem'* pallour of the place; something inside of her snapped, and gave way to regret.

A ghostly hand rattled the old gas lamp near the temple as an empty milk bottle jingled poignantly across the cobbles in the wind, and Mathew wished that he was holding an argand for her troubles.

"Everything's turned out all wrong again," she wept. "Don't you worry about a thing mammy," he said. "Everything's going to be alright. We'll soon get a council home just you wait and see. Then you'll know that this was just a passing phase!"

"Oh! my Mathew," she sighed. "What would I do without you. You're going to have to be the head of our family now..."

"Beggars can't be choosers," she'd said. "You'll like it or lump it!" Mary had another suspected bout of blackwater fever on the horizon.

What a rotten place to be. He wondered if he'd be staying there for any duration. Spotted in the bush the Marshall gave chase. Must have been on the job...when Mathew was sent to market there was no need for a shopping-list.

In a uniform begged beneath the scoffing eyes of the shopkeeper he shuffled through the quagmire of forest junk towards the sneezing *Conch carrying the box camera.*

He knocked timidly on the shingle and stood well back
to observe if there was any sign of life at half past
eleven. There was a groan...

Danny stumbled to the dawn and beckoned like a gate
across the seven seas. 3-day working at the foundry...

Through the portal dwelt a jungle of decaying
artifacts strewn haphazardly over the earth of the
mangy establishment.

A squire of Cognac still nuzzled between the unmade
bedding with its neck resting on the pillow and a
perfect charcoal drawing by his prodigious young
daughter was pinned proudly on the tinker's opposite
escarpment.

The heirloom of a broken egg-timer. Never lifted a
feather-duster. Toes like a crab.

The once proud perfectionist could not understand
his wife hesitating by the edge of the hawthorn.

He had no option of course but to sell the property
for only £400 to Paddy Mulligan. He added.

Said he was thinking of migrating to a permanent
placement where no-one could ever find him. It was
better than a poke in the eye with a sharp stick.

"Do you mean to say she still doesn't want to see
me?" he asked with surprise and jerked his head.

G-Whiz! He's finally getting the message?
His eyes began to water and his heart seemed to sizzle
with the *Oil of Ireland.*

How about another sojourn to the Outlaw's stone?
Mathew clammed-up.

He presented the stock-in-trade and quickly
scampered through the bushes hoping the rustic could
not catch him, though he could hear a voice calling
full of heaviness from the cave of Aeolus...

It was Sunday and Gretel had been invited to the
pantomime.

All day long he moaned and griped about her
considerable absence. Bitterly nibbling at his gum he
interrogated him once again.

"And what party is "this you say?" he'd baulk after a
few moments pause, determined to uncover her true
allegiance.

Father and son halted at the junction of *Showfield*
where the luminous virtue hovered succinctly on its
rocky column.

Each passing pair of headlights burst clouds of
cotton wool above the rainbow's arch.

His skin-grafts were ridding their fulvous fluid
down the bite in his limb but he still insisted on
escorting his 'second best' over the uneven length of
Hussy street.

With the sensitive hands of a Cyclops Danny held his
sons tiny mit like a sublime collector of words. As
they trundled slowly past Walter's abode he could see
his friend's mother come over to the window. She
pulled the curtains of their lanterned room but she did
not smile.

At the greenhouse Danny suddenly halted in his
tracks.

"Don't forget what I told you my boy," he swished.
"Let me hear you once again."

The physically retarded child rehearsed once more
his vulgar lines. Practice makes perfect they always
say.

"Daddy says that he loves you more than all the
pretty birds in the sky and that he'll never love
anyone else as long as he lives." repeated Mathew
methodically.

He released the grip from his father's stronger
brooch and prepared for a showdown with the *Babbitry.*

But what could this be?
He stammered with grief and his body seemed to shudder
under invisible weights. His face seemed mortified
with chagrin as the little son wriggled his hand free
of pins and needles.

Mathew pored over the great drops of balneation
which bounced in disillusionment.

"What's wrong daddy?" he asked. "Have you been
peeling Onions?"

"Life's too short," he said...and melted into thin air.

Beside the garden shed he could see Alice-Eva frying their muck through the murky diaphane. He could auscultate her muffled recitation of 'the Captain of the Buffs.' It was a favourite stand-up piece when her squaddies resided at barracks in the *cultural capital of Guardhouse*. Had a pair of drawers they used as an 'out-rigger.' Always had her curlers in.

As she packed the razor-edged weapons into bread-and-butter sandwiches her flesh obscenely swagged from the ripples of subcutaneous waste.

The walls were thick with grime and several skins of paper jockeyed for position at the skirting board. They must have had the dust shipped-in especially from the Luggins. Pus-bag crunched a slice of gristle in between their legs. The lop-sided jaw of the floor was iron-clad with crustaceans. If you'd accidentally spilled some blow-bubble it would have left a dewy patch on the fringe.

Her corpulent 'washer-woman's' cheeks flushed with mauve as she discerned who had dripped in for a whirl. The many faces dropped, but she decided to take her time anyway...and she usually rushed to make a fuss.

"He's here again look!" she loosely mumbled and glared distrustfully at her husband.

"I wish you wouldn't keep encouraging him. Doesn't he have any friends of his own age?"

When the dartsman turned the clavis his grandson floundered on the brink...the slob pretended to jump back in fright as if she'd seen a duffy, although the boarding had been pre-arranged.

She tossed the pillowcases carelessly to one side and wouldn't look at him. Ogger still had that clothes peg stuck to his jersey. He had once been swept from the riverbank by a marauding troupe of rodents. Stung by a mosquito on his backside once as well.

"He scares the living daylights out of me!" she whimpered morosely feigning a cold shiver down her deleterious spine. Something wrong with his sugar; he drinks fizzy pop! Canyons scalded into his skin.

"I'm completely at a loss how she's going to cope with him. He'll probably grow up to be a *juvenile delinquent* at this rate." And his eyes were too close together for words. But for the grace of God.

It was manifestly plain why Ogger always kept her safely hidden from the wider world. It was correctly attested that she had never even visited a public house. Ogger *camera buff* nabbed him with his Leica lens. Always record your vital moments!

The Enviromental ledger demanded that the matresses should be gutted! Bobbles on the bedclothes.

She had escaped on one previous occasion only to be discovered in the fruit shop narrating to perfect strangers the gruesome details of her myriad pregnancies. Her most consumate skill was in playing one family member off against another. The male members of her line were particularily prone to this trend. Blummin 'ummer, he'd see spots in the sun!

The gathering positioned him on a buffet in the centre of the hot house. For an hour his relations persisted in telling tall stories and made as if to hug him. Somewhere over the rainbow...

"Has the cat got your tongue?"

"If this is the way he treats him," they complained..."then he won't be allowed to take him out in future." What a fuss-pot she always was.

The mug-worts prolonged the inquest with a lukewarm cup of tea in a brown stained jug. Had he beaten him up again they asked...but Ogger still wouldn't let him eat the cream bun lying near the pastry hatch. For some reason as yet unexplained margarine was superfluous to requirements in a bacon-butty. Did it have a fat of its own? She said. Grovelling from staunch Quaker roots the gump rolled his bogie's in a ball and flicked them in the butter dish. When Ogger scoffed his grub he flailed like a Combine harvester. Don't let his sugar get too high! Tommy Steele was the best guitarist in the country.

"I know things about you," teased Stanley. "Look how many ticks I have in my exercise book." Why do you always take your socks off every night to wash your feet, and sleep with your head under the blankets?

"Now who's got the scruffiest hair?" he smirked. "You can't even make it into the lowest of the low." (She'd once been a fetcher on the warp.)

'Swapper' had once arrived at school with a solitary glass marble, and by a crafty process of augmentation returned to the hatchery in possession of a brand new train set.

His father (Ogger) always forbade him to fratinize with the Indians, otherwise he would go on the warpath.

His appointments at the dentist were cynically brushed aside but his teeth were never droned. Only the rub of the green. Just like a brother to him.

She assured her youngest brat that he wasn't really that short in comparison. Although his shoulder blades were brindled with pock-marks.

Then 'Ogger' zoomed from his miniature rolling stock dusting a *disagreable* duffel bag.

While the *shite-gobbler* snorted another plate of tripe he offered him the grist of boiled sweets from the back of beyond.

Day excursions to Margate or Masham. Trailing down the corridoor...to Ostend?

Plop, plop, (no 2's) went the pleasure ground amid the blowing of his foghorn in the dead of night.

Mathew fished through the mucilaginous wax of treacle in fear of the dreaded lurgy as Pus-bag coughed up a herring bone.

"He thinks the sun shines out of his arse," she tinctured. Well, shuffle in your brothel creepers! Suddenly Mrs. Gummidge went mental! Never even been to *White Hart Lane*. That word *suddenly!* again...

"Oh! take him away," she agonously screamed with horror and revulsion. "I never had such a damp squib in all my life."

She proudly boasted that she couldn't even boil an egg when she tied the knot, but she could certainly bard the life out of a can of baked beans.

"You and your Irish father!" she raged (perhaps she'd mislaid her own family tree.)

She charged across the arena like a penguin stormtrooper and for no apparent reason tried to turf him backwards. Once poured a boiling hot kettle over her! At 16 Ogger had put her over his knee!

M-alice could have strangled him with a blue-and-white scarf. Fans of the ukelele playing semi-moron!

Too much of a shrimp to angle in our big drink. Hadn't even the guts to attend the soccer trials with no kit...

* * *

"How much further...how much further must we walk?" pleaded Gretel.

The triad crossed the cemetery road from the station beneath an arch of many colours.

"We must have landed at the wrong stop," said Mary. "We can't have far to go now."

When they entered the male ward of *the Big House on the Hill* Mathew could see his father in the distance hurriedly relaying all his buttons.

There was a rusty erubescence around his oaken finger as he straightened his toupee with an excessive sense of nostalgia.

As the family drew nearer the Slasher began shaking like a bull before the slaughter and hid his wrists from view.

"Hello Danny dear...how are you?" gleamed his wife. She'd just torn-up the photograph album before setting sail for the hospital during the heat-wave.

The children visioned from the fly-past. It had been touch and go for a long while but he was able to weather the storm.

"Don't get the wrong idea. I've certainly seen the Canon; but nothing he said has caused me to have second thoughts."

"I told you what I'd do if you didn't come back to me," he mustered.

"I'm extremely sorry," she countenanced, giving no inch or quarter. Good will and love towards all men!

"I've decided to go through with our final separation;
and you'll be receiving the *divorce papers* on Monday!"
He's 'guilty' of divorce then?...

The night before her wedding, to Esmerelda;
"I don't want the house, I don't want Danny, and I
don't want to get married!" That she didn't love him.
But just you try and prove it!

IX
THE HOLY FAMILY

The undefiled flock recorded the juncture bloated with
pomp and frippery when the little tin gods laid the
foundation stone dipped in the charity of their
inspired benevolence.

A change of scenery was as good as a cure? Who in
god's name can turn wine into water? You can't
unscramble boiled eggs. She rasped.

This magnificent white elephant would no doubt
guarantee them a bumper crop of foison come judgement
day. "Mansions! Huge big mansions filled with jam-
dough-nuts when you get to the pearly gates!"

No stilleto heels to be worn on the gaming-preserve
thankyou very much m'am. Cock-a-doodle-do!

A whole new chapter in their development was just
beginning.

That was prior to the auspicious hour when the
entire hemisphere turned niello and the tuneful nine
engulfed the heavens with their 'golden dust of
laughter.' Lucky to be alive.

D'Artagnon rushed from the fray to flay the line of
daffodils along the beds of the castle with his sole.

Emerging from the canopy of sorts coughing and
spluttering from the flocculi he would smart at the
diorama which sometimes winced his vision. Birch,
slipper, cane, in that order!

Deep in the heap Blinker would recount his
experiences with the headless fisherman who would drag
them from their sleeping bags down to the quayside.
But if Mary could not even afford a packet of sanitary
towels for Gretel what chance the Junior Explorers?
Old MacDonald had a farm, and on this farm he had a.

Haggard faces drew back their tardy curtains or
faded further into quarry if bailiffs were badgering up
the Ichabod.

The *bitches of Eaglesfield drive* had an army of whelps who were permanently on heat and a cluster of snotty kids circulating in constant companionship. Dyestuff was sprayed on any tidy piece of brickwork. On firework-night bangers were delivered through the letterbox. Would it ever be possible to live down the stigma? Prezulis had brought a sample of something in a test-tube, but it certainly wasn't cow's milk.

'His' highly acclaimed faculty was to drink the dirty water spoiled by their myriad paint brushes. The deviant craft gained him a breathing space from oppression but he didn't half look peculiar wearing purple lipstick...serves him right for being ginger.

When the classroom thugs commended him another 'poisoned chalice' the teacher was already on tap. He anchored overhead before pouncing on Mr. Hyde from behind. If the slaphead did not do them justice his glasses would be smashed at breaktime.

Blinker often walked out in front of traffic just to see the driver's anguished expression as he skidded to a halt. On the last occasion he had been extremely fortunate. And Blinker wouldn't even hurt a fly.

The photograph of Hiroyasu was snatched roughly from his grasp. Had sent him a manga.

"Are you a puff Monaghan, writing to another boy...where's Japan, is that another country?" he asked in all seriousness. The dunce couldn't even spell his own name properly. Already had a sprog on the way.

"I don't like you Monaghan!" snapped O'Brien viciously. "Wog-off!" he snarled. The primary parent.

"Why do you look like a girl?" he said and mocked the coloured squeeze. "'Gift of the Gab!'" he snorted. Mad dog O'Brien. Now what's his claim to fame?

With his firing pistol Jake McCrombie could shoot the sparrow from any telegraph line you'd like to name...he only did woodwork. Sounded his T's like F's.

It was impossible to retrieve the correspondence by diplomacy. What was he doing out of his seat...rescuing his pride?

Destined for bigger things...

74

Doing time. Copied his home-work straight from the book. Micro grammatica under the desk.

A blackboard rubber was aimed across the room by Mr. Devlin while he attempted to intercede. The projectile splattered the pupil's nodding snout making his eyes sparkle in a daze. Ran like a bloodied piglet.

"I'm sorry," he said. "But that's the last time you disturb my class by chattering...you'll be lucky to be sent to the Grammar school since that prank of yours with the *hydrogen sulphide*!"

When the fire alarm bell sounded they assembled in the top playground for the register. After checking all the students were accounted for *Sister 'Tampon'* decided it was nearly time for home. Her methods were a 'credit to society,' she presumed.

"Just going to the 'boggotry,'" he said. "I'll only be a minute."

He waited in the cloakroom for Fatso to finish his then casually entered the lavatory. Unfortunately the kiosk was engaged...but at least Blinker had stayed on the outside.

It always took a few moments for the liquid to burst forth into the piss trough from the delicate tissues.

Through the perspex Blinker's silhouette was pummelled against the wall by Irish 'Rentagob.' The Arsonist even alleged that 'he' was a 'Brown and Muff.'

They had already thrown him down the banking once, at noon; for no other reason than that he was...the 'Blinker!' And the fact that he had just suffered from ringworm. Hair like a garnet.

Aaagh!

What must the Ugly boy have thought of him the previous down tools when they had both stood side by side at the trough?

Since then he had avoided the third former like the plague.

Mathew flushed when he recollected the borderline case.

75

'Boggie' had come to stand beside him as he tottered
for a slash. With peripeteia and dismay Mathew noticed
his fuzzy-wuzzies, further to his bushy sideboards,
frozen like a statue.

"Just like Danny!" he'd panicked. Hermetically
sealed he had shrank like a wilting willow. 'Boggie'
must have had an ocean for a bladder. He seemed to
continue urinating splendidly for hours!

A few 'dribs and drabs' had begun to splutter with a
mounting sense of relief, prior to proper urination,
when Mathew heard another active member enter the
closet from behind.

He heard a sigh and slowly turned with trepidation
to see who had arrived to relieve himself so urgently.
His rigid body shuddered. A failed opportunity to gain
admittance to the tub was to blame.

Once more 'Boggie' socled confidently in line. The
young man soon began to urinate powerfully down the
drain but in his own case nature simply wouldn't
operate. To 'fall into the sear and yellow leaf' he
was the 'Spitting image' of Uncle Stanley.

He could hear Carmello now. "Monaghan can't have a
piss miss!" Corleone said he was a ding-bat. Alice-
Eva regularily accused him of drinking gallons.

'Boggie' shook his penis by the hand and turned to
leave as if he didn't have a care in the world. He
back-kicked his zipper and abandoned the late developer
in peace without washing his hands.

Perhaps he had a bladder retardation or something?
He certainly couldn't pass water like any other.

As 'Boggie' departed another boy stepped across the
threshold to stand in the shanks. Mathew decided he
would just have to hold on until he could box the
compass. In future he would just have to excuse
himself from lessons.

The pair of merry men dawdled down the dusty lane to
feast upon the pictures of Barbarella daubing the
facade. The sea of faces had drifted from the gate and
there was no sign of trouble near the peacock cage. He
had a whole half crown in his blazer.

Crazy-horse-McGhee the Pumpkin-master had rejected his
lines from the school libretto on account that it must
have been written by persons unknown.

Preying sublimely on the skyline O'Brien tested his
Dock-Marten boot against the sphere...and went on red
alert. Not much else to his name.

"There's still time to turn back!"

"If they see us running scared."
As they approached the park entrance you could hear th
skinhead chanting the palace anthem and see him waving
his Arsenal scarf in the air. His ranking was forever
rising among the *hard-nuts* and he had even threatened
Billy Garvey. Face like 'Captain Hurricane.'

"You're gonna get your fucking head kicked in!" he
yelled at the height of his pitch to the beat of
'Jumping Jack Flash.'

"You're gonna get your fucking head kicked in!" he
trilled in a double bass voice well and truly broken.

O'Brien and '*Rentagob*' were grinning on the wall
beside him, drumming on the asbestos cover for suppor
Y.O.B. and a flying pig tattoed across his neckline.
Must have been a stake-out.

Perhaps the lout had gained inside information abo
his mother's private investigations for the D.H.S.S.?

Mr. O'Brien had recently eluded a custodial senten
by the narrowest of margins after mowing down a child
on the Zebra crossing while four times over the limit
A petition for leniency on behalf of the sponger had
been signed by none other than the Canon himself.

"If you'd only tell me what I've done," he argued.
"Perhaps we could parley?" Search his pockets!

"I want you dead," he retorted. He waited until h
was just removing his jacket and ripped the Osprey fr
his lapel. Hand over the loot!

With his cosh of billiard balls tied in a sweaty
sock the *Zulu* drilled a hard right home to his head
catching him completely off guard. Snatch his
telescope! Quick. Lets scarper.

After that it was childsplay.
O'Brien easily gained the upper hand without any
resistance whatsoever.

This pleased him no end and freed him to probe his
burgeoning puissance to the boundary, and the gang of
five. The wizard wheeze.

"Come on ya spas!" he roared. "Fight me...fight me
if ya dare! I've waited for this ever since the day I
first saw you, short-arse."

"Why can't you pick on someone your own size," cried
the wimp. But this only provoked the bully enough to
land another series of direct hits.

With one last shove, and a trip from Gennick, Mathew
hit the deck. Blinker ran forward to retrieve the
battered corpse of his defeated arch-protector.

In the same instant he was knocked ruthlessly aside
O'Brien instinctively drew back his shin to level a
kick at the jabber lying on the ground. He connected
perfectly with the jaw-bone.

Everyone heard his bowsprit shatter. The force sent
him sprawling dangerously roadwards where a passing
articulated lorry missed his head hanging over the kerb
by a whisker.

The spinning *Juggernaut* raped the finer strands of
his greasy mane from their roots...

O'Brien was unable to suppress a cheerful smile. It
seemed as if all his Christmas's had come in sight at
once. The lord said.

Rentagob hooted like a foghorn...his gingervitic
mouth was 'caked in blood,' he indicated.

Even in their wildest dreams the gang had never
perlustrated such a nirvana. The spectacle was
positively fascinating.

There would of course be no point informing the
school authorities. They would simply punish them both
'equally.'

"See the error of your ways Maffew."
Moonighan cut short without a squeak!!

Alpha Centauri, with 'golden eyes'

You cloak me in winds
where the secret world spins
and vessels climb storms
above the river's red gorge.

You cover me with flame
where the pageant unfolds
distant ages unborn
on the lava's live rock.

You choke me in blood
which rained from above
whose path beats a hush
from heaven's haughty hub.

You fill me with must
where clouds shift their dust
for my inquisitive eye
from the earth's blue sky.

You find me in stars
where the summer snow falls
on the Argo of fort
among gold doublet glows.

I'll meet you once more
when the plane greets my name
on my happy return
from the light never fades.

Mathew Moonighan
The Holy Family School
May 1967

X
THE STARS THAT PLAY WITH LAUGHING SAM'S DICE

Would you like to read the route map of the space-time continuum?

Bonanza didn't play tonight; it was Friday and the President had been purged. Fading were the tender days of pucelage...

Even the Vicar knocked on the latch and offered his hand when he saw her lilliputian figure struggling at the window rail of twenty Park View Drive, with the curtains undone.

Mary had a way of rubbing herself against the glass for every passing male to stare across the avenue. Why when the telephone rang would she suddenly spring to life? It could have been someone else. Fred Bloggs.

Mathew lay back on the floor and wondered where his sister had been all night after they had been to see Jimmy Clitheroe in panto. And she'd been seen loitering on the beach as if she was looking for a lift.

When they had approached her she had axelled out of range. Caddying a cheap reticule slung over her shoulder she had entered the amusement arcade and slipped out the other side without a trace. Stung by a sea creature? She had bigger fish to fry. Could win every game of Poker.

Why had sleeping at her friends house resulted in the stiffening of her gait...and what was *heavy petting*? Memories came flooding back as he casually glimpsed up his sister's outspread gymslip and realized she wasn't wearing a stitch.

The stars beside someone's moniker in her tally-book...Don't keep diaries under the bed!

"Mum, our Gretel's got a hedgehog at the top of her legs," he shouted with alarm. Then the eleven year old girl had snatched his tiny penis until he squealed for help.

Mathew had *absolutely no idea* what the crude jokes made by some of the local scum referred to.

He had a brief recollection of her being passed around the older lads and crossing the field with one of them toward the beech with the knickers in her hand.

THEN there'd been that disasterous holiday on the coast when the two females had jibbed like a two-edged sword at his budding prominence...taking turns to jab and doff his kittle, and deracinate his inadequate redoubt.

The landlord's daughter Catherine who had swooned romantically at his feet when she heard what he had to offer was on the way.

"I'm not going to touch any little ten year old!" he'd shuddered. "Even if she will do anything that I want." His sister had kindly declined the inducement for him...

"I have!" she pouted.

"You haven't! Girls like you don't do that sort of thing," he assured her.

"Oh, yes I have!" she said. But still he wouldn't believe her.

"You can't have!" he insisted...she didn't look any different.

"Well I have anyway," she bragged with supercilious satisfaction. "I lost it with a Policeman in the donkey's shed at Woodhouse."

"I've been doing it regular ever since! You ought to try it sometime, buddy."

When he first encountered Sophie at the church hall dance the awkward squad agreed how lucky he was to be courting the Ambassador's daughter.

"So Susan has a girlfriend at last!" teased Fatso. "At least now we know he's one of us, even if he has the longest hair in the fifth form! Looks just like one of the *Partridge family*."

From the party at the broken-down potting shed called the 'Pits' the couple departed from her families estate down Ramscott lane. They were still in mourning for the prolific left-handed electric wizard. An invitation to the Isle of Wight-

Not even two shillings to rub together.

'Just imagine escorting her to the shambles
inhabited by the seething midget running amok,' he
ruminated. On the cards.

Martin's father had dragged him from the opium
filthy doss-house to complete his meditation in the
brig. 'His wrangler jacket belonged to Billy Bunter
anyway,' she scoffed. Every man to his humour.

They even snogged in the hanger on the road from
the bacchanalia. But the sun was held in chains.
'Sweet as nine.' Too delicious to touch.

There was a dischordant break in the clouds. You
could hear starlings jingling amid the Oak leaves over
the dry stone wall and the call of the hay-makers
chasing down the runnels. A shower of Perseids
dropped like an untimely candle to their bed against
the murmur of the universe.

Her blue-grey eyes sank reminiscently to his chest
as she invited him to rehearsals at her little theatre.

"I used to be very shy," she remarked. "But I'm
sure I'll be alright when we've known each other
longer." It was downright impossible to harness his
energies towards a closer encounter.

Like a miniature Chaldean Mathew revealed the
mysteries of creation with the stars sparkling
overhead like a ceiling of marble mica. He began
with Syrius which was the brightest, and Orion...
sadly missing. Impossible to say.

He instructed her in the use of the two pointers.
How best to capture Hesperus; at sunrise. That human
existence was linked to the phases of the moon...
Aquilla and *the Archer*. He even compared our entire
hall of fame to this vast array of splendour.

'But aren't all the proles exceedingly special?'
There were times when the source of light seemed to
speak. Catch a falling star, put it in your pocket.
save it for a rainy day...

"We have a thief in this school," sniffed the Monsignor,
flicking the ash of his enormous cigar into the
yawning depths. Emblazoned on the beam above him hung
the motto of St. Chads: '*Planan et conquaerere.*'

"A prize 1925 Bugle has been lifted from a secure
school storeroom. I need to denude the culprits
otherwise I will have no option but to call in the
C.I.D." A sacrament the outer sign of inner grace?

The poker-faced audience gasped. The pawnbroker
had just replaced his receiver to the station.

A comedo on 'Moggies' brown paper face projected
its mountainous features to the flinching mass and
touted for a retreat in the autumn.

Frieze adroitly spun his reflector to the correct
position as cool as a cucumber. He balanced the
mechanism in his hand carefully affording a glimpse
of Miss. Fit's suspenders. His favourite blow was a
spur to the groin in the dinner queue when demanding
money with menaces. Woe betide anyone who let the cat
out of the bag about his exploits. But he had a
cutting about Mr. Dinsdale for them all to chortle
about. Just the tip of the ice-berg.

Leaning right over the chair top he accidentally
touched the back of her leg. The young school teacher
diddered and quickly swung round. She caught him red
handed and warmly smiled. Ought to be a satist.

He dead-legged the diffident drummer boy tapping
with his foot. "You little runt," he hissed. "I bet
you're still a fucking virgin!" With what he's got.

Beneath the ebony recesses of the stage claustral
excommunicates peered through the single narrow strip
of light from their pillarbox. From the upper cubicles
of the complex a ragged pack had been chased by the
Black Friar into the yard.

As the priest blessed the 'bread and wine' O'Hurley
ejaculated in the darkness...

"Call this homework laddie?" Is your periodic table
a herd of crapping *elephants*? Fatso denied the very
existence of heavy metal.

Bay City Rollers; flavour of the month.
"Moonighan!" he screamed. "How many times have we
told you to get your hair cropped? You are a disgrace
to the whole community."

"If you wanna be in my gang!"- Gary Glitter.

Beyond the marionette's irreverent education they
departed from the Ram's Revenge discussing the new
band revolving on the wheel of fortune.

As they floated to the painted wagon some of the
guys from Greenhead opened and shut their raincoat
standing in the doorway.

"Quick flash!" they tittered.
A snowdrift of dung gleamed from the highest ledge
of the swaggering colossus. The procession festooned
stem to stern.

Quavering in his crushed velvet bellbottom loons
he mingled with the throng of fans with his birth
certificate hid under a bushel. Very little
improvisation called for. Roadies brought the gear.

Fulfilling their greatest expectations the group
performed the complete corpus of their first album
climaxing with the superb *Phoenix*. The amaranthine
warriors returned for a further encore. They were
certainly on eagle's wings that night and soared from
the platform to tumultuous applause.

A selection of mediocre songs followed by the
bedrock rooted to the flying ground. The crowd were
gleeking after the preceding *Utopia*. It was a hard
act to emulate. Although the rockers had a loyal
stream of supporters who were not to be overwrought
it seemed as if the sleeping lion heralded a final
curtaincall.

Below the gallery a choppy sea of venules summoned
the necessary dynamism.

From the crest of a quasar the main sequence plunged
into their swansong and the venue trembled with the
impact of the Second coming.

The powerful oscillating chords of *THUNDERBUCK RAM*
hissed through the ballistrade in a projectile of
coloured lasers as the mighty classic exploded like a
bombshell, and pulsed throughout the entirety of the
furnace restoring their fame to favour...
crystallizing time in the quiescent quelling brain.

Between dusk and the dawn the fortissimo thrust the
web of Gypsy signs deep into the heartbeat of a thought.

As the intruder pryed from the bridge the *starmap
unfolded* below him; guiding their progress
telepathically across the void.

Diaphanous multi-coloured beings hovered near the
uninvited guest shivering in their midst. Their volant
frocks shimmered like a fumid *Jellyfish* as his ka-ba
swooned along the *Borderland*.

This shadow cabinet looming on the knees of gods,
transmitted from Alpha to Omega webbing the unestimiable
cosmos of ubiquity...the hypersensitive darted faster
than knowing itself as they mobilized the pyramid on
board their timeless vessel.

Deserting the giant saphire of space they drifted
past the red dwarf toward the *turquoise* luminary.
Long millennia of track andanted by until they
approached the candescent disc.

In the twinkling of an eye the extempore was almost
bourn on the highway of the exterminators.

It was a warcraft, an invasion fleet! Their
destination mother Earth gathering cloud and rain.
Contraband spells danger.

Slow inertia chained his rotary as he motored to
the launchpad in the blinking of an eyelid.

The deafening hum of their war machines crammed the
livid lamps above the dado.

Heaven's eerie messenger of doom split the atom of
the ear-drum with the high-pitched wailing of their
nauseating Toledoheads.

Let the people know. Terror from the sky my friends,
terror from the sky!

XI

KOYANISQAATSI

Powerless to touch their tender surface he held a
mirror beneath the uneven baggage. A sinuous red line
threaded along the mottled underbelly of the troutbeck.
Judging by the documentary evidence it must be syphilis
at the very least. His penis projected well through
the empty toilet roll though. He repacked the
candlewax cast of his nose carefully back inside the
drawer, and crept slowly through his brown study on all
fours. Lovely bunch of coconuts...On your march, GO!
M. scribbled a message in a bottle to 'Claire Rainer'
and threw it in the pin-down, left of starboard. With
'Love like a man' burbling beneath the stylus she had
scorched him with the nozzle of her suction pump-lips.
   "Sometimes I feel so randy I could kill..." she had
confided.
   "Jesus Christ, hold on a moment," he'd protested.
His gums were actually bleeding.
   And there was hollow-eyed Desiree wandering up to
the bathroom. Up periscope, down right rudder. Always
said grace before meals. He hardly had elbow room.
Felt about as turned-on as a vinegar whelk. Tried to
psyche him out.
   "Don't you have some funny records?" she scraped.
"Where are your tapes by the Four tops?"
   "Please take your hand away one minute...I'll be
ready in a moment," he quirked.
   With the tweed skirt rucked around her waist and her
chasm bubbling like a red-hot ulcer he hesitated to
walk the plank into oblivion. If he touched her hand
she wailed 'Ouch!'
   "Aren't you going to fuck me then?" she'd finally
hissed. "I like you, but I don't fancy you."

86

"Wouldn't you rather discuss the Glass Island, or the
Lion, the witch, and the wardrobe?"
   "There are only two things to do when it's raining
and I don't like playing Patience!" She grinned.
   But the Shuttlecock had lost any interest in the
Xala. At fourteen her knicker elastic had already lost
its tautness.
   "Tea children!" She barged in.
Said she'd stop when she got to a hundred...

The kitchen knife stabbed unerringly at the handle
wedged against the outer cordon and eventually clawed
the catch apart, reeking vengeance on the mass of
unruly hair still fribbled at the top of his pillow.
Time he got his act together.
   The tip of his glans was glued with the remnants of
'flour-paste' to the pink fabric of the stitch.
   She ripped the bedclothes from his richly acned body
and demanded he divulge the origin of those sleazy
smears diffracted over the entire region of that
rheumy-eyed matress.
   Why did he suddenly stir during seed-shedding? She
tore the pin-up into shreds. 'But nobody could be
exactly five feet?' he quizzed her.
   "You lazy good for nothing idle sod," she shouted.
"Why aren't you at school again?" she screamed. "What
do you mean there are no clean clothes; I've got better
things to do than chase about after you!"
   "Get a bath," she shrieked. "Certainly not! What do
you think this is, a Hotel? You've had one this week
already and that's enough for any normal person. I
don't want to hear any more about a...*rhinectomy*?"
   When he answered her back the faggot biffed him in
an instant with her broom.
   "Tell them you walked into a door!" she laughed
disdainfully.
   He forced a retreat from his private area and set
about curing his socks of 'riga mortis.'
   She led him by the ear to scrub the poxy blemish
starched in the bath enamel before she loosened her
grip.

87

He proceeded to comb his hair back in the mirror in the hope that it would detract from his expanding snout. She clonked him with her copy of 'Sigmund Fraud.'

Mathew deliberately bombinated and sprinted past the fulguration. Inside leg 28. Can't take a shower with the rest of the squad. The silver screen flickered images of the masked Avenger. Usurp the throne.

The agoraphobic youth dawdled uncertainly at the exit before his mother jaculated him down the road in no uncertain terms. Who wears the britches.

"And I don't want to see you tomorrow evening. Gretel's friend is exchanging visits."

"Why didn't you keep your big gob shut about my boyfriends?"

"There's plenty of dripping in the grill tray to spread on a loaf."

It was a tale told by an idiot, full of sound and fury, signifying bugger-all.

With summer crashing into quicksand the Clockword Mouse could not approach the gate of Holycroft where hostile forces gathered at the bus stop. He would just have to approach the shelter side-on if the hackneyed tribe were anywhere to be seen.

At least three single deckers zoomed past him before he was able to take the plunge. Then there was the long climb up Beacon hill to quell his hard-on. Should he fly down the catsteps? A line of vehicles at the traffic lights made him see red. Another half-hour diversion via the boating pond. Surely he didn't think they were looking at him? Send the nonce on jankers!

As he entered the sixth form entrance of the Boy's Grammar School his little finger lifted quaintly from his briefcase.

The priest held the instrument of torture above his head...'No, I mustn't think about it.'

"Don't make me blush more than once today," he palpitated, and then he coloured at the thought of the inevitable, as he digressed the darkened cloister. On the starboard tack the mere speck of dust drifted to report his presence to the headmaster.

Hearing Mr. Henry sneeze and blow down half a wall he paused before taking a deep breath at the edge of the Common room handful. His legs turned to jelly. Not a squeak issued from the stalls. Never since Senlac.

With the prickly heat bruising like a scarlet fever he plummetted down the wooden steps raising his simple eyebrows. Screwball, Queer cunt, mutton-head.

The in-crowd supining egocentrically in relaxed conversation was interspersed in isolated groups by 'dolly-birds' from the nearby college. Word had quickly circulated of his surreptitious entrance. His perambulations seemed to course on an altogether heterotactous flux of film.

"Cuckoo! Cuckoo!" tittered the peer group. His petrified face jerked fitfully down the spiral rungs to lesson. Then there was at least two sides to every picture-book? Didn't have the brains he was born with. Too lazy to scratch his own arse.

Squealing on his ratchet Fatso mimicked his queer expressions and appeared to scratch his head just like Stan Laurel. No longer looked like Bryan Ferry.

"For Fucks sake look at his hair!" someone mocked. "What's he done with it today? Moonighan you remind me of a Penguin the way you waddle," burped the rugger captain. Flawed in every respect. "Looks a bit pastey? Sure you aren't anaemic?" "Johann Straus the elder!" "Uncle Fester!" "Your flies undone!" Sure enough he fell for it..."Hey sexy!" teased one of the hostesses. "What an idiot," they moaned. "What a clown!" "Dick like the jib of a crane! Playing pocket billiards?" His back was even-covered in cuckoo-spite.

As he froze outside the master's office where the seminar was in progress a blow from the cricketbat made him see dog-stars. Completely scuppered. Lost for...

By the time that he had rotated everyone was sitting innocently with their arms folded as if the undertaking was only partially completed. Held down with the sense of Justice and fair-play.

"Do you think he could be mad?" asked the psychology student. He struggled garishly with the knob; honestly, it was better than any slapstick.

"Ah! Mathew, you've arrived!" sniffed the history professor glaring for a prankster.

With his head bent against a torrent of stares and his hand held up to his face the pupil lurched across the Axminster to find a seat.

Twirling the large moustache twisting in the overcast he marked the rumple of the 'egg and bacon man' with a length of yellow cane. Jacob Buckhart. Damned good egg! Hadn't anybody told him it was rude to pull faces?

"Will you be joining us for dinner tomorrow?" he cajoled, flickering his eyelids open and closed. "Don't you know what day it is?"

"We will be discussing Charles the Bald and the break-up of the Carolingian Empire due in part to outside pressures."

"And where did you get that black eye! I hope you haven't been brawling Moonighan, huh?"

More than a self-conscious mumbled monosyllable the semi-moron suddenly found his voice when the expert cleared the stage for his reluctant curtain-call.

"Thou art a soul in bliss but I am bound upon a wheel of fire that mine own tears do scald like molten lead," gingled the clearly spoken character actor.

"Mathew could I have a quiet word with you? If you're not too busy?" he asked. "I want us to be on first name terms."

Mr. Buckley removed his spectacles and began to clean their rims on the desk with his neatly pressed white hanky.

"How are you feeling dearheart?" he soothed. "Where have you been hiding during the close season? Have you managed to finish reading 'The Plough and the Stars?' Why do you persist in keeping company with the likes of Ryan Starbuck?"

There was a glimmer of background radiation as he began to fiddle with the mechanism of his platinum alarm. Star pupil. Off his rocker. He really was a 'laugh-a-minute.' Could drink like a fish.

"Everything hunky-dory at the prefab?"
"Certainly is," purred the lunatic.

"Any problems?" Flaking his four o'clock shadow. "You can always confide in a friend."

"Is there something the matter with you?" This statement was loaded with presuppositions.

"We consider you to be potential Oxbridge material. Please do not disappoint us when you apply as a candidate."

"Nothing!" he grinned.
Followed by a sigh. Nothing will come of nothing.

They even positioned a chair for the beetroot-man at break-time and prepared to keek the dizzard. But Sharkey always cheats at poker that's expected. The smaller they were the harder the humiliation. Black and white are not colours!

Must we presume some sort of mental deficiency? "Tell him Spike," urged the advocate. "Don't keep the dolthead hanging in suspense." F. looked as if he had poisoned the reservoir and was waiting for him to drink. By Jeeves!

And why had they recently sent him to Coventry? By outstaring a stray he could make anyone crap in their trousers.

"It wouldn't surprise me if he suddenly snapped." A malign and sadistic smile snowed his pock-marked summit.

"I fucked your sister at a party last night!" he lewdly whispered. There was blood and snot in the garret. A gross generalization.

Frieze taunted him with some pornographic literature and pressed the disconcerting images against his gangling skin.

"She was an excellent screw while it lasted," he sibilated. "Hard to believe she's related to a little runt like you!"

"You didn't" "You're lying." "She wouldn't." He blushed. Never even asked him out. Oh, Lydia.

As they played slaphead over his molting dome a soiled jam-rag was slung down the back of his collar.

He was tossed like a bag of shoddy rags into the
comfort area. There was a large disparity in weight
beween them consisting mainly of water.

After a severe beating by the creditworthy headboy
his neck was pushed in the septic tank by the rat-pack
to fry his bacon - Cable is Not a transvestite. Flush
the fucking chain on him.

"I'd like to do something with disadvantaged
children," she said.

XII
THE LEAVING PARTY

The dissident wench was just departing to the Fair-
ground debauch when he tackled her about why she had
donated his entire stamp collection to the kids at the
bottom of the street *and* burnt the catalogue of his
early balladry. The counter-jumper had sold his *Black
Swan* for a sizeable profit to a dealer. His Conch had
been thrown down the river. Serves him right.

The young woman towered above the buffoon in her
high-heeled shoes. His whinging words were just enough
to swear by and he had a face to stop the clock.
Gretel could get away with bloody murder now!

She'd rushed down from her convent school to set the
operations in motion first thing on the bed spring.

"You must feel really small and inadequate compared
to all the other boys. Which 'Eagle Adventure holiday'
are you going on this year?" she jeered.

"He's the spitting image of Sid Little," she
sneered. "My dad's good looking but Mathew is an ugly
toe-rag."

"You English guys make us sick," she said.
'You're a wad of feckless oafs who wear white
handkerchiefs on their loafs and never see their
shrivelled-up dicks due to the extent of your beer-
bellies.'

'And Lydia is going steady with Frieze.'
"But what about that trick with you?" he stammered.

"That was ages ago!" she murmurred impatiently.
"He forced me! He raped me when I was blotto," blurted
Gretel. To bow and to stern.

She suddenly kicked him on the shin..."Mind your own
damn business!" she sniggered. "I hate Steve anyway."

"Hurry up. I think the Old Cow is coming down," she prosered. "I wish she'd leave us fucking well alone."

Mary entered the hall-way on an air note of despondency. She curtseyed obsequiously and nearly wet her underclothes.

"Mother, take 'it' away!" Gretel demanded. "Make 'it' fuck off or I will be leaving here for ever. Get him sorted," she blared. "There are patients on G-wing in a more sanitary state than that little drip over there." A dead parrot.

Then she slapped his face for good measure.

Did Ogger realize that his number had just been called? The other wood resting was his trident of prize crown green bowls.

His widow lolled at the book and candle as Mary sanctioned the proceedings with a toast. Kicked the bucket. Hell for leather. Shuffled off his mortal...

"You've always been very special to Esmerelda," she assured him. "You are the son she never had. My sister thinks you still have some good qualities remaining...but she's entitled to her opinion!"

"Our little princess!" smiled Alice-Eva. Why were her nut-hazel nylons always so bruised and out of skew?

When the time was right for the offing the blushing adolescent was summoned south to be directed on his proper course of life.

She kindled an increasingly provocative attitude which made him sense a trap.

He timidly approached the gathering and perched awkwardly on the edge of the pin-cushion.

Mathew went to turn the light off...Mary turned it back on again, though one could not see what she possibly had to gain.

Stanley urgently insisted that he inform all those present just what his exact plans were for the future, and how he expected his poor suffering mother to provide his upkeep for very much longer. Her maintenance of five shillings-and-sixpence had now expired it seemed. 'Kick him where it hurts.' Working men were the salt of the earth!

"Have you no idea which line of track you wish to travel in? She can't possibly carry on supporting you on a paucit student grant. I understand she has even had to plead with the *Samaritans* to make you see sense. How can she expect to be herself when you are permanently quoffing underneath her snout?"

"You young upstart. Isn't it about time you shaved off your bum-fluff. Why not spread some cream and get the cat to lick it off."

"But human beings don't voluntarily become *lighthouse keepers*," he scoffed. "You'd live like Robinson Crusoe. Can't you think of something else you'd rather be? If you go on like this you're going to turn into neither fish, flesh, fowl, nor good red herring. No absolutes! You deny the dead certainty of common knowledge? What do you mean there's no such thing as 'normal.' How can a little squirt like you ever hope to improve on nature. I'd go banana's if I kept in my room for as long as you appear to do. Look who's been drinking the beestings."

"You're blooming Crackers!" agreed the assembled multitude firing on all fours. "The buck stops with thou." 'Talks like a twat!'

The corpulent washer-woman's cheeks puckered with ridicule. Alice-Eva could even remember the pitiful spinster before she dropped from the railway bridge.

"Who does he think he's saving it for anyway," she asked them. "Go sow some *wild oats* why don't you? What's this about blaming our family for not being nice looking?'. He's as nutty as a fruit cake," she whispered behind her mit.

"Oh, he won't take a scrap bit of notice...he never does anything I tell him," smirked Mary. "So perhaps he'll listen to someone else instead. High time you 'bucked' your ideas up and tuned in to some sound advice. We're only thinking of your own welfare," she added. "I actually caught him sunbathing on the steps!" she promulgated. "He eats me out of house and home. Where he puts it all god only knows. Must have a tape-worm. A chip on his shoulder a mile wide. Doesn't know his arse from his elbow for sure."

Aunty Esmerelda dusted the crumbs from her digestive. She took a sip of liquid from the fake China mug and cleared her smooth white throat, before adhering to the hard row to hoe. She pressed her finger against her stiff upper lip...

"Children should be seen and not heard!"

"We've thought this one over very carefully," she sniffed. "Your nearest and dearest have arrived at the only fair conclusion in this case. Why not model yourself on Cliff Richard."

"With the best will in the world we consider it prudent you clear your room lock, stock and barrel to join the *British Territorial Army*. Surely you don't want to outstay your welcome?" Wielding the surgeon's scalpel.

"Now that you are finally sixteen it's essential that you fly the nest. You never know what you like until you try it."

"Experience in the forces will make a man of you and enhance your feeble prospects. You come from proud working stock. So don't let us down."

Esmerelda ostentatiously opened the thick brown envelope marked 'Army Career's Information.'

She grinned charitably towards the grotesquely indigenous youth. Mary salaciously licked her plate.

"You'll meet with everything you require in there love," she spoofed.

"It's just what you need to get you started," they urged. "Mary has slogged her guts out to fill the place of your father but more discipline to keep you on the straight and narrow is the order of the day. You don't want to turn out like him do you?" How much better you will feel when you've been neatly ironed-out and iodined. Cleanliness is next to godliness.

Reeling beneath the hair-lipped logic of their black propaganda he slumped from every expose of his blink. The family hierarchy gained extra strength and succour from his deportment.

"But I never had a father..." he suggested.

The entire wagon-load rolled with ridicule. Was he a complete nincompoop? Of course he had a *paterfamilias*.

He tipped his cup like a mechanical crane while they toyed. "But I came top of my form three years running," he stammered.

"Then go and fall from the roof. You must have cheated. He did, I know he did."

"Mathew must think we were all born yesterday," she hooted. "This has been a joyride for him so far but the holiday is coming to a rapid conclusion. He was only born that way," she lamented.

"But my sister is being encouraged to stay on for her retakes," he whimpered. Accused him of trying to rise above his station. Tried to put him in a bad light. Easy for some. Couldn't sell ice to eskimoes.

"Gretel can loss and find him," she explained. "Her behaviour has always been immaculate." Ramekin.

"And he was such sweet child," effused Esmerelda sonorously. "Always laughing and full of jolly fun. I can't think what ever happened to him..." Hadn't a clue how to talk about his feelings. Mat was quiet as a mouse. "Well, I'm not having any more shilly-shallying about!" she cat-called. "You just don't like to see anyone else enjoying themselves!"

"Poor Gretel is having to leave home because of scatterbrains," she drilled. "He's made her life a complete misery. A Sunbeam for one's birthday. I've never heard so much silly twaddle," she tweeked. Just how many of our ancestors sinned to survive?

"I'm surprised that you have any friends left. If you want some pocket-money you can get out and earn it the way I've always had to do. You'll not receive any hand-outs from old muggins here," she promised. "He's even too lazy to scratch his own arse," she twittered. Blood, they said, was thicker than water.

When he mentioned the ten lost tribes peering intensely up to her silhouette his aunty reacted with typical party spirit. The charade was hardly ever interupted by his dissimulation.

"Oh, Mathew...I think that you must be jealous," the
schoolteacher condescended. "Take some vitamins."

"Pretend you never noticed them...moderation in all
things," she strongly advocated. "How can a tulip grow
if you constantly remove it from the ground to examine
its roots?" That was a new 'un.

His mother glared at the *chopping block* and willed
him to swallow the bait. "You can't believe the word
of a seven stone midget," she hissed. The sacrifices
she had to make so he could go to the Grammar school.
She glowed with pride.

Her friends were always thundering into the dining
area.

"But can't my exit wait until I meet a nice young
girl to settle down with?" Let me see now. A son is a
son until the day he is wed. A daughter is a daughter
the rest of her days?

"You've been reading too many sloppy stories,"
confirmed Esmerelda. Her sister's sunrash was steadily
accelerating. How long until the donkey dropped for
his carrot?

"Married!" she snorted. "Married?" she sneered.
"Mathew dear 'some kinds of men' never make a good
enough match."

Eventually he asked the grandmother to mention by
name a single member of her kin either past or present
who had achieved anything truly outstanding.

"Timothy is a 'Chartered Accountant,'" she cheered
gloriously – *in medias res!* "You walked right into
that one," she fizzed.

"What makes you think you're so bloody special."
"Have I outgrown my short-trousers then?"...the *arch-
deceiver* leapt to her own defence.

"Don't be *mental!*" fumed his mother. She had been
determined to put a lid on his troublesome slander.

"On the contrary...oh don't bother trying," she
irritably snapped. "Anyone can see there's something
wrong with him...just look at the funny look in his
eyes. What have I ever done to give birth to a useless
sod like that?" she moaned. "I never had any
stretchmarks until he came along."

"Have you seen his chin...what he really needs is a
bloody good hiding!"

Mother Mary, meek and mild...
In a pocket of Ogger's morbiferous kitbag festered the
remnants of his most recent indigence.

This magnificent find consisted of a tin-pot jerry-
can into which was deposited an enormous metal razor
germinating from the Normandy landing and a half-stick
of shaving-soap with the silver wrapping-paper imbibed.
The rusty blade was still packed with gunge and had
sandwiched the debris into a repulsive wafer of
lobsterflesh.

Mary fitted him up with a pair of the sweaty
slippers. "Now there's no excuse for wearing your
waders!" she stipulated. 'He'd try to exonerate
himself until the cows came home.'

"Foot slogging to the bathroom? Don't forget to
wash the dirty bits," hollered Esmerelda.

He removed his threadbare pullover. Mathew was
marched to do the dishes while the dunkers lay down
their arms. Never lifts a finger. Needs his backside
tanned...school-blazer ripped first day all his fault.

Mrs. Hogwash arrived in her daughter's quiet bedroom
just as the scoptophilbiac was driving himself up the
wall.

Why couldn't he engage her in a modicum of polite
conversation? Did he really have the gumption to
change his farcical behaviour? That'll wake his ideas
up.

"Do the decent thing! It's about time you went to
your own sing-song."

The attractive middle-aged housewife loitered
lovingly at the sewing machine as she arranged the
tresses of her sultry daughter's bridal gown.

Chastity often crooned for hours at the dispersive
oracle across the way.

The woman glanced occasionally in the direction of
the quince where the strange young man appeared to be
tinkering with his champion moderator.

What if he attempted the totally unthinkable rising of
a curtain?

He taped the broken piece of mirror to the stand and
adjusted the tailor's dummy at regular intervals.

Inch by tantalizing inch the ritual soon developed
into acute tight-rope walking. Take deep breaths. A
cold shower and a bucket round his bell end. Boggled
into shape.

Every so often she poked a finger in the corner of
her cornea. Watching like a hawk she rested on her
elbow and blanched. It was a real turn up for the
book! Time for a wave?

Alternating the direct current he swanked his
intromittant organ in front of the window lace.

She opened her arms, smiled amiably and... *Shazaam!*
The minister entered.

XIII
MIDNIGHT PROWLER

As Pan's people danced seductively on the television
screen that Thursday night Mathew burnt his fingers
with a totally innocent compliment. Mary was gurgling
with a glass of TCP at the time.

"Don't you ever make a sexist remark like that
again," snarled the two women. He was treated like a
viper in their bosom. "Only wants to oggle them!"

When Alexis Korner appeared to mime his number one
hit record with that deep bass voice of his grinding
like a sack of old nails...

"Peep through the bathroom door, did you ever, did
you ever, see your sister in the raw, did you ever,
did you ever?" he decided to flit hand over fist where
the frowzy air was less curdled.

"Good riddance. I hope you top your blooming self."
"Why don't you start acting your age not your shoe size!"

He ascertained that the emersion had been 'unconverted.'
With his ears pressed against the lining he audiled their
charge and flow unearthed conveniently out of range.

"My God, what's that?" screamed Mary.
They bent over to examine the denuded floorboard in
closer detail. If you cupped your hands around the spot
it afforded one a tiny chink of light shining in the
blackness down below.

After this horrid epistemology they relocated the
dresser away from the fan heater. He could hear the oak
base grating over the ceiling. Lo and behold here was
another fissure in the buildings' Victorian
infrastructure, which if you pressed your eye against
the tube offered a limited glimpse of the ceramics above
the bathtub. 'Hardly capable,' they sneered.

'Had the log-cabin always been intramural?'
He shuddered and shook in the recess as the two women
investigated further and found the whole residence to
be riddled with holes like a giant block of *Austrian
Emmental*. Persistent vegetative state?

"What are you going to do about him mother?" he heard
her bray. How could she ever forgive his 'speech from
the throne?'   Animal, mineral, or vegetable?

He wrung his hands in grief. What now...flaying
alive or bow-stringing? What an imbecile.

"Leave it all to me," barked Mary. "No son of mine
is going to turn into a nasty depraved individual."

A noisy argument erupted concerning the most
opportune moment to pounce on the pest. And birds were
not to be referred to as chicks.

Gretel seemed convinced the execution should be
announced immediately by a phone call to the station
but Mary seemed keen to postpone the event until they
had gathered more concrete evidence.

A violent scuffle began in the hallway which spilled
over the drugget. The weaker sex.

Mary swiftly punched her daughter to the ground but
it was not all one way traffic.

To his surprise he discovered that the warring
parties had triggered a mysterious phenomena in his
trousers. Inappropriate behaviour!

His sister hammered up the stairs in tears and
slammed her chalet door.

At last it was bathnight; he'd been ho-overing since
dawn for the object lesson in hydrodynamics.

The hippodrome opened and the aqua vitae whirled to
the brim, rising with his sense of jubilation until his
weary self was almost sea-sick.

To add amphetamine to his boozing veins the visitor
descended calmly from the stratosphere; a signal to
raise his expectancy more than ever as he spun in
rapturous circles and punched the air.

Major Tom stumbled wheezing from his dorp to dampen
all the shackles fraying on his patchwork.

Drawn like a delinquent moth towards the distant
spark he quivered over the seedy lino in order to
inject his dose of kief into those drowsy neurons.

A kaleidescope of colours unfolded for the satellite
fibrillating on all fours. He attempted to release
the straining metal with no immediate success.

Meanwhile the exhibitionist paraded her wares
before the congress. Perspiring in steam she vainly
mauled her butresses.

Major Tom almost swooned with apoplexy. Her minge
was like a shaggy mound of peacock feathers.

Razzled wildly to the rhythm of the carnival he
nearly split his drumsticks.

Proudly prodding the marsh gas above his feet his
painful six-shooter throbbed like shooting iron.

He steadied himself for her removal from the pool,
and the excoriate Grand finale, as the soft drink
gurgled down the plugoyle.

While she powdered over every follicle he was able
to observe her most unconscious aspects, griping with
the tenseness in his ciliary, and the numbing cramp
which all too often shot across his stern.

The scopolamine mouth hung on the clothes line as
she knelt to open the packet and raised her legs onto
the toilet seat for easy access.

Was the purdah about to light up?
He mopped his brow with the towel from beneath his
single tenament.

The tormented Tom trembled like a pillar-monk as
the woman administered a stick of gelignite into her
flourishing Vulva.

A piece of primus served as the reminder.
His whole body convulsed like a fever pitched caldera
and his lungs finally gave out with a clatter.

The impact of his spasm rattled against the ramp.
Her gaze whistled to the interstice with a mixture of
dismay and outright loathing.

The sheep-rustler stumbled verbosely back to his
nefarious kingdom as Mary arrived like grease
lightening.

Glancing hungrily through the palings with the prong
in her hand the gradgrind hissed abuse as he limped
semi-naked over the threshold, and *whipped down* his
drawbridge.

A fracar developed in the living-room that
summer's afternoon...

Her robust thighs soon straddled across his skrawny
chest.
"Worry, worry, worry...that's all you ever bring
me," she fretted.
She tugged up her skirt and made the dog beg for
mercy. One thing led to another....
"This meat tastes awful!" he cried. But she still
forced him to eat her revolting *dungkebabs* from the
dinner plate. Cornflower blue Pretty baby.
"What did you say to me? What did you dare say to
me?" she fulminated. With gyring eyes the she-devil
thrashed and nevelled on his bole. Her hair-piece
nearly slid-off in the struggle.
He winced against the source of the adamantine
which shone from the bay window above him. Was he
becoming allergic to high frequency interference?
"You will go to the toilet when I tell you!" she
fumed. "How dare you call your own mother a blot on
the landscape! I'll teach you to answer me back."
Her dank and lifeless roots hung like a cobweb.
A freckled face appeared from their modest garden
tottering on the brick and whispered words of
childlike censure at the glass.
Mary continued to pull his hair in clumps completely
unaware her niece had been knocking meekly at the latch.
"That'll teach you to retaliate!" she blasted.
"Come with me up to the bathroom where you will learn
to do your business properly!"
When Mary instinctively turned the girl slipped
hurriedly away, feeling guilty for intruding on their
family's secret ritual.
"There, you've gone and shown yourself up once
again!" Just typical.
To cover her tracks Mary raced for the mouthpiece.
Yolande hesitated on the cave of Adullum with
'Swallows and Amazons'- Arthur Ransome.
"What on earth was your mother doing? I'll go
straight home if I've arrived at an inopportune moment."
"I'm afraid that I broke wind," sniffed Mathew
despondently. His cousin drifted down the avenue with
her head bent.

In a matter of minutes the heavy duty Joiner was
pelting over the log-jam in a fit of moorish temper.
He dive-bombed his nephew with an ash-tray from
his flying carpet. Another flashy motor.
"Just wait till I get ahold of him!"
Mary spectated on the step above him as
trumpet-tongued Uncle Bobby targeted his man.
'Kick seven bells of shit out of him.'
He rattled the blackball venomously against the
fake wood panelling above the gas miser. His
dovetail-joint was completely turned to stone beside
the vulgar print. Hark the kettle calling the pot
black. On the never-never, off to never-never land.
"I'm so glad you're here," she sobbed.
"I'm terrified he's going to wind-up just like his
father. I'm not going to be treated like that in my
own home," she sneered. "I'm the boss around here,"
she hissed. It's as plain as day.
Mathew's paltry frame shivered like a matchstick
kite as the circus strongman battened down the hatches
with his rigid torso.
Gallant Sir Gal-a-had Woodentop gave the sub-human
type the third degree with a lighted brand. Have you
been doing anything you shouldn't have?
Taking Mathew by the throat he mummered the rag
doll with the blonde hairs bristling on the back of
his bulldog neck and threw him single handed over the
sofa by his scruff.
The tongue-tied adolescent could feel spit
showering down his cheek and flower petals capsize
from their stalks on the windowledge.
"After all your mother's done for you!" he railed.
"If you touch her again I'll bash you so hard that
what grey matter you do possess will run out of your
ears."
His teak finger prodded at his clavicle.
"How do you like it!" he screeched. "Not even worth
a fucking wank," he snarled.
Gloating with undisguised glee the little concubine
emerged from the closet on the day her master is
pleased.

"You're not a man!" she ridiculed. "You're
inadequate in every way!" Must be half-fairy?
     The second-dan blasted out a hundred press-ups on
the spot to emphasize the point. Leaning with only
one arm to support himself on the floor he lifted the
matchbox from the carpet using only his two front teeth.
     "Until you can find some digs of your own treat your
mother with respect!"

Brazenly supining in the armchair Gretel considered it
rather strange that her brother was so enthusiastic to
brew a pot of the brown liquid when they usually fought
like cat and dog.
     She scanned her latest copy of 'Mind' on a rare
parochial cadge to wet her social graces. He counted
the ear-rings on her lobe as she drew on the stem of
her weed.
     She dredged her first sip from the firebrand to the
frou-frou of his silken utterances.
     "Uugh! tastes a bit funny!" she cringed. "What have
you put in it?"
     "Arsenic!" he joked. "Something to make you sleep
better."
     He gnawed impatiently at his fingernails.
She seemed to be ready for bed until a klaxon awoke
the echoes.
     "What are all the curtains doing on?" she spluttered.
"It's still daylight outside and they'll think we're
rather quaint. I'm feeling well and truly fucked."
"I'm going up to my room. When the bitch comes back
tell her I don't want to be disturbed."
     After only twenty minutes the intruder streaked
in hot pursuit.
     He entered the ensorcelled nunnery in the coolness
of mid-day having negotiated the creaking of the
tollgate.
     A gluttonous twinge knotted in his stomach as her
arm dangled limply over the abyss. That awful
stillness dug a pit in his cranium as he knelt beside
her soiled garments. Try one on for size. Couldn't
care less where she dumped her chattels.

He congratulated himself on his chicanery and ventured
to check her pulse. Thank the unknown god for
Alice-Eva...and her Temazepam! He paused.
     Even as the crumbs still lingered in the lining of
her belly a drop of his fluid suffered death and was
buried.
     With the levin neatly in his grip he lurched toward
the furnishing deep within. The most well-endowed
sneck dipped its wick.
     'God bless mummy, god bless daddy, please forgive
me when I'm bad.'
     Suddenly she stirred from her kip.
She fixed her features in a mosaic of absolute
repugnance.
     "What are you doing in here without my permission?"
she sobstuffed.
     "The Fire Engine is making overtures!"
he stammered.
     It was indeed true that the atmosphere had become
densely nephological.
     "I left the chip pan unattended!"
"Piss off!" she stonewalled. "I'll never forgive you
as long as I live," she promised.

Buckfast Abbey had been the village school for over a
hundred years until it was obtained for the Grammar
school out of Catholic funds.
     The wizard wheeze quickly peregrinated the
refectory at tiffin.
     "Moonighan can't eat his Cornflakes Miss! He's a
fucking headcase!"
     Staff and students alike sniggered the length of
the hippophagy. Even his oral vibrator had suffered
a technical hitch.
     A loud roar erupted as he tipped the contents of
the spoon down his chest and dribbled the cereal
over his spotty chin.
     "What is wrong with you Moonighan?" leered Blondie.
"Are you off your bleeding rocker?"
     Fatso placed his arm around his neck and
pretended to smooch with the grey man.

The clockwork hand sprung mechanically to his
defence as he blushed down to his ankles.

There had been a short-circuit in the master's
study and a heap of *faeces* had been found centred
on his matress.

When the Cyclop's jeep departed for the country all
the windows had fallen from their mountings.

The garvie's name was of course only obscurely
linked with this at first, but the tenuous gossip soon
became a natural reality.

The clansmen charged to wet their lips while he was
left to write a hundred lines.

An hour later Ryan returned with a pint of mother's
ruin.

He apologized for spilling some of the contents on
the two mile trek Ogging from the *Roebuck*.

"Still, what's normal!" he interceded.
"But what is normal?" he asked. Then there was Mary...

In the very beginning there had been those high noon
excursions sprinting from the shower area in her
birthday suite...until it seemed perfectly normal?

Then there had been the clamorous fizz of her
poppling bladder and the smell of her emancipated urine
permeating the neon as she squatted with her legs wide
apart above the scullery bucket. She always emptied
the contents down the sink.

"Do you have to relieve yourself in the kitchen when
we have a perfectly functioning toilet in the
bathroom?" he'd asked her.

"Oh, you are a prude Mathew," she laughed. "You'll
never be attractive to women while you still hold with
this puritanical attitude."

But it was still a shock to rouse oneself and find
her fopping over his headboard. Was Mary going slowly
potty; she hid it under her pallet?

Ryan repeated the words of the pretty schoolteacher
reclining in Blondie's lap.

"Miss Nowall agrees with everyone else. You need to
see a shrink. She said that you have *'all the charm of
a country yokel combined with the sexual allure of a
maculated scarecrow!'*"

When Mathew crossed the parlour a pair of Picasso
nudes were lounging on the mugwort with their crayons.
His immediate impulse was to bolt up the stairs to his
hide-out. They had been out climbing Capel Curig.

The belly-dancers continued their dissertation as
if he were almost invisible. 'All night long,' she
sighed. Ran like a stream down her leg.

In her self-communing hagiography Mary adumbrated
the immensity of her leakages lying on the level
beside the pottery tutor.

She bared her teeth and congratulated herself
once again on the perfect splendour of her spotless
dentures. Apparently 'he,' Mathew, was no oil painting.

Chance and contingency were luridly linked to
some other casual acquaintance. Allergic to every
brand of perfume. Lived on a pittance.

There sounded plenty of opportunity on the campus
but the *ne'er-do-well* wavered on the horns of a dilemma.

On the *feast of Ramadan* while the spirit of Ganesh
trampled the shoots beneath his bulk the restless
insomnia gradually subsided into real estate.

As the luminous hands of the Westclox decoyed the
conscious senses he leap-frogged the portcullis of
the sandman.

Suddenly he awoke in the black night with the sweat
pumping between his rib cage...the moon was white hot
silver and the sun was dressed in weepers.

The hideous sound of retching down below threw him
into a gargoyle, as the shape of a midinette wailed
like a bat out of hell from his sluice.

The sluggish eyes of his unfocused gaze
pandiculated her endeavour as the duffy cascaded over
the tampon. Needed an iron for its skin.

With a guilty curse Grendel's mother disappeared
into the woodwork clasping nothing but her nipples and
her tonsured crutch. Her dank and lifeless hair
slumped without its blow-dry.

"Oh! my God!" the hag lamented.
Antelope flying express train.

He reached for the *precious thing* perched in the corner
of that sombre iron lung.

Undisturbed beyond the ochreous newsheet rested a
teeny-weeny smattered tinderbox.

Its vignette was still patterned by an engraving of
mute white swans.

He scratched the faded enamel and finally sprung
the catch.

On the head of a pin the chintz caspsule was
removed and pedantically unwrapped, so as not to
disturb the delicate contents preserved deep within
doors.

A nostalgic momento since his first growth of hair...
curled in a chestnut wisp as fine as the day it was
cleaved.

He gently lifted the Baby curl and placed it into
the palm of his hand, appraising the vulnerable
threads which reminded him of blighty.

At the twang of the charwomen's undercurrent his
ticker raised the alarm.

He bounded down the basement steps and clambered
over the crape to peer up the coal-grate.

XIV

THE WHITER SHADE OF PALE

A knock at the porch caused the greenhorn to rise
impatiently from the wainscot and a break in his
solitary star gazing.

He answered the persistent interloper who simply
wouldn't see sense and dictated once more to the *cuckoo
clock*.

"It's only half past ten," he stated. "That means
that you have only been gone for five minutes when I
specifically declared the minimum period. I'll play
with you later when she has passed water. You can only
return when the big hand is at twelve."

Time dangles and the pendulum swings, but still the
boy looked puzzled. Why was she always the lucky one?

"Are you blind?" he chided. "Can't you understand a
single blinking word?" Stanley had always compelled
the little one's attention to detail.

While the three foot tall minikin reclined on the
ermine her brother was escorted safely towards the
neighbourhood fence.

In the hallway the Joiner's plane and spirit-level
angled up the skirting.

Her snow-driven bloomers were hung on a twig of the
vibrant asphidistra soaring at the weighing scales.
Eagerly anticipating the belated guerdon piecemeal the
numinous host squirmed and gleamed in thrall-like ways.

He immediately ordered the removal of her dummy.
"Good girl Pixie!" he grinned. "Are you going to be
well behaved today? What a little treasure you are;
Mummy will be proud when she arrives home from the
little hours."

"Tail!" she whinged. "Touch him again...will you?"
Dash! Dash! He was just about to...

The flat leather football crashed against the garage
door and rebounded against the pebbledashing showering
its chippings onto the window ledge.

He flogged on the frosted glass.

"Lie across the deck!" he vituperated.

He lewdly lowered his garments once more and resumed the hourly routine in the missionary position.

Her naked matchstick legs opened instinctively as his gorgon penis throbbed excrutiatingly with the iron.

Its bulbous knob jowled assiduously against her scarlet orifice. Never again would his wand of office pulse with such an excess of brazen vigour.

"Nice!" she shivered. "It feels lovely."

She tilted her head from the fundus cloud.

"Put finger in hole?" she asked. His fledgeling twitched.

Pixie twisted the dark strands of cotton elflock between her tiny stubs and removed her other hand from where it had been hugging the greater thickness of his stem.

She placed her loving arm around the teddy bear lying snugly at her side as he paraded full frontal along her length.

"Put it right in there!" she smiled.

Her exiguous nippers raced to fan out her moistened piss-flaps. 'Her clitoris was shining like a runny nose,' he observed. How in damnation at that juncture when she hadn't even started term at the kindergarten.

He glared at her with a shy disapproval.

After only a few seconds he removed the antenna glistening with warm aroma and utilized its properties as a barometer. 'An easterly breeze,' he deemed.

Pixie's bright blue eyes clouded over and twinkled wetly with a grateful resonance. She sucked the bitter pill with avaricious buds.

His bald penis jinked like a marking buoy as she noted the strawberry stain. All good quacks take their temperature?

She toyed sentimentally with the ear of her favourite plaything.

"Rub!" she cadged. "Rub me with your tail until he spits." Where had she got that from?!!!

Pixie was never content to play second fiddle to 'his' sheep's eyes.

Stimulated by her delicateness he leaned forward to sniff the pungent odour of her puerile crevice...suddenly the alarm bells rang!

The ridgel hand of Gordon cranked down the tollgate in their rear.

"Why is she taking so long for a *wee-wee*?" he barked.

At the same instant his auntie's car skidded to a halt on the tarmac.

The timekeeper scurried to place their house in order.

He led Pixie quickly into the playpen wearing only her shirt top and threatened her with the fires of Domdaniel.

"No tell-tales!" he sponsored.

She chaffed her eyelid with the back of her paw. With real tears flooding down her cheeks she swayed and nearly lost her balance.

Pixie was subpoenaed on the banks of the Lethe that the *age of innocence* was still on the cards.

The youth bustled her brother out of the room and ordered him to watch *the deliberations of Dougal*. He flung on the micro-wave oven.

"No tell Mummy...no tell Mummy lies!" she whimpered. "Never dare to talk to strangers," he scowled...

Heroin addiction? Temporary abhoration. I can handle it: identity crisis.

What if she should spill the beans? So many *good intentions*. Summer holydays. Skeletons in the cloakroom.

"Have I committed a mortal or a venial sin?" he wondered. "I'm sorry Jesus...but I hate you God!" he blanched.

Paroxisms of fear. A vague idea pollinated on the pangs of boredom...the *lost tribe of Tyre*.

His aunty came giggling into the bungalow while her toyboy from the playscheme drooped on the passenger seat. Worn out we should imagine.

"Boys will be boys," she joked.

Esmerelda mark 2 returned with the fried chicken and her gift of a smutty Aubrey Beardsley.

"Can I get you anything else? There's a kipper in the
freezer. You only have to ask."

On the first catch of his maiden voyage he avoided
the daemon's rich temptations presented to himself and
resigned his lucrative perquisites to old Blinker.

The fun-loving dental nurse fidgeted nervously beside
him on the sofa.

Suddenly there was a cry. Mathew heard his auntie
call as she fell headlong to the floor clutching the
ironing cover.

Lifting her dark head to rest gently in his arms the
tentative hero closely scrutinized her baby doll face
(like a juvenile lead).

Beads of perspiration formed below her hairline.
He noticed almost at once how the top two buttons of
his auntie's blouse were undone, revealing the white-
plumed cleavage rising and shivering with her breath.
They pressed together like a pair of generous twins.

Her buxom load slid urassailably down to the carpet
where the plump eisteddfod remained there pretty
motionless.

Her red and pouting lips, smothered with a fresh
coat of paint, slowly carte-blanched wider, the crust
clinging slightly as they parted, and a dessicate
dribble of saliva from the corner of her mouth
glittered suggestively as he hesitated.

Should he fill it with a bulbous type of wedge?
The open hold offered itself seductively to his
thoughts as her insensata hand tugged the skirt of his
toga virilis. He glanced uncertainly over her span
where the line of teeth had been ripped asunder. 'That
was a fine heap of bullion,' he had to acknowledge.

Still the woman forgot to stir. Mathew fumbled with
the rip-cord of her Levi.

Should he just shout for a real life doctor?
The wench began to make sounds. Her eyes gazed back
into his like a lost echo. She must have been codding
all along by the compass of it!

"I've been feeling dizzy all morning but don't let
on to Harold," she murmurred.

He woke beside the gas miser with his head buried in
the armchair to find the winter gloom had already
darkened the living room. Gland fluid had trickled
embarrassingly into the crease as Mary and Gretel
taciturnly counted the cost. He attempted to disguise
the hard-on which always mysteriously erupted,
especially on the bus. Squeeze her zits. Chlorinate
the looking-glass with scrim.

"Get a move on lazy bones!" she snapped. "My friend
is waiting and she's already rung up once."

Dashing for his jacket the "ugly long haired lout"
hurried over the threshold. With *the 'Best of Cream'*
tucked underneath his arm he fled from the lair of the
pea-worm. He rocked unevenly over the cobbles of the
ring towards the large Victorian quintain.

To be honest Mathew had been taken aback by that
bizarre story which had reached him on the grape vine.

Apparently she had suddenly decided to scythe her
chignon with the dress-making shears.

Pixie had been discovered trying to thumb a lift to
town with a trucker. Surely they couldn't connect
anything with him? He'd grown shifty-eyed. Perhaps
the dye had been cast from the word "Go!"

Wetting the bed, again. Gordon. Mary said.

"Hiya, Archie Passwater..."

"*Drugs Overdose!*" he stated categorically and rapped
on the latch.

The actress of the house offered him a Special Brew
from the cabinet in the meantime...

In those days a strange metamorphosis was occurring in
the young man. With unwelcome side-effects the youth
soldiered on...loitering like a Pigman on the stairs
with the lustful water drooling in his funnel and
swelling his turgent penis.

By demon theop-neustry he listened fiendishly at the
nadir of the shaft to their voices whispering urgently
with the pangs of thirst. From down below something
rotten gripped the bannister rail with a creak, a
cringe and a curl...

"I don't like him do you?" she wailed. "He comes when
we're asleep, and stands at the side of our double.
Don't go to sleep will you?" she begged him. Her
brother assented and agreed with her whole heartedly.

"Put a knot in your pillow and don't forget to look
out." Give him a thick ear...

Who was that trembling at obscure heights? Who
dared to crouch in the basement prowling deep in the
fog? His huge pointed ears flapped like a spanker as
he curst for them to slumber and flesh come into
season.

With baited breath the white-faced ghoul climbed
with extra caution the creaking steps to Eden. His
foot hovered above the penultimate obstacle before
ploughing over the abyss.

Under the torch in the dark medieval cellar the
German shepherd sniffed adroitly at the banana door.
She was safely chained below the salon so there would
be no 'tender mercies' from her hastate fangs.

Cerberus shook the spectre with a hideous howl. Her
groyne was longer than a length of soggy bog paper.

On the level from the fusty pristine hills of
perdition the creeping thing scrambled over his
mountain pass towards the Green Goddess.

He traversed the Gamehunter's cobwebbed trophies
glaring amid the battlements where he was born that
chilling night. His eerie shadow humped along the path
until he discovered the gem of a second water for which
he had been dowsing.

Through the eye of a needle Grendel's enormous beak
and uncanny grin loomed over the lintel and peered
round the cream faced surface of their chamber.

His precedence was followed not long after by his
sickly bloodshot eyes and albino palour.

The vile shape-shifter entered beyond the Pale of
their portal and floated over their slumbering bodies
in the full moonlight to place the powder mirror to her
nose. Look behind you!

His silhouette chuckled delightedly on observing the
reems of joyous censer (using scotopic vision.)

He turkeyed beside their delicious purring to broach a
victorious snigger before mounting the pile of
catalogues carefully laid out as part of the course.
The familiar perfume which andanted their girdle seemed
to torque a flock of seagulls fluttering round his top.

Flinging away the redundant motifs of inhibition he
rapidly increased his pace from reef to whirlwind.

Like the shade of a submarine pilot his malicious
haunting often lasted for imagined eons.

Grendel 'Noseforartil' breathed a sigh of relief
through his quivering nostrils and semaphoring with
glee carefully rolled the sheet over Benny's pigment
deficiency.

"Come on my beauty," he lewdly whispered and weighed
her corpselike limb like a trough.

Foaming at the mouth the lurid Clown with a Talcum
mask of white tugged the remainder of the nightdress
from inside her anal crevice.

With a faint simper he removed the raven cloak which
flowed like a lunar gale around his skrawny frame and
danced as if his feet were capped in acid.

Like a 'praying mantis' the midnight necrophiliac
leant over the ripe fruit fallen from grace which
submissively supined for his obdurate mausoleum.

The sconce of pearl cascading through yonder
skylight illuminated his naked body into flakes of rice
and flour. White pride, worldwide!

With keen appreciation he discovered Brigitte's
genial plasma to be surprisingly warm and accomodating.

Between the gemini knolls of her cushion his cutlass
throbbed from the new sensation, clinging to his weapon
under the dulcet moon.

It beat seeing her clip-clopping round in high-
heels. Any-day.

As his incisors of chalk chattered unstoppably with
'Huntingdon's Chorea' Grendel redirected his glance
sharply toward the innocents appealing visage.

He placed his hand over her eyes.

He combed her darling hair with his long goarish fingernails, titillating supererrogatively with the argentine chudder and patting her affectionately on the shoulder with his clammy device, before boring deeper into her behind.

But what was this peculiar tingling sensation germinating near the neap in the pits of his groin? The feeling spread and centred on his glans...as la dolce vita pressed ever more enjoyably into the plump vices of her blistering skin.

His organ peeled back similar to the fleece of ripe fruit. Who in heaven's name ranted in the pulpit and how in Gimle did the Cabalust wamble in the dreamtime.

A teratitical craving deepened into a piston pumping, and before the daviant knew what was transpiring a bounding spurt of jissom exploded from the tip of Gae Boleg.

He leapt in the air like a startled rabbit. The guardian hollered from the nether regions as the planethood moaned southwards.

His skewer showered through all points of the globe. Splattering each article in rapine; the engine running exhaustively until the fuel subsided, the monkey speeding rapturously up the chimney like cork from a gun. "So who's the Governor now!"

Convulsing like pulp in a blast Grendel cautiously returned to scoop up his oil into the rightful capital.

He had a good idea what the emission might be, but by no means was he certain of the connotation.

Scurrying from the limelight the rabid monster discarded his magic talma at the foot of their post where the prints were completely white-washed.

Brigitte stirred and turned over to pull at Benny's share.

She gave a low-key nag and whimpered tiredly until eventually she obtained her desire.

From the corridoor their *Dark Angel* scouted back and forth on tip-toe. In loco parentis.

Grendel hankered for a chance to rematerialize and sponge away his crime.

Like a sea constantly trying to make its bed he fretted ill at ease in case the couple should examine the snitch baby is under torchlight.

With his garments at half-mast he vowed never to relapse while the house was still blighted and thin at the roots.

The salubrious arrival of their car headlights careering up the drive forestalled the second helpings which this further mumbo jumbo warranted.

Stealing grist from the mill he grubbed the disturbed filaments of the occupation until the inebriate newlyweds entered along the landing.

'Had he been in a hurry from ablutions?' she procrastinated, staring in a downward manner.

The mistress of the establishment relaxed in Fabian conversation while the lambustrious 'Braddock Bull' attempted to stampede her up to slats huffing and puffing in his Boxer shorts.

"Don't get shirty with me!" she railed..."Are you so fucking cocksure?"

Checking that the babes were safe and well he returned with Brigitte who couldn't sleep. She was dressed in her pink-frilled nightdress and her cheeks were glowing with incense. Often had 'bad dreams.'

"Mummy I've just seen a ghost at the bottom of my bed!" she insisted.

Her father assured her that everything was splendid in their turret. The token white gay-guy.

Lifting his daughter for a fond hug from his wife the sleepy-eyed girl was then encouraged to give Mathew a kiss. She thanked him for his fourth dimension until he could come again.

"He's got one just like my dad!" she suddenly blurted with absolute certainty. Oh, crumbs. Husband and wife began flirting. Then the daughter was carried back up the stairs on her father's pigtail.

Mathew reclined beneath her like a scalped royal. "Did we have any unexpected callers?"

"Do you have a girlfriend?" the woman meekly enquired. She seemed amused as Mathew coloured.

"Why ever not?" she asked.
"I can fix you up with my assistant Annabelle," she offered..."Shall I arrange a definite date then?"
"How would you like to begin an apprenticeship in my hairdressing business?"
"She's not pretty enough," he sneered. "I don't fancy her! She's only seventeen and I prefer older women..."
However much he admired the blonde in her short mini-skirt it did not entirely justify the founding of a traditional new sect.
"I'll run you home love," she insisted. "Of course it's no trouble when the Rakehell is over the limit."
They strolled to the white 'Roller' in the silver edged mist, ploughing through the centre of town and into the seedier regions.
"Well, aren't you going to give me a goodnight smooch?" smiled Edwina.
He reached quickly for the handle of the buckboard and slammed down the catch.

Intoxicant! Cyanide of Cythera; corrosive sublimate, tempter God, corrupter of the hundred percent. Why once captured can you never release the milksop?
Even when 'nanna' was called in to replace him many moons later he connived his devious entrance with beansprout. How philanthropic was the magic mushroom!
The 'washer' woman with puckered lips assayed for his erogenous zone as he knelt on the carpet below her thrashing tongue.
She could stroke and fondle his neck while he buffed his gnarled cat's paw over the raised purple ridges of her *varicose veins*.
Alice-Eva pitched like a corsair before accepting the red-hot neve as tolerable. 'Cold hands, warm heart' etc. She whispered like an old tart in a pub doorway...
"You don't look at the mantelpiece while you're poking the fire!" she suddenly counselled. And then..."Many a good tune is played on an old violin..."
What in heaven's name was the fatty suggesting?

Her awry profile just reminded him of *Mother Shipton* as the bulbous dome shivered over the obtuse trunnion of the alimentary canal.
"You're exceedingly lucky to have a best friend like Ryan Starbuck," she enjoined.
The nervous cadet feigned a flimsy palliation to mount the forbidden string of scales up an extra storey. Was there no end to this audacity?
"I'm just going to see a man about a dog. I won't be long!" he promised. His grandmother seemed to sense a rat was cooking...

The creature sniffed impetuously at their thin red line as the yellow rectangle below the border revealed they had not been long hitting the matress.
Alice-Eva hobbled down below as he shuffled urgently forward with his prayer-mat. The low-flyer pressed his palm over his mouth to prevent further sibilations.
Under the blistered craters of the argent plane Grendel 'Brass-hat' executed his meanful trick.
He perused the pillowmorph joined at the hip with the stealth and hypnotic stance of a bummer from the black lagoon.
Closing the vault behind him to shove the world of men beyond he peeled the blanket from his favourite breeding place. Hard fast asleep again!
Brigitte's cerise and pouting lips offered themselves to his unbridled lust, but first he gently removed the restrictive practice of her thumb; there was no room for foreign objects when Nosferatil's cartilage ached to stuff itself inside the limited recess.
With the bluffened pencil-point he drew her breath while infanta grumbled and protested in her bye-byes.
Hook-nose prematurely celebrated. How peaceful he would subsequently snooze for once...the rising scent of their rich bouquet blurred his brain and made his senses reel.
With an adroit flick of his tool Grendel jammed the weapon into the beckoning gap.

She yawned and gripped his gorgon stem in her mumbling
entrance.

She gipped and struggled with his increased tunnage.
A line of consternation creased across her brow.
Motioning her lips to the rhythm of the wands she
tightly squeezed his creaming gondoliers and admitted
half his plum by gradual consent.

Throwing caution to the wind Grendel gave a gleeful
shriek. He charged once more against her echinate
dentures which tickled his oversensitive glans.

While she chomped around his choking trunk he
patiently climaxed in a matter of seconds for a full
two minutes riot...

The starry eyes of Little Bo-Peep quickly ate their
flame as he laid a shilling under her hassock.

His nectar cruised along the crotchet and cascaded
over the corner of her mouth before dripping into her
ladle.

With obvious disgust she laundered the stub of orts
on her sleeve presuming it to be a jam of her own.

Through the candid rails of their cot her large
brown eyes rapidly clicked their shutter.

She jumped like a parched pea to discover it resting
against the woodwork.

Something in the nature of the beast alarmed her
fixed attention. But her eyes could not draw away even
slouching on his lap. The family pet laid a lick on
his bell-end.

Brigitte grasped her tentacles close against her
chin and attempted to break the spell by tapping on his
shoulder.

"Go to sleep!" he heckled. "Daddy will be back soon
and mummy will be cross to find you still alive and
kicking."

He tremoured silently to the bathroom for a cold
rush of spring. There was the patter of tiny feet.

Suddenly her micron was standing in the doorway
pleading for a drink.

He'd lucre what he could and see if nature careened
its seedy course.

There was even an attempt to rebuff his slide between
her rug.

Meanwhile an oven fire was creeping up the
wallpaper; the supper had caught alight while Grendel
enjoyed his spurious banquet in the bowels of the
Alpine earth.

He came bolting down the fire escape whipping up his
flies. Would he still be committed for arson if he
relinquished ownership of their inner sense?

The Iron lady was adamant that if it had not been for
his mother she would have called the Flying Squad.

The estranged family had recently retired upstairs when
Eileen Fairchild offered to watch the late night serial
with him...even though Mary had summoned him early to
bed. Riding on the crest of a wave.

'It's far too late in the day for swotting.'
In those Halcyon days she appeared extra grim in the
presence of this loving Catholic household although the
long separation was still hanging in the balance.
Danny had been moonlighting at wise Arthur Browns.

The four-foot eleven-inch elf curled up happily in
the armchair as Carmel proceeded from the lounge to
wish them both goodnight. Seventy moons Swalabr.
Never in a million years.

"God bless and give heaven thanks."
She dipped her hand at the door and made a sign of the
cross through the back of her bone. Her sister would
be returning later from the Ram's head.

Somewhere in time her daughter plunged into the
waters of oblivion beside her near relation. Her
defunct remains were about to have a close encounter of
the Grendel kind it seemed.

Her bell, book, and candle flickered like a sanguine
creature as the television screen turned into ether.
With a raidate 'ping' the imprint fell dark with his
hand on the remote control button. Application tended
for growth hormones.

Past like a summer cloud the dermatologically
disadvantaged youth had overcome his grit in the
ointment.

Uncatchable as the Surrey puma he tamed the hissing
babble to focus on the piece of primary lamb...and
entered the twilight zone in seven league boots
sporting an unfashionable skinhead.

He swiftly assessed the tweed texture of her grey
schoolskirt between his fingers before hauling the
material slyly upward. Her cover was rucked so far
that he could squinny the great beyond. Her pink
thighs were riddled with goosepimples.

A slight trace of emotion rippled over her otherwise
motionless exterior as he prodded and poked in her
levin.

He struck his telegraph pole on the cohering skin of
her form and percussioned over the cheesegrating studs.

To reach her mouth drooling toward the flying geese
he would have to kneel on the rickety stool. He always
rose to the top. The caped-crusader.

Suddenly the back gate slammed and footsteps echoed
down the passageway. Fingers tapped on the window
where he had forgotten to pull the curtains. Why did
he just stand there frozen like a lump of lard? If
they caught him he was likely to be struck-off.

He feverishly fished out the keys from the drawer
and fiddled with the light-switch.

"I can explain," he coughed. "She is suffering from
a clear case of mental amnesia."

Mathew jolted awkwardly to the hatch holding a
magazine to furnish his gross embarrass-ment.

The Doctor shook her violently from the deep
hypnotic trance and she slowly regained consciousness.
But the beast was not to be thwarted...

Hidden deep in the wardrobe Grendel perlustrated the
princess as she undressed below the two-tone highlights
of the stroboscope lamp.

He peered into the vertical slice of icterus
striking down his forehead, and only when her chamber
was painted over did he emerge dressed in blue silk
gown and turban.

He paused above the pallaver once only for voices
raised in anger to subside once more to calm...

and woke to butter melting on the two tablets of toast.

His eyes skated quickly over her occurance and
casually nodded his absolutions.

Eileen's smooth fingertips had been drenched in the
waters of life.

Not a blotch nor a smear silted her virgin white
epidermis.

She giggled immaculately and trotted gaily from his
room with the tray.

Now a member of the exclusive troupe, the membership
fee of which she was totally unaware...

Lord of the flying trap-eaze!

£   £   £

'Swallows and Amazons forever'

There was hail shower stunning the opening...it was
four o'clock and the bell had just sounded its spell
down the river. Its ring sent the girls racing over
the slipstream from *Holy-croft*.

She rested her arm on the wire.
"Is it alright if I bring my little sister to play with
you. She's got a new pencil case and wants to see your
puppy so long as we don't miss our bus again."

Mathew smiled. Cross-eyed Mary would be another
twenty minutes arriving home from Temple street. The
sorority dorm had been prepared in ready expectation of
their wager.

From that very first instant he plotted their escape
together and chose rake-boned Stella to do all the
counting.

"Hey, no cheating!" he ordered. "Face to the wall
and do it properly in *elephants*."

With high anxiety he marched the young one up the
winding spiral of the tower. In the *wonderful land* all
dreams could be made possible; that much was certain.
He led the soft and tender thing gently by her hand.

"If a body catch a body coming through the rye," he
chachinated. How did that old song go? "Let's go and
see what Santa Claus has brought you for Christmas," he
jested. Let's play 'Bless your neighbour?'

"Do we have to go all the way up here?" she stilted.
Gerda stood on tip-toe to reach the door knob....the
more distance put between them the better. He could
still hear the whippet methodically verifying her
numbers as he closed the escape hatch securely behind
him. And living right next door to you!

His tongue dragged over the stairs as he followed in
her wake and his breath scorched the roof of his mouth.
The pretty wood nymph hopped those cedar steps to the
top of the world and entered *Hy Brasil* with *stars in
her eyes*. Lord of the 'flying-trap-ease!'

126

As the twilight played tricks on the wardrobe mirror
shadow fell in the early glimmer of the fall. By a
slip of fate the *prince of spades* was aided by a
fracture of the space-time continuum. The motley youth
demonstrated to the miner his *compendium of illicit
instructions*.

Garlanded she knelt before the royal personage, the
innocent, the sacrificial offering, eager to please and
drooping her head as he commanded...ducking down lower
towards his lap where the dragon-head rose above the
surf like a gorbelly of gnarled oak. The 'Chargeman'
tensed as he noted Stella calling distantly below...at
the bottom of a well.

"Coming, ready or not...! Are you safely hidden
yet?"

Her crackle of musketry plummeted helter-skelter
back down the stairs to the sandy embankment leaving
them to their communion in peace after admitting defeat
with the stiff iron lock.

"That's the last we'll see of the chaser tonight,"
grinned the overman. He pressed his hands flatly
together.

"Shall we say grace?"
A sparse gush of flame groaned from the Gothic window
brace nearby as the *Top 'Odd* fizzled squeamishly then
gave up the ghost. He positioned her closer to his
rule and screwed the words ecstatically from his
throat.

"Decant, and slide it through your fingers," he
softly stipulated.

Her yellow mop sank deliciously to make contact.
She sneezed...

"God bless you!" he hailed. "Remember that your
saucer eyes should be shut and your warm hands should
be pressed around the hod like so."

She settled for one of her mits, finding it
necessary to use the other limb to martial her support.

"Keep your head still," he earnestly directed...he
struggled to straighten the deviator whose feather soft
cheek rested tentatively against the purple plume of
his pimples.

127

"Now turn your head slightly...no! Back another inch."
he remanded. "Put your lips directly over the
spot....yes! Just like that!" He brailed his lids and
quacked-out gratuitously.

Somewhere in the restaurant 'Freddie' was surveying
the menu. "Lower down the drawbridge." he coarsely
muttered. "It's open!" she reported.

Should he ask her to perform the ultimate task for
her *grandmaster*? Well, he'd journeyed so far, so why
not go the whole hog?

"I can feel you now." he felicitated. "Lick the
hood and taste the crab-apple." Her sensation rattled
the flag. The vertical range of the depth charges were
immeasureable.

Her white unblemished cornea loitered over the
erection awaiting his categorical imperative.

"Place me in your cavity!" he suggested rather
matter of factly.

Gerda swallowed the hulk right up to her hilt and
coasted him to the back of her gullet.

But the immediate stampede of horses heralded the
emergence of the richly saturated soup alive with cells
and vitamins, and that would give the game away.

She suddenly raised her angel head and squeaked. He
cursed her frustratingly short attention span.

"I know what this is!" she blurted
unequivocably...but it was too late; she'd *swallowed
the evidence*! Bad digestion?

"How old are you? What sort of music do you like?"
she inquired.

The chinky-eyed manikin with libidinous eyes focused
insistently on his hirsute pouch, curiously awakened,
and rolled her giant tongue lewdly around the wooden
edge of the measuring stick, before penetrating.

Mathew could not help noticing a 'bleg' which had
lodged itself in the entrance to her left nostril;
although it was not this unsavoury aspect which damned
Stella from ever obtaining a visa to his tunnel of
love...

128

He observed with incongruity that the senior citizen
was now wearing a tight fitting pair of blue jeans
inconsistent with her status. He detected a crooked
outline similar to her mother's shabby coathanger of
ribs.

There was a flapping and beating of wings.
Mary arrived carrying her easel with the identical
twins swinging their rackets. One 'has been,' and one
'may-be-was,' it transpired.

"Anyone for tennis?" called Marissa on their way to
the courts. He answered in gibberish.

The manikin was far to plain. Worse than that the
minor girl appeared far too bloody eager...

He listened in the hallway as Mary bellowed down the
phone to her mother.

"Well then, don't send her again," she screamed.
"I'm far too busy and I don't want them here e-v-e-r-y
single night. I've more important concerns to cope
with."

Mathew raised his hands as if he had been held up by
Dick the highwayman.

'I'm sorry but what can I do?' He postured to
communicate in makaton.

Stella pouted sulkily, blushed, and with a wide
friendly grin exposed her finely-chiselled viaducts.

The 'leudes' swooped down from the steppe where they
had gathered round the band-stand like a tribe of
desperate Huns.

Attracted by the distinctive hum of the fan belt,
and the tryst they had agreed the previous evening, a
fresh horde of disciples entered the *Milky Way*.

The *immortals* landed spitting and fighting in the
yard. Who was going to be the first to put their hand
in his pocket this time?

Scouting furtively across the street the *old hands*
gathered randanly in the doorway with the pile of wild-
eyed new initiates who seemed curiously disorientated.

The hazy mob with milkmaid eyes settled like a row
of 'placebo's' for the entertainment to be inaugurated.

129

Ryan craftily sanctioned the proceedings. It was
agreeable that Mary had been invited to a rally or she
would undoubtedly have been rushing down the stairs for
him to pull up her zipper.

"I've got a monkey tattooed on my chest!" he
chuckled..."If you put your hand in my pocket you can
feel his tail!" he whispered.

Lucinda reached forward to plunge her hand deep into
the cunningly punctured inlet.

"Open your mouth and shut your eyes I'll give you a
big surprise!"

"If you give me a candy you can show me your
'willy'," she said.

The burlesque continued by a process of common
menticulture.

"You've got a bigger dick than him!" ,
The fair young elf blushed at her friends
precociousness and accepted his bribe of the 'Galaxy.'

"Oh, no he hasn't!" protested Mathew: but that had
always been his downfall.

"Do you want to play 'Doctors and Nurses?'"
The scruffy young urchin ran to wave at little Joe the
skipper. Conformed to fact.

"Stop peeping!" he concluded. "Close your eyes
tight shut! Do you want to do the same as Lucinda?"

"Yes, please," she meekly rejoindered. "Exactly the
same."

The passenger instinctively encroached towards his
potion.

"No, not there!" he exclaimed. "Do you want to
cause an explosion? Only further down the stem where
you can sink your teeth into the side."

"She never told me about this part!" Even though
they were from the same regiment?

The Comus grinned. There was no doubting what she
said was down to earth.

His Bobby's helmet met her with a bow.
"Hey! stop peeping again!" he warned her
angrily...well, what the eye didn't see, the mouth
couldn't gab about!

She lolled on him with penis envy flapping her arms
defiantly on the up-draft.

Again she rose from the wood. Had she had her fill
of board and lodging? Was the acrid odour repugnant to
her senses. Don't forget the tickler.

Larissa rubbed the back of her neck and straightened
her collar. But life is a roller-coaster ride!

"Can't you do anything to get a bit higher?" she
whined. "I like everything else, but all this bending
over is giving me a cramp in the neck."

Mathew pretended to strain himself upwards,
adjusting his position slightly, and returned to the
level he'd already occupied on the toilet stanchion.

"It's the same for me!" he protested, raising his
haunches as if he had back-ache. It wasn't anything
significant but the effort seemed to satisfy her. She
continued to mark the unplumbed depths but he was still
much too afraid to extravasatate.

"Could you slurp a bit harder?"
The placebo responded with increased vigour. "I'm
doing the best I can," she choked. "I can't take any
more of it!" Her eyes sparkled open once more as she
did so. As good as his word.

He thought, Oh! damn it! Forget it, just forget it!
Then he suddenly spotted her long pointed ears.

The *Comus* was on the edge of a premature ejaculation
when he burst into a fit of laughter. For they were
brighter than the burnished bulb.

He grabbed the creature roughly by the hair and
spurted repeatedly into her *auditory auricle*.

XV
GARBAGE

The school-leaver sauntered to retrieve the mail from
dakwallah, and opened the final notice from Alma Mater;

*'We wish to remind you that on leaving the sixth form
your copy of the Browning version was not returned on
clearance day. If this is not forthcoming soon we will
have no option but to prosecute. You have been warned!'*

Did this mean that a satisfactory reference was in the
pipeline?
     The Clockwork mouse had accelerated from the
catacombed building...feast your eyes on that!
     "Don't you think Mathew's rather odd!" a voice was
heard to speculate from the staff room orifice.
     "His behaviour has been most strange recently."
Maurice twisted the finger on his temple and chuckled.
     "He's turning into a real Jekyll and Hyde
character," he hummed...but one swallow didn't make a
summer! "Great job for him," he guffawed. "Down at
the poultry farm...taking blind turkeys out for shit!"

One aspect about dustcarts was the bitter taste they
drafted in your windpipe. 'Shove that in ya flipping
cakehole!' A crunt on the breastplate. Sighed Sid.
     Especially on gristswept mornings when the pack of
council tubmen ran to starboard as the lead twisted
among the cobbled streets ahead. Or hanging on the
cuffs like a clutch of bed-rabbits.
     Minced with all the foul debris and slurry the
loving spoonful felt like swallowing a containment of
red hot mustard powder.
     Every payday when it rained a paste of mud and glue
formed upon the face where an impetigo happily festered
round the eyes.

A kick from their hob-nailed boots sent rats the size
of cats fleeing from their bread-baskets on the second
layer straight into the iron-mincer's gullet.
     With rancorous greed surly General Regan gathered
all the finest mullock; to be weighed in at the end of
the week, and divided among the fortunate few on the
summit of the refuse tip.
     "We've 'ad little 'uns before who learnt to pull
their weight. Where there's muck there's brass," he
snarled.
     While the crews dashed for last orders the pariah
was still hosing down the yard at half-past three...for
a wage of nineteen pounds.
     Up in the messroom they had even thrown him in the
broomcupboard with old Ernie the 'Ratcatcher.'
     The heavy breathing faggot had begged to swallow it
in return for a fiver rolled round his...
     In a meteor flash the binmen had discovered Mathew
was still a little virgin. Then you could really hear
a pin drop!
     "Never been laid?" someone laughed. "Nobody will
ever drop them for old Snozzleconk! Who was it then?"
     He turned to ask Mathew if he was settled in his
fond vocation.
     "This isn't the job for you lad," he
cajoled..."There's a vacancy at 'Whipsnade Zoo' which
would suit you down to the ground. Why don't you apply
to go training?"
     "Wanking Elephants!" screamed the faggot grinning
caustically. "You ought to see the size of their
blooming pricks! Tha'll need a bucket for 'em." But
there were other snags...
     "You've been reprieved," snarled the cleansing
department super. "Get ya rubber gloves on!"
     Funny. Never had piano lessons like Gretel. Always
poking around in something.

It was usually only drizzling by the time they passed
the affluent 'White horse.'
     A terrace of dry stone cottages frowned from the top
of the flagstone causeway.

"Come on fucking Mathew!" groaned the old iron driver.
"Don't let Selwyn do all the frigging work again while
I'm mucking-in. You 'aint got time to spend a penny."

From the frosty pleasure garden he carried the leaky
pail tottering over the uneven steps to the *Shitwagon*
grinning on the opposite side of the wall.

The thin steel handle bit into his grip. As he
lifted the pan numerous lakhs of bran began to slide
over his bloodied hand and trickle down his neck...the
whey wheedled through the shaft as the curd churned
with ash and cinders during centrifugal motion.

Mathew covered his mouth and tried not to vomit.
In the doorway the hoary haired spinster smirked adieu
to her stools. Corn on the Cob!

"Nobody likes emptying them there *piss-pots*," he
tiraded; "but someone has to do it."

Climbing in the cabin door of the *Shitwagon* moody
old Selwyn slammed the door purposefully on Mathew's
fingers.

It was a revenge attack for an accident which made
his eyes water.

He returned once more to the primrose path of his
dotage. 'Puts fucking years on you!' he spagged.

Selwyn shook his head regretfully and romanticized
about his youthful conquests when his spike would never
mollify. His spouse had become infarcted with her
second skin. Three score years and ten.

Trundling in through the yard Mary approached along
the street ceiled in her shabby leathers.

"I thought it was a frigging fella when we edged up
really close!" he scowled. Bun-brown wig.

"We'll give you one last chance before you get the
sack. Here's a brush and cart!" said Jack. "Clean
around the marketplace and along the filthy kerbside."

Mathew slowly motored into town trying to appear
incognito...what was he? A Plumber a Painter, a ,
Candlestick maker? Doing something useful;..thats
fine! Face like the back of a tram smash.

"Have you heard that Moira has gained a place at
Oxford?" she gaily squealed. Cutting up snaps.

But just as he was searching the church green for
public droppings a familiar pair appeared lugging the
shopping.

It beat being loaded in a dustbin and tossed down
the chute by the snoops.

From the direction of the Piece Hall a couple very
similar in age to his mother hitched to converse beside
the lampost.

Mary nattered as if she were stood at her
schooldesk.

He watched in disbelief as the woman suddenly threw
herself into a frenzy.

With hair on end she tore clumps from the wench's
frizzy coiffure, and punched her deep in the mid-drift.

The *human beings* seemed like interlopers as his
estranged sister careered anxiously to the rescue.

Mary's former associate from Bagcraft gleamed like a
Cheshire cat. 'Don't you dare wolf-whistle!'

She continued to lambast her opponent even when the
fight was virtually over.

Mary attempted to straighten up the mistake and
dusted her stumps. She always ordered a pint.

"I can't believe that you're still talking about the
past even today," she flared.

Had she conveniently forgotten leading him on? He
laughed, and *then he called her a 'liar' too*!

"Just look at you!" sneered the barmaid. "You're an
absolute disgrace; whatever did he see in you?" Lost
her hair having a bastard child. She said.

She'd said "Oh! don't be silly! You've had your chance
and ruined it. All you did was sleep all day in bed,
and you'd only do the same thing again. As long as
your housekeeping money is on the table on Friday
that's all I care about. What do you mean you haven't
been out looking for digs? If my brother Bobby comes
down again to turf you out you know what will happen
next! Why are you always up in your room? Are you
sure that you're not a *Brown and Muff*?"

"Don't make me angry!" chided Mary. "How could you
treat your own mother like this?"

"I've never spoken to my mother like that in all my
born days and she's got a damn sight less to be proud
of. Don't you dare give your job in without a better
one to go to. No son of mine is going to be an idle
unemployed layabout! Gretel is sitting *her* retakes."

"At last you've found your true vocation," she
sniggered to her accomplice. "I might have known you'd
come to no good...he's found his own level." She
tossed the poster disdainfully in the container for
collection. Another slap on the wrist mi boyyo...

Then Mathew came back to his senses; they were
whispering in the front seat. He buckled under the
weight. Most definitely into porno.

"We'll drop you just here," he grinned. "Remember,
I want all those plastic bags filled to the brim, and
no skiving."

They sped unhesitantly down the bank having expelled
the oddity in nowhereland.

Dumped on valley road in the middle of a *foreign
landscape* Mathew laboured for a while at the edge of
the leafs.

He couldn't see why on earth they had tied him to
the string of the gridiron waste...it wasn't as if the
area needed cleaning very much; all he could find was
the *gutter scrofula* which needed scraping-up. Hardly
enough for a mornings work, never mind a whole
day...bringing into focus. Call him dirty names.

The eight-stone eleven-pound pocket-Hercules
scratted through the gum with his prong. Then he
sheltered in the shade of the electricity house groove
opposite the British Legion homes.

At near on four-o-clock he noticed a young couple
moving towards him hand in hand, and recognized them
both instantly.

Fatso strutted confidantly linked-up with Genevieve.
He showed definite signs of having entered a health
farm. Been on holiday.

"*Mooncalf*!" he grumbled. "So this is what you're up
to?" He howled at the top of his hooter so that all
the neighbourhood could hear.

The cadet was full of sparkle since being accepted by
the Bobbies.

A van pulled up and Cappy drew down the window.
"Come on *Baldy*!" he shouted derisively.

"You've just been reported for *loitering with
intent*!"

When the rank outsider paraded past the archer's board
and into the foyer of the Roxy nightclub that evening
he was feeling crammed with giant optimism; a couple of
tarts pussyfooted at the door to place on their scales
the nuts of each new masculine entrant. A bottle of
fire-water before leaving had nicely done the trick.

As they meandered numbly across the dance-floor Ian
dropped his pin-stripe trousers.

He displayed a naughty 'Mooney' to the grogs in the
upper galleon where they prospered in robes of
sartorial elegance. The third member was reputed to be
as crooked as a ram's horn.

"Don't *you* try pulling a stunt like that or they'll
lock you up in clink," he teased. Ryan had suddenly
spurted like a flagpole. "I could shag the arse off
that!" At first he would appear coy. Then keen.

The cloven hooves of the cattle market herd sounded
heavier than the band as the strutting '*fanfaronnade*'
casanovas ensnared her with a Snowball. She led him on
at first just so she could slap him down.

A conveyor belt of waxwork dummies manoevered before
the mirrors as Ian dribbled slurry down his chin. She
gave him the glad eye. Mathew blundered in his Buzz
Aldrin platform shoes. Shaken not stirred. Three
hours in the offing. Gave her a turn.

"The closer you get the better you look girl..."
blared the speakers. 'Disco Inferno.' Tina Turner.

"Who do you think is the best looking in us four?"
he cracked. "Am I the hound?" sobbed Ryan Starbuck
appearing to rub his eyes in grief. "Why am I always
the ugly one?" he whimpered. He'd never had a spot of
acne in his life. Rutger Hauer lookalike. Distantly
related to Tyrone Power?

'He' looked like 'George.' Who was married to Mildred.
"You aren't!" railed the girls in unison. "In fact you are the handsomest dude in this joint. But we don't like him!" she sneered. "The one with the bent over nose...why do you bother buzzing around with dopey? Little pricks are neither use nor ornament. Alright, keep your 'air on," she assayed.

One and all agreed that Ryan was a very lovely person. Charm oozed from him like syrup down the staircase. He'd charm the birds from the trees. "Never had a wicked thought in his head."

"Have you ever thought of a 'dating-agency?'" asked Ryan resolvedly. "It's the only way you're gonna get a screw if you don't get a move on. I bet you never chat up a bird in here tonight. Never in a blue moon unless I'm very much mistaken. I'll just let them come to me..."

The *odd couple* wedged on the tangent of the palais de danse made long faces...Ryan crooned for the inevitable. It wasn't many minutes until a few approached him giggling from the aisleways. Stuck together like fly-paper. Shite on a shovel.

"You'd be nothing without your big mate!" she scorned.

The girl appulsed who Mathew had been attempting to hypnotise at a distance. Got up in a trendy cheesecloth. Tickle her tummy from the inside. Made her skin crawl though.

"Is that a ladder on your tights, or a stairway to heaven?"

"Excuse me," she scowled. "Do I know you?"..."I don't think so." Accused him of cradle-snatching.

Ryan Starbuck gave his silly friend a bit of practical advice.

"GOOD LOOKS or MONEY are the only things that really count in here!"

"You will never get a second chance to make a first impression. Just go for the one with the biggest tits. It always works!"

"I always let her do all the running. If she takes a fancy to you she'll bend over backwards."

"I don't have much of a personality so I have to rely on my strengths," he insisted. Believed in 'ethical cleansing.'

The body of evidence was based on his own experience...

After her roll in the hay below the walls of Jericho he attempted to palm Julia off on the rebarbative rogue. Ryan had money to burn; he often threw small change from his jacket pocket.

She called Ryan pompous, arrogant and conceited, but that only made his head go through the ceiling. He was an expert in taking the urine out of people.

One endorsement for having bald tyres. Leg in a pot from the smash.

But Mathew had really fallen for her and that simply wasn't cricket. She pleaded with him to put in a good word with no strings attached. Apparently they had the same eyes...

"Whatever you do, don't tell Mathew," she said. The vamp casually emptied the contents of the glass down his shirt and cursed the casualty for when they had been on the Broads robbed of her oats...

Those were the days when Mathew played the field!

Lost in space the time warped youth wandered distraughtly from room to room on the stock exchange...he was turned down more times than a hospital blanket.

"Did you hear about the Irishman who thought Muffin the Mule was a sexual offence?" he joked.

"And what career do you intend to follow?" asked the trenchant secretary.

"He's a 'refuseman,'" jeered Ryan shining a tercid face. "And he hasn't even dipped his wick yet."

She expressed her condolences, even though he *definitely* wasn't her 'type.' At least she would let him down gently.

His deferring movement suggested an untried astronaut walking on the moon. Come on, put him out of his misery someone.

"I certainly wouldn't employ that ugly bastard," sniffed the Executive officer. "He's just not that fuckable."

'Now for something completely different,' he thought, as the model shuffled her feet, and hoped it wasn't her he was aiming for. A young man like him ought to freshen himself up.

It was before she was banned for using Monopoly money at the Pile bar. She had even appeared full frontal in the *Levin*.

Candy had never forgotten that dusk in Ryan's beach-buggy. She was horrified to find it was not his little finger she had been holding.

"You remind me of an apple," he gawked.
"What?"...she gasped and pouted like a Barbi-doll.

"*Gold'n delicious*!" he simpered jubilantly. But she still did not give him her full attention.

The wench was reaching for her handbag to disappear to ablutions when he caught her with another original straight from the archives.

"My name's Mathew," he stammered. "I'm supposed to be good at chatting up chicks. How am I doing then...(and, with enunciation) Alright?"

"Do you want to dance?" Her eyes glittered cruelly.
"He's got a nose just like *Concorde*," crabbed her friend disgustedly. "Shut your fucking gob up!"

"Just Piss off!" she hissed almost laughing.
"You're rubbish...stop molesting me."

She pranced forward to report him to the bouncer for bottom pinching.

Why did she always find it necessary to snitch in Ryan's ear lug?

"At least he's got something to be big headed about," she jiggered. Could 'outstare' any silly cunt.

"Take a good look at his face!" she hissed. "My six year old son has a bigger dick than the *Raincoat man*. It's just like polishing the coal skuttle when there's never a fire in the grate."

Fatso had been observing his peerless performance. He arrived on a tidal wave to give the birdbrain his heartfelt goodwishes.

"If it isn't little fucking Moonighan!" he leered. "I thought they would have had you in the *loonatic asylum* by now. Glad to see you've still got a spotty clock though." He feigned to stroke his remaining hair.

And where was the 'Billiard Ball,' jamming cheek to jowl with the pretty girl in the lebensraum? I bet! '*Slaphead*' they called him, and '*Slaphead*' it was...

Following a vindaloo at the Taj the lads rovered to the engagement party at the sergeants. Ryan disappeared to get his leg over. He'd mowed down a mouser in the turbulence. She wasn't going to speak to him ever again...

In a sleek pair of black nylons his wife chatted to Mathew on the sofa. It looked like a glass of water, but it was really something much stronger.

He was warily watched by her husband as he sneaked his hand up her skirt. It was almost broad daylight. What could he have been thinking of?

"I'm a waste disposal engineer!"
Her husband stared through the crowd but could hardly lend colour to his prints. Another assault and battery in the quod seemed imminent. Wait till you get copped. 'You'll cop it!'

Like a raging bull the irate eighteen-stone ex-con charged across the room to head-but the head-case. His wife insisted she had not realized where his creeping hand had been profiting.

"I'd like a word with you mate!" he slavered. He invited the madman for a showdown in the hallway...but he was soon a zillion light years away from their company.

Beaten black and blue Mathew clomped down the stairs from their bathroom. He hesitated over the final step and entered the living room with his ears ringing.

"You've been a long time upstairs Sneck," muttered Tina. "What have you been doing?" In his absence the boys had ripped-off his dosh and stolen his silver cigarette-case.

"Nothing!" mumbled the harlequin as he shrunk on the strand of their rumble scratched by milk teeth.

His buddies kept glancing askance. Ryan gaped towards
his trouser leg. Always said he was a D.I.Y.
enthusiast.

Mathew slowly shifted his gaze...he hoped that he
had remembered to shut his zipper properly. Flying low?
"Thank God for that!" he murmured anxiously. Then
he crossed his legs toward Sally. He flopped lower
than ten ton of whale-shit.

A great glob of semen dripped down his suit flair
after his recent clandestine activity.

A sea of surf was lodged on the outer surface of his
material. Ryan turned a *whiter shade of pale.*

Which auspicious name had been drawn out of the hat
this evening?

Horace from the office?...Gerry the milkman?
That nice man from the Garage who had filled her petrol
tank...or Braddock? His wife was away visiting a sick
relative. Slimey Sid the insurance broker? Ray or
Dick or Colin Creep? Capt. Webb the Scoutmaster? He'd
discovered a way to turn the Sahara over for productive
agriculture. Or Tony Blackhead?

The unmuzzled harlot could amuse the entire squad
now that she had collared a suffrage...all *except the
Pigman.* He definitely wasn't on her menu, and had been
given his marching orders in no uncertain terms before
the fall. 3 chips short of a happy meal.

Shivering with Morton's fork he shinned up the
scupper leaving a trail of keck from the 'parve
componere magnis.'

Even the *Fatgirl* hadn't fancied him.
"Why was your friend blubbering in the back seat of the
car?"

Ryan had other more urgent business to attend to.
"I'm not putting my neck on the line for no cunt," he
expressed.

The 'shiner' crawled his way into the pit. Quiet,
they're coming back; I think you can hear her slinking
over the landing? She entered first to check the coast
was clear, followed not far behind by the Creep still
smoking his cigar.

142

He'd ditched his ring on the dashboard of the jeep.
"I think he's already asleep...he's always asleep;
we're home and dry." You could never really blame a
hot-blooded male.

There was no mention of that sordid little scene
inside the parish. 'No floor too low to scrub for
her.' Slack-Alice.

Aroused by his curiosity the whirr of Mary's sex toy
probed through the light tin walls to Mathew's garret.

He closed his proser studs and prepared for the
crescendo with hands pressed tightly round his lobes.

Orgasm after glorious orgasm rocked the rejuvinated
woman. She climaxed repeatedly and gripped the wooden
headboard.

Her bed rattled noisily across the numdah like the
skull of a pneumatic drill. A family heirloom
regularly employed.

Sighing grandly she begged him to stay the night
even though half the neighbourhood had already been
woken.

Hidden in the props his garlic smell of 'Brut'
grafted the tormentor to her ageing feminity.

Beneath his sheets the *Clypeus* twitched like
nobody's darling...never even thought of turning
himself in!

143

XVI
MOTLEY COLOURED CHOCOLATE BROW

In their tiny tenement below the summit of the town's
new tax centre the gang of hungry workmen slammed their
fists down on the slab.

"Hey there, Smelly!...you're slipping away earlier
every day...so why aren't all our mugs rinsed out and
the tuck on the table? Joe wants to know how many
years it is until you retire. How old are you anyway,
sixety-four? You'll still be in this job when you
reach the bitter end," he conjectured. "Hurry up you
dozey twat-head bastard!"

Their 'mate' in the piping-shed recited an
incantation...He emptied the slops over the rigid
organic remains in the kettle and said nothing. Having
already brewed his own char he gave it a little stir,
and rushed along the planks with his widow's mite at
arms length.

As he entered the dusty old cabin the packed crowd
were already starting to riot.

Had he "been for a crafty wank in the basement?"
Drinks were served luke-warm from a lingering spout of
smog. 'Didn't think his balls had dropped.'

"What do you call a coon wearing a balaclava?" asked
Tim. "Anything you like, cos the cunt can't hear
you...and what do you call a coon with a machine gun in
his hand?...Nasser!"...even the gaffer chortled at that
one. Completing the crossword...to egg-on - toast!

"Hey, Joe, look whose here with the grub!" sniffed
Tim. "Nice body, shame about the boat race...where did
you, where did you," he sang, "Oh! where did you get
those spots, Muldoon. Well?" he grinned in
anticipation. "Well, did you find it?"

The shifty-eyed stooge managed to remain silent
between the carking lot of them.

*

"Aaaagh!" sighed Joe rubbing his chops in a satisfied
manner. "I had a really good jump last night...how
about you Mathew?" All the workmen nudged each other
and winked; this was the prime time for the hammerheads
lampooning to begin and trigger his blistering prickly
heat. Joe lovingly stroked his multi-coloured
moustache with fake affection.

"You know how it got like this don't you?" he
gleamed..."Muff-diving with the wife on a Saturday
night. She's got a clit like a red hot poker!" He
bellowed furiously and smatched the air with relish.

The workmen carefully watched to see if their sport
would start to blub today. "Look!" someone cracked,
pointing rudely at his humbling. "You are blushing!
Why are you blushing?" he demurred. "You are!" he
exulted. Red-hot-twopence.

"What on earth's the matter with you...is it your
heart? Have you got *high blood pressure?*"

As Mathew began to lift the sardine sandwich
tentatively to his gob Tiny Tim stood beside him with
the builder's tape measure. There were scratch marks
on the back of his hand as if a squirrel had been
clawing. Another searched his spine for insertion of
the clockwork key.

"You could make five of ours from the stuff that's
in yours!" he whooped. "Have you ever thought of using
a demolition team to blow your snout to pieces...Ha!
ha! Did you not realize that you're right shoulder
blade is higher than your left?" he junctured.

"I know who he looks like!" snapped one of the
backstabbers, holding aloft a copy of the *Levin.*

"Cardinal Basil Hume!" That sent them rolling over
the shed. The gobby bastard!

"Go on, tell us the truth then shorty," jabbered the
Gaffer. "What do you think about all day if it isn't
screwing, or do you play with your nuts when you get
home and are lying down in bed? Er, how big is your
dick really, just as a matter of interest? We've seen
how easy you press the potato weights overhead, so why
don't you have a regular *piece of cunt* to shag?"

Tiny Tim jumped from his seat to mimic the Swapper's
self-conscious gait as he negotiated the building site
rubble. He reckoned to trip over a scaffold pole he
hadn't seen in his path. Barney Rubble!

"You know. I'd love to see him on the job. I just
would....if he ever gets a solid stalk-on that is!" He
burst into a loud and obscene guffaw. "She'd suck 'im
in and spit 'im out," he declared. Whatever turns you
on. If you've got it flaunt it.

"Boy, but I can't wait until I get home tonight!" he
revelled. "I'm going to shove it up her arse just so
she can't sit down for a week! It's not how big it is,
it's how you use it!"

"Stand up while we measure how tall you are,"
demanded Tim. "Precious McKenzie was little too, and
he was powerful with it."

He pretended to scrutinize his head. "Hmmm! lost a
bit more since yesterday. Why don't you wear a wig if
it worries you so much?" he asked. Joe cunningly
disturbed his dome with a dexterous sweep of his arm.
Grab him by the short and curlies.

"I bet his sink is full of molting hair," jibed the
older cognate. "Can't you take a joke? We're only
knobbling, god does he bite easily. His tash'll never
grow in the shade."

The stiff wooden puppet retreated into his familiar
carriage...then they uncovered the pad in his boot.

"Look at you, the way you are...are you 'simple' you
ugly cretinous dork?" he bawled. "If you fancy a pop
you better make your first punch count."

"Grass doesn't grow on a busy street!" he mumbled
half-heartedly. Get a rise out of him. Get a pair.
Play on a flush. Skin cream like *Diarrhoea Spivak*.

It was Joe who first noticed the tide mark round his
cup. "What did you make this from, dishwater?" he
hissed. Kick him in a place the sun don't shine!

"Witch's piss!" screamed the Pumpkin eater, as one
by one the workmen slung their pots through the open
door and into the sun drenched savanna. Flash the ash.
Flick it in his bristles. It's how you use it!

146

"Pooh! You don't half stink muscles. Don't you ever
change your socks?" he gasped. Suddenly they tumbled
out of the portacabin.

A greasy brown carton was tossed under the table and
the door was slammed shut as the beetle-brain sat
locked in the dark. He listened to their yells outside
the hut from where the *smoke bomb* had been propelled.
A cunt had some uses afterall.

The bank of thick yellow fog wound around his ankles
as he anticipated his indecent antics before the
riverbank...

When the kink returned to the house Mugabe had already
finishing flailing his tooth-pick, and was preparing to
put his feet up. That cold stare was a warning sign,
and Gretel had a complacent turn to her cheek. He'll
take you to the cleaners. Married women were always
fair game. Five year olds' already in films.

While Mathew hovered over his dried bread and
dripping the dry-eyed medicine man scowled with
derision, twisting his *swaggering* dreadlocks
reflectively in the maw, and bugging the square-shooter
for signs of brinkmanship.

"So you say you saw Steve with another woman on his
arm in the nightclub?" she nattered...Mugabe
concentrated intensely on his lame dog with looks to
kill a convict.

"You liar!" she spat. "Steven would never be
unfaithful. You're fucking history."

"Well, actually, there were two of 'em," he grinned.
A sterner expression than before crowded the chocolate
metoposcopy. The head perched like a rotten coconut
began to steam from its ears. His eyes began to pop.
Look out son! Here's Johnny...

"Hey! That's my boyfriend you're talking about!" she
hooted. You know how she worships the ground he treads
on. "Admit it! You were wrong!" she said. "Shit
stirrer. I hope you get your come-upance. I'm
beginning to think the old cow was right about you."

"What i-s he on?"

147

The woman suddenly burst into hysterics, and her boyfriend had to hold her back in case she spoiled him.

"It's not a question of kinship," she fumed. "Blood loyalties mean nothing to me! You should judge a person on the sort of character they are, not the colour of their skin." She squeezed his padded thigh. "He's just a warped little sadist," she grinned. "And a filthy sex pervert!"

Mathew was just going to say something different when his sister cut him short.

"You wimp!" she pilloried. "We know that you're just no good with women."

He was going to say 'but don't you think that all men have the capacity to behave upright.'

"What about *black rights*!" she clamoured. "Society has failed the oppressed minorities in the matter of life and death. Look at the situation overseas. There are our obligations. Well, at least he isn't going thin on top," she sniggered. "It's highly immoral to discriminate(etc)."

"Such a nice young man!" Mary concluded. "Mathew leave this room at once!" she ordered. "You've caused enough trouble here for one night!" Admiring her sculpture of the bushman...

As the delinquent crept by Second Avenue he saw a walker from the dim and distant past edging down the road towards him. Perhaps help was on the way then?

She stopped and paused for breath resting on her cane before muttering vague reproaches to the wind.

So frail, so frugal, yet so enduring, the sprightly griddle had confounded expectations to receive a telegram from the Sovereign.

In her succinct and sugar sweet utterance the *woman-child* spoke to him as if the intervening years had brought but little change.

"Hello, Mathew love," she euphonied. "It's been a long time since you came to see me. Why don't you pop round one day with Gretel?"

"Do you ever see your dad these days? Eeee...he was such a handsome lad. We felt so proud. I remember when he first came to lodge with us before he got hitched."

"Have you seen him recently?" she asked.

"You were such a sweet little boy," smiled the trow-woman. "I've still kept the first poem you wrote at Saint Sebastians; 'Fairies on the surf' You won't remember my husband Jack...are you doing a bit of courting yet?"

As he traipsed by Oxford fisheries the fully grown hoodlum approached him from between two parked cars.

The head-hunter curled his lips and flashed his teeth as he offered Mathew his clasp.

A queue of onlookers outside the Bingo Hall had ringside seats as Steve Mugabe let fly.

His first blow knocked Mathew clean off balance. Then the martial arts expert set on him with a further flurry of shots which sent him crashing against the cordon.

"*White Trash*!" he shouted. "You're a fucking freak! I'm going to turn you into gingerbread." He clocked him on the snout with the ridge of his knuckles.

The *aspiring pimp-and-lawman* continued to supply Mathew with the thrashing of his life until he had him laid out on the ground for a further sting of his brogue.

Knocked the wind right out of his sails...Said he would. Said he could.

During a lull he managed to scramble to his feet and take it on the chin.

Hobbling down Victoria road with his mutilated platform heel he begged for mercy from his pursuer. A spirited fightback gave the pusher an added bonus.

Running like the clappers and shaking like a leaf Mathew flew in their front door and quickly bolted it behind him.

He pounded up to his room where he fretted in the tar-barrel with a stink plugging his nostrils.

"How dare 'you' lock my door!" she screamed. "Who do you think you bloody well are?"

They invited the *good example* into the honeymoon suite. He was gleaming victoriously, almost mocking, and bragging it had been money for old rope. Bees round a honey-pot.

With true love, patience, and understanding Mary ran
to..Steve Mugabe, and flung her arms around his neck to
ask if he was out of breath. Gretel hugged his other
shoulder and had a crafty feel of his weapon. In her
new black-and-white frock.

"Well done!" grinned Mary. "He's had a good hiding
coming to him for a long time! Let that be a lesson.
How could he expect otherwise...and there's another one
coming in his direction. He's just a bloody racist!"

The maggot's heartbeat had frittered considerably as
he cottoned-on to their footsteps, stomping noisily up
to the place.   The ultracrepidarian intercepted his
brutal foreplay...surely their heads could nearly be
squashed by an elephant's paw.

Then the telephone rang just as Lora-Lee was
standing against the wall. "Close your eyes and take
deep breaths." She was firm for her brood, but not
particularily for a daughter of Adam.

"All alone?" giggled the Fatwoman. "We'll have to
meet up one full moon." Wouldn't touch her with his.

"You can't make a silk purse out a sow's ear," she
pandered. "But I have one or two things you might find
interesting."

For hours the primary school teacher chattered and
grunted. The claver of lips shrivelled his scheming
proboscis.

After finally giving her the elbow he cut the wire.

'She' was crying when Mary answered the late night call
from her flat. He'd never heard her sob before and it
sounded quite pitiful on the extension.

When she mentioned the word *dentist* his heart
skipped a beat. Mathew realized the pretty elf must
have told her everything about the knitting bee.

"I've never seen her in this state before. You're
son must have put the fear of god in her," she said.
"Should I call the station? She's bawling the whole
house down." Jody, head-in-the-air!

"Stay right there!" loured bloody Mary. "Don't do a
thing until we get to the bottom of this."

150

Trust his luck to be nabbed on a perfidious line of
questioning.

Then he distinctly caught the *renegade* attempt to
describe his organ-loft.

Fortunately she recanted and burst into tears again.
"No case history!" Close escape? Phew! But don't
count your chickens just yet..."I'd only taken her
temperature."

There was a hard thud on the wood and the dark
foreboding presence of the *Marshal* passed over the
threshold with his greeting card.

Though he was not dressed in black a fowl of
mourning disfigured his Judas kiss.

He was offered a seat in the living room so he could
go into details. Bit of a bright spark.

"We have received an urgent message on the
transmitter," he issued glumly.

"A local Catholic priest recognized your son being
involved in a very serious incident. Apparently there
was a fracar outside the bingo hall."

"I've checked with his former Grammar school," he
flushed.

"They say that Mathew was not just bright, but very
bright," he gaped. "We take a very dim view of
brawling in the street and Mathew is lucky he is not up
for *disturbing the peace.*"

"I'm sure they must have switched cots at the
hospital...you do bring shame on me." She gave him her
blackest look.

Then she whispered in the *Marshall's ear*..."If I
have any more trouble can I count on your assistance to
evict him?" She pleaded helplessly. "I'm sure he is
heading out of control."

"I suppose I will have to do the best I can with
him." She bowed and shook her head regretfully.

"At least he's found a steady job to aid clearing
his name! There's never been any sign of it in 'our'
family," she fumed.

Tall and thin rose to vacate the establishment and
was gratefully passed his hat and coat.

151

He said 'pull yourself together,' she said 'tighten up
your clockwork.' His powers of deduction were out of
this world.
     "I've had a word with my super. We have decided *not*
to press charges - on this occasion..."

Sometimes when she weeps, she thinks the worlds not
fair...and sometimes when she cries, she thinks that
no-one cares.
     He'd wanted to be free; to sow a few more 'wild
oats!' "There's plenty more like you," he'd scorned,
"who want to go the distance." But there'd soon be
another following close behind...

Since the embryo had been annihilated her lover had
departed...deserted, the plucked pidgeon lies with an
empty vase by her bedside...and stabbing pains in her
abdomen.
     A stretcher-bearer holds her fevered hand to the
watch.
     The woman arrives to play at loving mums and
daughters.
     But it's all a farce! A dirty rotten sham.
There's soughing in the cough hall...'Would she be
spared?' she asked.
     The after-effects of *Paracetomol* can be quite grim
even in the prime of her life.
     The colour of death she dappled the softness of
light.
     Her taciturn visitor impersonated the correct
bedside manner on such an eleventh hour.
     She decided to give him the mushroom treatment; keep
him in the dark and feed him on fertilizer.
     "Should I tell buggerlugs?" she torpidly mused. "So
far he's totally ignorant about absolutely everything."
     "Don't tell him anything at all!" she spluttered.
"Mathew's not my brother. He's nothing to do with me!"

XV11
THE IMPOSSIBLE DREAM

Ever since that vacation visiting the naturist colony
at Torcross, Julian Biggs had been prone to expose his
'Baby's arm' when 'over the limit.'
     The blotchy beanpole with a wiry-thin physique, and
pig-like snout, crowed over the increased status which
this new notoriety brought him, though he never forgave
his two persecutors for feeding him *dog meat* from the
unmarked can at the camping stove that long hot summer.
     His prolific stock and trade, apparently a family
trait, began to alter the quality of his entire co-
existence.
     His irascible integument angrily reddened in the
stream of light, to bake still further in the
blistering and damaging rays, until three hours later
they roused him to take a gander at the enormous
emerald freckles smeared across his skrawny shoulders.
     With his discarded wench sunbathing on the rocks
Ryan Starbuck contemptuously threw pebbles on her
midrift...standing alongside Julian flexing his muscles
like the before, and *after-math*...he had decided not to
remove his trunks. She eventually took the hint, burst
into tears, and roared off in her Triumph *Stag*. When
Sarah was gone they focused on the exception, and
mocked poor Julian's big toe which Ryan said he would
have been proud to deploy during *sexual intercourse*.
     Julian's mother, a local Yoga teacher, had confided
in the bleached blonde Adonis...
     She begged Ryan not to tease her teenage son about
his appearance any longer if he valued his friendship.
Apparently he had been having nightmares about Ryan
stealing his girlfriend. When he had one.
     On his first day at work, as a Park keeper mowing
the *Sanitarium* lawns, the tall gangly *Biggs had* managed
to chop his big toe clean off.

He was rushed straight into *Outpatients* with the bleb
wrapped in a bloodied handkerchief.

The novice began to take lessons from his idol in
the art of 'taking the urine...'

Ryan could mount two in quick succession. He said he
would probably never 'tie-the-knot' though.

He pretended to preen his hair in a fictitious
looking-glass held in his hand.

No woman had ever failed to achieve orgasm when he
was planting the crop.

His prick had always done its duty even when he was
the prime candidate in a rough and tumble gang bang.
His mother never failed to sing his praises. He had
recently proved his claim that such a handsome rogue as
he could use *bestial force* with impunity.

"By laughing at someone else's misfortunes, we can
best learn to laugh at our own," Ryan remarked.

"If you were ever inferior in something you will
always have a complex no matter how much you break with
the past," he admitted.

"Anyone who doesn't take someone on *face* value must
be extremely shallow...Bobby Charlton would never get
selected these days. Even if he played like a dream he
could never be the subject of schoolgirl's fantasy."

The great Ryan himself had once been called a
shrimp. His T-shirts were always allowed to shrink.
His mother refused to let him go and travel down-under.

"You'll be lucky if you manage to make one or two
genuine friendships in a lifetime. Don't even trust
your own brother. One man's tragedy is another man's
gain. It's not the taking part it's wearing the crown,
and romping home." Nights were spent locked in arm-
wrestling at the bar. 'Would pumping iron work for
him?' he asked. "Will I be able to knock-off Miss
World one day?" But the penny hadn't dropped...

"Just imagine if you didn't even know how to toss
yourself off," winked Ryan. "It would be impossible to
know how to use it properly before the dinkum oil came.
Get out in the fresh air and sunshine. That'll leave
not a rack behind of your ugly zits Popeye."

Bunny had already offered them the barn for a kip as
they fagged around the drinking table after rambling to
Buckden Pike...

The deep sea diver besieged Ryan to *'Sham the Ram'*
again since it always had the band in stitches.

But Ryan could not perform when anyone was watching
him. He waited until the packed audience were turning
a blind eye before attempting his ace in the hole.

A child's baseball cap which the gifted mimic
insisted wearing was pulled down tight over his head.
He continued grinning as if he'd just been taken out on
a joyride.

The assistant herdsman mulled silent as a lamb with
his wild infectious smile growing slowly more animated.
His huge pectorals braced and tensed... then, just when
they weren't expecting any such drum his lungs
discharged a bass vibration which shook the glass from
their tables.

Rising on the surf the tide of laughter spread
infectiously round the *midnight congregation.*

"Baaaaa!...baaa!" churred the rippling chords once
more.

Then with a brainwave of improvisation Ryan
duplicated the echoing bleat of a Ewe, wandering lost
in the fog across the fenny; the fiery audience erupted
into another spirited cachinnation which vibrated
beyond the burning stove.

"Cut it out!" entreated Froggy, whose face was
turning mulberry. "You're making my sides ache! I
can't breath anymore!"

The deep booming fathom emanating from somewhere
near his tonsils was so realistic that you could have
sworn there was a real *Ram* hidden somewhere below the
tap room.

A student of dernier cri rubbed her nose against his
as she asked him to pass on his digits.

He placed his hand over hers and then apologized.
Never-never-land. Crossed purposes. Trick of the
sight. They say.

"Oh, I don't think he's so out of the ordinary," she
mused.

"You hardly ever see him with anyone respectable. He's
nothing but a self-opinionated bucko!"
    "Has anyone ever told you that you have the bonniest
blue eyes?" smiled pendulous melons.
    "But I intend to be *absolutely perfect*," insisted
Mathew. "I've always wanted to be the cock of the
walk."
    Then Bigsy went and spoiled it all by drawing
attention to the size of her *Ibis* beak...

Lumbering up the galley past the old cafe the mixed
party paraded back to the Youth Hostel at after one in
the morning.
    Margot alighted at the brow but he wouldn't go
inside for coffee mate. Ryan was disgusted.
Apparently 'his' father had been something of a
'Ladykiller...'
    He dead-lifted the side of his jeep with everyone
crammed in the snood...those rude words drawn by the
imps on the rigging had become practically invisible.
    He'd even been prone to shouting 'Cripple' through
the window. A coat-hanger served as the ariel.
    "I'll rip his flipping coconut head off if I catch
him!" he promised. "Why don't you get out and push!"
    The pock-marked trull from the annex suggested
climbing in through the lady's lavatory.
    To hoots of *Sherwood* laughter they all followed in a
chain in case the weather took a turn for the worse.
    As the *motley crew* filed cautiously into their
dormitories the 'bit-of-a-charmer' pushed her up
against the cubicle wall.
    He'd sworn never to wear a 'French letter' and
certainly kept to his word. Soon it was Mathew's turn
to 'dip his wick' in the dark. Down to her whalebone.
Beast of 'Old MacDonald.'
    "It's now or never, or you'll always be a bilker,
Pops..."
    "Are you sure you haven't done this before?" he
asked repeatedly.
    Her pointed teeth drilled into his flesh like an
extinct *Bird of the Plains* while Ryan coolly drew on
his Dunhill...

156

Pleas to mash more gently were contemptuously denied,
until someone turned a light on and huzza pelted down
the passageway.
    "Who's that? Is anyone there?" called the bronco-
buster...
    "I wish you'd hurry up!" she screeched. "I'm sick
of trying to screw this useless oik."
    As the ball-breaker rose from the gutter she vowed
to inform them of his *virgin incompetence*.
    "What an Achilles heel!" And they said the devil
never changed his melodic lines.
    He struggled for the latch with the monarch bleeding
profusely. What a place to give a lucky 'hickey' the
refugee conceded. Bit of a dark horse wasn't he?
    Racing rapidly to his bunkbed Mathew threw himself
in without bothering to get undressed, throwing the
sleeping bag over him and pretending to be deep in
slumber.
    "Let's just try it once and then forget it!"
suggested Ryan...

The warden marched out of the porch and snatched the
brush and shovel roughly from the Fools.
    "Don't bother coming here again," he vituperated.
"I do not think that you are Youth Hostel material.
You are banned!"
    As they walked down the lane Ryan Starbuck stripped
to his waist.
    Dazzled by day. Could swim like a fish. Had an
iron clamp grip over his state of affairs...
    Could roll his eyes like a Catherine Wheel.
Composed of the particles of stars. Loved by the
optical lens.
    Crossing the river-bridge a group of cyclists
spurted past like a flock of *wild geese*.
    As they rose in their saddles *yellow-back* motioned
towards the bronzed hulk peeling away his final
inhibition.
    "Good God! It's Garth!" he jeered, which only made
Ryan's head swell even larger...
    Bigsy said the *Fonz* could get *any* bird he wanted,
but Ryan disagreed...

157

"If I do get reborn," he joked, "I'd like to come back short and fat; at least if they didn't agree with my opinion they would tell me straight."

"Do you remember the day at Buckrigg Brow?" asked the late-developer. "How long ago is it now, six months?"...had it really been the birthplace of such a bell-ringing?

They speculated about that moment when the reigning Mr. Universe was placated in the ordinary wooden chairs below the ring of coloured lights. Jealous as hell.

The rival American gave his four hour lecture on the *new philosophy* while his attractive young wife waited coyly in the wings. Never had a single grain of sand kicked in his face.

Sitting relaxed and confident before his audience the articulate and intelligent suzerain was not so massive as the other, but had finished third that year due to his poise and natural posing skills.

Steve Adonis declared that there was no real substitutefor *Pumping Iron*.

"The *more wood you put on the fire the greater the flame*," commented the pedagogue. "The higher the load the greater the temple of fame. Healthy body, healthy psychic organism."

He went on to discuss the importance of Amino Acids, and bulking-up on protein. Supersetting and burn-outs, strict regimes. The danger of overtraining; split routines; getting ripped. Reaching for the elusiveness of *perfection*.

The unnecessary use of *anabolic steroids* which he had managed to repudiate; a credit to his methods. Their introduction ended with a brief penultimate question and answer session which was well balanced and informative.

"Have you ever taken drugs?" asked a rough diamond. "How many times a week do you masturbate?" replied the host...

"Now I'm going to pose for you!"
His fans warmly cheered as the muscleman disappeared backstage to transfuse wild-fire in his veins.

After about twenty minutes the well-known signature tune began, and the tardy curtains were pushed aside for a strapping *young God* to take centre stage. The world came tumbling down...

Amid a burgeoning sense of awe the supremely sculptured body mounted the platform of a plain wooden boom as an astonished gasp sounded from the gob-smacked multitude, cursed by mediocrity.

Transformed in his nakedness the *physical culturist* displayed his versatile wares before the spellbound converts: contrasting sharply with the dilapidated interior building of the *old cabinet*. Nature had certainly smiled on him. *Pops* stood about as much chance as a snowball in Hell. Ryan went berserk if you so much as mentioned his calves!

The bunching tissue of his thighs and calves threaded like a sack of freshly strung grapes; the whippet which struggled to be free from his chest; the magnificent striations when he tensed his squamous triceps behind the V-shaped retinue of steel...every aspect of his Everest was demonstrated from each angle, as the grateful complementary clapped and applauded each new variation of a chiselled burin.

Dazed and confused they acclaimed him in long eulogy until all their fevered hands were numb and cramp convulsed their arms.

That climacteric afternoon both Mathew and his friend were captured and enslaved forever by the *Impossible dream*. A chance to kick the ball himself.

Three times the triumphant *magician* returned for a glowing encore summoned by their pious chant...and thrice the tearful audience nearly brought the house down with their ecstatic drumbeat of plumage.

A flood of warm emotion filled the town hall as emphatic new disciples struggled at the rear for a glimpse of the classical Athenian.

"What do you make of that?" he asked, in a hypnotic trance-like state, munching his dessicated liver.

"Well, it's certainly something to be proud of," said Ryan Starbuck. "In any case complete perfection is a very rare commodity."

XVIII
CHICAGO

When Jennie retired to ablutions the guy in the
pinstripe pulled up a chair. 'Typical of the clientele
who frequented the '*Muff-diver!*' he thought.
     "That your bird mate?" he whistled. "She's a bit of
alright then." Was she a supermarket commodity?
Perhaps her packaging had been brighter than he first
realized; in retrospect it may have been wiser to
introduce her to a wider circulation.
     He noticed Jennie returning through the smoke-cloud
of Yobs in a slough of despondency...
     "What's wrong with you Mrs. Glum?" he asked. "Has
your cat just died? Is everything okay, twinkletoes?"
     "Of course," she insisted, "but could you stop
burning me with your cigarette everytime you move. Do
you have to have a fag? I would have thought it could
interfere with your training."
     He smiled and attempted to inject a spark of
nostalgia into those dour proceedings...
     "Do you remember that night at the *Ram's head* when
the landlord emerged round the corner only to see your
hand in my belt? He dropped the wine glass he was
carrying. And that afternoon in the development area
when we were petting against the desk....after twenty
minutes we looked up to see X-Ray Buck's study group
with their heads pressed against the window on the
third floor. Didn't we split our sides. Like two
tomatoes! Did you hear about his American campaign by
the way? I felt very close to you in those days..."
     She looked kind of sad. "You asked me not to get
too keen, that other girl, you liked her too?"
     "Do you remember the sweet little charmer...Kath,
Kathy...yes I did rather like her, but she wasn't like
you..."
     "Are you sure that you like me? I know that we've
travelled this route?" On the eve of St. Agnes.

But I simply have to ask for the last time. Did you do
it before with your other girlfriends? How many
times?...Are you sure? Absolutely certain...
     "Don't keep on!" he clammed. "It will be alright on
the night. I'm just waiting for the consummate time
and place that's all." Sweep it under the carpet!
     He quickly changed the subject...a spark of summer.
"We're due back the second week after Christmas. Did I
mention that the Principal tooth-dragon has halitosis?"
     "He was standing next to me one afternoon in the
sculpture pen wishing he had such a good rapport with
all his other students. I had to retreat from the
stench of his issuing firebrand. Then it's on to post-
modernism next spring!"
     "The rock singer, Sian...she asked me to pose for
her book of still-lifes. I wonder what marks she
received without me on the front cover? Partly through
jejune. That creep Dougal was in! Did you see it? I
noticed he didn't hang around long on the night that I
arrived late to the shag."
     "My sister said that you were the nicest girlfriend
she'd ever seen me with..."
     Warm kisses all the way to the Queen's Hall...Then
someone must have read his thoughts. They put that
damned record on the jukebox once more!
     "It's our song again," he said. "It will always
remind me of the bottle party when we held hands
underneath the table. They teased us both for being
such a pair of lovebirds. Kelvin didn't believe me
when I said we hadn't yet. What a face he pulls,
really odd, as if it were a crying shame...and he says
that you are much too fine for me."
     The slave of his erection rose to leave the *lounge*
and presumed to walk her to his heart.
     "You gave me the idea your parents were rich," she
said. "It was rather a disappointment, but it really
doesn't matter."
     Should he come clean about his antics in the
churchyard, and what he did behind the gravestone when
he should have been sketching the clocktower?

Would she fall around in stitches if she heard that on
that very first day the late starter had carried his
house door key gripped tightly in his hand all morning?
Should he risk another slap in the face?

'That weekend stay in the Capital, when you hid me
in your wardrobe. Farhat the 'Cat' thought the whole
fool thing was hilarious.' Kiss and tell.

'But why did you tell me about the Milkman who
screwed you in his truck on the way to crammers? Why
did you go into details (even when I asked you) about
the curtain-raiser when you copulated with your older
cousin? The ruffian at the piss-up...was that another
opening premiere? And did you have to tell tales out-
of-school when befuddled with dipsomania. The *devotee
to Iacchus* with the milk bottle in his trousers? And
all the rest of them ever since, who have formed a
queue from the steps outside the door...leading from
your boudoir where you'd wiled the porno books to read.
Found in your father's potting shed when you felt the
urgent need to *masturbate for England!*'

'Yes! You were filled with false expectations. You
were very disgruntled, that time when we were left in
peace at the Shambles.' That knocked the cup from your
lip. My dear. Into your pile of leaves, Mr. Pogle!

'You said, "Is there anything you want me to do?"
'And I said, "Is there anything you want 'me' to do?"
And the answer to both questions held no brief.

'How could I match up to all of that?'
'Oh! I made plenty of profane excuses! You have to
give the devil his due. I'm good at excuses to excuse
the *poser* which ached from deep down below.'

'Playing politics with the truth.'
You said, "I thought we were going to make love?"
Make love? Don't make me laugh! Make love? By what
means do you expect? How could the *monitor* admit he
was just an innocent tourist. While you were...*not a
white virgin*...and then 'he' felt 'guilty.'

'I'm good at passing the buck, but perhaps it was
just the jitters. All I could think of was to deposit
you on the first tram home.'

Just trying to explain a little. My heart had leapt
overboard.

'You asked very gently, but I was too proud *ever*...a
complete washout.'

'Do you want me to hand you over to the Yardie
Mugabe so he can satisfy your unbridled lust from now
on?' And Ryan could drive like a demon.

From *Misery Inn* the odd couple dawdled along the row
of market stalls from the Penny Arcade along the main
street.

At the iron drawbridge of the Castle Gates they
parted for the final time below the watchtower of
Little Washington.

"I feel a rising coming on!" he fostered. Was he
going to levitate? He flinched from her embrace.

The girl with the Germanic glance stamped her heel
as she prepared him for the short excursion below the
dark wooden chisel. The shadowland of flickering wall
gyrated like a row of *origami tigers* above the titles.

"A new velvet jacket just to impress me?" sniffed
the chambermaid. "You're shivering blue from cold,
never mind the fashionable image! I don't know what to
say...I'm very fond of you Mathew darling," purveyed
the well-spoken courtesan. "I like your muscles and
find you very attractive!" she insisted. "I do not
want to hurt your feelings but this is what I sense
must come to pass...There's this dishy Italian waiter
who keeps giving me the come on. I may not need to get
laid but just in case, I think....it would be best for
all concerned just to stay good friends. I find that I
have to put everything into a relationship, or leave it
well alone. Dear Mathew...I'm telling you this for
your own good," she cried. "I hope we can still remain
in touch. Some people are born to hurt, some to do the
hurting."

For the first time in light years he felt
unspeakably sad. His heart seemed to grind to a halt,
and a lump lodged in his throat. Tried and found
wanting was she flinging him out to grass? Should he
gallop along after Jennie, and tell her all the things
he'd been meaning to say before the *gegenshein became a
field of scarlet and black?*

XIX
MIGHTY JO YOUNG

Mary fussed around the *Lodger* as if he were the finest specimen that had ever trampled across her outer threshold and entered her domain...

He grunted coursely as he masticated his meal of *roast beef*, and when he bent over to lick the plate, dipping his thick dark sideboards in the residue of *sauce piquante*, Mary quite naturally copied his actions. Slob-o-dob-o-gobbing-all-over-him!

Tattoed on his forearms was a battleship emblazoned with the word 'Mavis.' He appeared quite satisfied with the flunkey. "Oh, I'm so happy," she sobbed.

"Now I can start to 'have a good time!' I've never been so happy in my entire life," she giggled.

"Isn't the real world wonderful."
Hugging the 'lodger' like a win on the jackpot she caressed his neck and fondled him suggestively.

"Oh! I'm so happy everyone! Can I have a lick of your ice-cream cone?" She chuckled salaciously.

Then she proudly bared her clear white teeth which she always claimed were her most outstanding feature.

One could not deny that her stern despotic glare had grown less tense now that she was once more in lucre of a regular supply of 'wild oats,' yet Silcott appeared far from thrilled and the *purlieus* remained constant. Avast, buckle-down, all hands on Dick!

"It's a '*business agreement*'," he stressed; they'd only known each other for a fun packed three weeks until she popped the question. Alive to opportunity.

The slovernly wench slavering in his earhole had not mentioned the old hobbledehoy in their prior negotiations. Shoulder to the wheel son.

"How am I supposed to bring him home with a lout like you still gadding about the house," she scowled.

"Too late to do anything with!" stated the 'lodger' categorically and refused to speak to him directly.

"He's the simplest 'prick' I've ever known," railed the bellicose 'groundworker.' But she had a mind to throw him into science. No relation. Thought they could be pals. Assumed responsibility.

"Where did you find him; the *abortion bucket*?" he asked ridiculously. She sniggered and touched his leg.

"Don't you think I haven't noticed that tribe lurking around outside!" he sneered.

"I've told you where the muttonhead will spend his bottom dollar. Just you mark my bloody words."

"I'm on 'cloud nine,'" she rambled. "I've never felt such a full dinner pail!" Her besotted eyes sparkled as she admired her new engagement ring. "You'd better bugger-off now Mathew," she said. "You've finally run out of rope. The 'lodger' and I will be starting our own family soon, and we don't want you hanging around to spoil the atmosphere or be any part of it. We may be considering adoption, in which case I might eventually have a son to be proud of. And get those stupid weights out of here," she snaked with absolute gusto. "You only eat to compensate!" Was that really so? His mother lolled dreamily over the newcomer's shoulder, teasing and coaxing the former amateur boxing champion to tantalize him further. She draped herself effectuately round his loins and whispered rude words in his ear to see if he would take the hint. The chaste bit of fluff gimmered to share some of their past secrets from the furtive *freak of Nature* opposite.

"If I might mention a rather delicate matter," he stumbled, caught between two stools. "Without meaning to cause offence, but those full-throated troats every single night," he flummoxed. "Could you please be a little more taciturn; it makes me feel uncomfortable."

Well...the schoolteacher gave her 'misfit' son such a *biff!* Mary looked as if she could have killed him on the spot. The lodger tugged on his thick patches of soot and angrily bolted upright.

"If you don't like it you know what you can do," he
growled...."Fuck off! You good for nothing little
twat."

To pacify her prey the woman continued to smooch
with him on the sofa and further embarrass the outsider
who was present also.

"Oh! I'm so happy," she wagged, nodding to the
stairs, as the 'lodger' bulldozed drearily toward his
heap of fulsome hardcore.

She rubbed herself against the anvil of the armchair
hose like a 'bitch on heat.'

"Why don't you just sod off!" Mary whispered
angrily. "Oh, I haven't done that before," she called
after him..."Do I have to tell you everything twice."

"Surely I don't have to pack my bags immediately?
There must be some arrangement by which we can go on
living with each other amicably. Why do you desire me
to vacate the premises so urgently?" Was he kidding?

"So that when you're gone we can screw together on
the rug in peace!" grinned the woman....and wandered
open-mouthed from the room.

"Is this what you want?" the domestic servant was
heard to reitterate down the passage.

She howled even louder than before as the itinerant
bedstead hiked bombilatively across the upland prairie.

'It's a knock-out!' Mathew turned the volume switch
to maximum on 'World of Sport' to drown the fan-fare
bursting along the wharfe.

'How could they dare?' he thought. In broad
daylight? A party of girl-guides past by...

The family pet began to howl in synchronized harmony
on the top step of the yard. Her devices were
proprietously promulgated to the lowest point. Were
you born in a field?

What could he say when they returned? How would he
dare look his mother in the chops again? Mathew
touched his neck like a *Downe's syndrome child*...

Sounds of her rising orgasm screeched into the
sunshine as the romping pogo-stick clattered
obstreperously against the bathroom complex.

166

The 'lodger' heavy-laden with animal fertilizer groaned
like an *extemporaneous* Bull and shot his load inside
the *happy humping heifer.*

§   §   §

With Skippy snapping at her giant heels and leap
frogging up her frock she came frolicking down the
Tulip steps from Holycroft, negotiating the broken
bricks, debris, scaffold poles, and timber, peering
inside the churning concrete mixer.

"'E lick me all over!" roared Lennie-the-labourer
toiling for the brickie on the platform. He mocked her
words as if she were an absolute jobbernowl.

"She's even bigger than the wife," he observed.
"*Jo-Jo* never be beautiful but just look at those lovely
meaty thighs!" he lewdly cooed. The girl arrived to
flit around the stanchion.

"Don't you think e's 'andsome Jo' Jo', don't you
think he's gorgeous?" Lennie teased the primary school
colossus.

"Pretty!" she said. "Just pretty." She shyly hid
behind her bushy chestnut mop of hair...

Like a fresh breath of ozone at the rising of the
dawn she appeared on the brow of the hill, waving
furiously from her parent's four-poster, or bounding
boisterously down the winding steps like a graceful
young gazelle.

The *Sand-fairy* always chased in hot pursuit to see
if she could climb the gate before her. The senior
never let *Jo-Jo* out of her sight for long just in
case...

Tying knots to the Ethiopean's skin Mathew lured her
into the hut when the *orks* had been spread throughout
the wide constructions.

The *Sand-fairy* insisted she should be allowed inside
the den after submitting the secret password;
'Candyfloss.' Jo-Ho! Hands over ear-lugs...

Sitting tentatively beside the *monitor* with her head
confined between her powerful arms *Mighty Jo Young*
revealed her sister's teenage crush.

167

"She dreams about you all night!" she
laughed..."Mathew, Mathew, I've heard her calling in
her sleep"...the *Sand-fairy bitterly* blushed.

But Jo-Jo was the tallest of her kind, and the most
intrinsically eleemosynary.

Her whimsical nature made the giant everyone's
stable companion. She could at this early age already
count the stars.

With her eyes tight shut they played at *pirates and
sailors*, but the *Sand-fairy* could not resist peeping
especially when Mathew sneaked his hand high above the
giant's hem.

His fingers sunk into the plump accomodating
softness of her skin.

Traversing the long bare legs by coign of vantage he
tenderly crept, until he finally made contact...

Suddenly the hut door was sent crashing against the
iron pegs along the rack.

Lennie-the-labourer seethed and quivered in the
doorway as a dust storm spread from the tin lampshade
above them.

He commanded them both to leave instantly. Both
girls turned to water lillies and fled back along the
path to the top of the field.

Then he threatened to inform the *Big Blue Whale* when
he arrived home from the station later that evening.

"I'm ashamed of you Mathew!" he uttered
pretentiously. "We thought you were a decent enough
young lad."

"Promise me that you'll stay away from her in
future. She's a dumb-bell for her age...Don't you
realize that? For two pins I'd have you exposed for
what you've done."

Touched to the quick they steered up the building
site together. He tipped the *melange* of compo into his
hod and tottered up the lower rungs of the ladder.

"He's only jealous because you got to her before he
did," mocked Martin. "You only want to make her bawl!"

"The wife isn't giving him any at the moment so he's
back to the old hand job again!"

168

His little pecker chipped away at the dry scumble on
Inga's bedroom chamber, while his faithful companion
loitered patiently on her three front steps, in the
bright red boiler suit...

The buxom blonde sloyd flexed her *gargantuan* chest
above his balding dome and continued to criticize the
Physical Jerk's poor performance in the bedroom.

"He's so out of condition," she sighed. "All *the
Naked Civil Servant* wants to do when he gets home from
work is go to sleep... why don't you pop around for a
coffee when there aren't any more irons in the fire?"

She scrutinized the *grenadier* of the girl who jumped
when he opened the door. Jo-Jo had just climbed down a
beanpole in the firmament.

"Didn't I see you two in the empty house below the
other afternoon?" she smiled. "What were you both
doing in there?"

The co-conspirator ignited and stared dolefully into
his buds. They made their silent way along a range of
empty windows.

At the end of *Greyfriars* crescent the line of
poplars swayed and jingled in the pastoral wind,
casting a taper, where she leant into a multitude of
spirals.

As he cleared the base she presented him with a
rocket-lolly from the small concern out of this world.

"I'm so shy," she said. "I'm so very shy!" *Mighty
Jo Young* buried herself inside the nearby masonry.

"They tease me at school because of my size," she
purled. "I'm an odd bird, but I don't mind," she
addled. "I suppose you've heard my nickname..."

As if to demonstrate her preternatural strength the
decajaar lifted the flaking cement bag above her head
in one easy swoop as if she was tossing caber.

She pretended to squint with her left eye in a good-
natured rebuke,..."I'll miss you when you're gone!" she
said, so incidental and unashamed. There was a fire in
her gauze and he waltzed with her head above cloud.

Temporarily choked for a second by this unprovoked
comment the corrupting influence hesitated for summer
lightning. She rolled back the delay of moisture.

169

"And I'll miss you too," he sadly replied...

"I'll return for you one day when I've conquered my mountain. Will you bide your time for me?" he asked.

"I couldn't bear the thought of you ever being touched by someone else."

"Don't keep me waiting too long..."
The dormer key slipped smoothly into the clavis lock and 'Mighty Jo Young' ran from the bushes.

For once the leeching skirt of the *Sandfairy* had been given the 'slip.'

She showed him some of the pornographic literature which the local tribe had found drifting around the workmen's *tamping Ark*...one of the specimens hung right down to his knees.

"Aren't we supposed to suck them?" she queried.
"No you certainly are not!" he stared aghast.

"Where did you get such an outrageous idea?"

She knelt in the murky corner as per her instructions while he nervously perlustrated the naked porthole.

Standing on a breezeblock Mathew shifted his gaze to the bollard fastened down the front of his *injured skiffle*.

"Keep your eyes tight shut. " he fretted.
He relocated her warmth towards the sharp *metal teeth* and carefully lowered her hand inside his choppermouth.

Her swanlike neck arched over, but her squeamish eyes could not calm, and flickered gently skyward.

"Is that the time?" she squalled.
"I don't know what is to be done..."

He checked the lie of the land again...but something was distinctly amiss.

At any moment Mathew expected the door to fly open and *the watcher* to come bursting inside the refuge.

Suddenly *her* calm demeanour evaporated. A single tear dropped onto the bridge of his hand..."I love you," she sobbed. I'm sure you did.

Mathew bent down and kissed her head.
"People shrink as they grow old!" she said...

Tabatha squatted down on the edge of the housing estate demesne and examined one of the perplexing globules of polystyrene which had been laid in a trail, and which she was collecting fastidiously in the polythene bag which the *bad man* had bestowed.

Out-of-doors she steadily approached from the lip, tossing the shards with fascination in the fanning and brewing them against the summer luminary.

There must have been a *Bank holiday*. It was so quiet they could have been in a ghost town...only 24 hours in a day. Better than collecting tab-ends...

Bird-lime, springled booby-trapped trip-wire.

As the sugar-sweet-shrew approached his snare her tiny bedding-roll was brimming, and her forearms had about as much as they could hold against her lucrative chin. Only a few morsels were left to dart from the plate.

She lapped on the doorway step mesmerized by the evacuee who was waving his favourite truncheon. He had been observing her gradual advance in the full length pane of glass at which he admired himself, resting a couple of yards away against the recent tender.

For eons at one hog she imbibed the solidly erect mass piercing her with its own timeless malice, rubbing her rich brown shoots every so often in case the *iron-gun* had been a *double-vision*.

She reached forward to retrieve the mug sent by Mrs Goldleaf and stroked the velvet surface of his triple cartilage moored on the jetty of his pubic bone, just as the shadow of the Site Agent joined them in happy re-union.

His rapid stride cleared him cleanly to the edge in a matter of milli-seconds.

Grizzled with his fly at half-mast he flew to face the wall and lick his wounds.

"Leave that bobbysoxer alone!" bellowed Paddy O'Brien as Tabatha raced for cover.

XX
FART

Paddy Nutgens 'Fine Art Fairies,' from the bottom of
the Polytechnic garden, gathered in the *Buck and
Brocket* for their inebriated conference!

Chatter was still circulating about that disgraceful
exhibition of 'Performance' Art featuring the gory
guillotining on the stage of certain 'vermin,' soon to
be mirrored in an actual courtroom case. One of the
lecturers involved had just been clapped for forcing a
student to drink his urine from a beer glass.

It was the days before the 'Sultans of Swing' became
match-winning, and you could present your 'thesis' in
the form of a local 'telephone directory' ('there's
the bastard type; now 'you' put it into words!')
expecting to achieve a pass with distinction.

Rumours that their guild was soon to hit a blank
wall were once again pushed confidently aside, as were
the tall stories that Kunst had lost his virginity; an
illusion which proved to be totally unfounded.

Little John was absent from the *bacchanalia* after
being arrested prancing through the arcade in his
pinafore and tutu. The 'singing policeman,' reciting
Under milk wood in the refectory lift dressed in his
birthday suit had been the subject of much heated
discussion by the dons of the college scrutinizing his
diction. A case for the 'happiness police!'

"If you've got it, flaunt it!" cheered Felix
Upstart. "A toast to Mammon!"

He still had the remains of his autopsy flaking on
his fingers. 666 was autographed on the bridge of his
skull. Poser! The *charismatic clone* in the lithe
leopard-skin leotard suggested they had a questionnaire
to discover if members of their clan masturbated more
regularly than other departments in the college. He
was the only creature in the known universe who could
drink his own weight from a *fountain of human semen.*

172

His *starting pistol* was certainly original...

This serious inquiry was resolved to some degree by
the pale frail little man with balding pate, who was
occasionally seen wandering the ghettos in search of
greasy combs lying in the gutter, with a flat cap
warming the nether cover of his piercing intellect.

The senior tutor contended that students in the
second year mistook a seminar for 'half an r.'

"Oh! I think you'd get a reply something like this,"
he smiled..."Yes! No! Yes! Yes!..No!"

"I believe that in *Egypt* there is an *old wive's tale*
it makes men go up the wall."

Then the almighty Nuttall staggered from his trough
with a radish in his eye.

He insisted that the need for popularity was a
flagrant weakness of his.

The Fat-tub insisted that he deplored the crime of
incest although researching his latest blockbuster on
'The Natural History of Fanny-Farts.'

'No man is an island,' he tiraded. 'We can learn
far more from you than we ourselves alone can teach.'

He stressed the importance of taking risks and
living dangerously, and guaranteed that rules were only
there to be broken.

According to Nuttall 'Floaters' in the basin never
flushed properly down the drain.

'Some of you cunts only come here to absquatulate in
a cave!' he baulked. Wankers of the world unite!

'Do the students consider it more appropriate that
they should be trained how to draw properly, or should
painting be judged by a more subtle form of criteria?'

'Don't we really know the difference between a good
pile of shite, and a bad pile of shite?' he frowned.

The *French Nun* was still pestering *Hinchcliffe* to
sleep with her in return for a high-enough pass.

"That's a load of shit!" he slurred...and tumbled
from his stool.

Said he would rather be digging in the 'Valley of
the Kings.'

173

Had throwing faeces at his audience, then masturbating
in front of them, to the annoyance of the *Amazon* women
craning over their seats, really been a form of true
Expressionism?

His 'Sighle na gcioch' dappering the gallery had
been admired from every possible angle.

Mathew retired to the bog to attend his fighter
pilot's moustache and apply another coat of
Silvikrin..."Mad enough!" ran his term report...."But
I wish he'd get even madder." Once more he returned to
the calefaction...

"I wish I'd had praise like that," sobbed Felix..."I
knew your sister at Portsmouth. Did you know her
sobriquet was penis-breath?"

At the opposite end of the table the enigmatic
charlatan glibbed in his scruffy Afghan coat concealed
himself behind a pair of dark *watch-lenses*, which
glinted oddly under the strip lighting.

Covered by a lengthy funicle of sable he gave a
high-pitched girlish titter, not too unlike the
intonation of a younker *seamstress*.

"Thought you were a Mr. Supercool when you trotted
in the bar with the chick," he tittered. "Everyone
here presumed you were one of the big-wigs. I always
thought that Vanking was the capital of China myself."

The *medicine-man's* black-and-white pen-and-ink
representation of karmic winds entitled 'Osibisa'
complemented Mathew's psychedelic watercolours. He had
previously been employed as a cabinet-maker whose job
it was to measure her body while still warm. Could
have been just like the lead singer of *the Faces*.

"Why don't you just shave your head instead of
lacquering your strands like corrugated steel?" The
art student pushed back his charlike hairline.

"I'm receding too but it doesn't worry me!" he
vituperated. Compared to the majority the clockwork
mouse picked self-consciously at his pork scratchings.
Chip off the old block. Will end up a headcase.

To make matters worse someone played the 'Vinker's
song.'

He stared aghast when he realized what was
coming...although the 'difficult one' was impossible he
squirmed like a rubric tom.

"What's the difference between an egg and a bloody
good wank?" asked the enigmatic circumlocutor, his
tinted glasses glaring queerly in the harsh overhead
illumination. The cast cogitated a second.

"You can beat an egg," he maundered.
"What are you then?" queried the *pongye*.

"I'm a green manalishi with a three-pronged prong!"
spurted Bates in thunderous response, straightening his
fractured spectacles mended with a piece of elastoplast
by an adept cross of his cranking utensil.

"Why don't fairies get pregnant?" he
asked..."Because they only go to *goblin* parties!
What's green and smells horrible? Answer...a boy
scout!"

"Did you hear the one about the nun?...got
excommunicated for doing press-ups in the carrot
field!" he reitterated.

Bates had recently tried to *hang himself* from the
studio balcony as a *sacrifice to Old Gooseberry*. The
stunt had backfired by the time they cut him down
almost comatose.

A docket underscored his tidemarked neckline.
'Always flow with the stream,' he whinged.

He swore that there was no such thing as an exactly
straight line although he had spent many years trying
to find one.

"I hear that you do *Pumping Iron?* Doesn't he look
sweet when he blushes," he chuckled. "Is that really
mascara festooned round your eyes?"

There was an invitation to the echo chamber but
Bates dampened the idea with another dram.

He'd once seen a billboard saying 'Drink Canada dry'
and he was determined to make an attempt before the
finish. On the turbulent crossing to Amsterdam he had
been the only one left standing in the bar.

"The only musical instrument I've ever played was a
'barley-sugar whistle' which I found in a lucky bag,"
he hissed.

After a break for last orders Felix drew attention to
the horde of entartetes.

"Has anyone seen those graven images buried on the
ninth floor...similar to the flour-faced *Bedlamites*
chained with spiked collars in prismed coffins?"

The queer cartoons tucked at the back of the drawer
caricatured masculine clowns with hideous hook noses
and protuberating lips engaged in fellatio and buggery
on an acrobat's swing. S + M.

Their glance fell towards *the Nixy* who had
hypnotized their heed. Had once been a Cellarman at
the Widow's Revenge.

It was the age of punk when Charlie Wax could
compose with a melted candle horribly deforming one
side of his face spitting like a 'wonder dog'...even
Nigel Bates trick with the Vesta's couldn't put a spark
into him. There was definitely something fishy about
his whole art of the possible.

"Look at that!" he slurred, rancorously pilastering
his 'pregnant' gut; "And I never eat anything! All I
want is to photograph beautiful chicks so I can fuck
with them afterwards!"

A *pin-snapper with Mohican spikes* arrived in the bar
through the saloon door wearing a T-shirt bearing the
logo 'The Police are Coming!' in black capitals
emblazzoned across her bouncing young mammaries.

"I hope someone cleans up the mess afterwards!" he
sniggered.

"This is how to do it!" he sneered in a mocking
'Punch and Judy' chant.

Bates continued to empty the magic matchbox
theatrically on the top so that he was not spoiled for
choice. The girls all turned their heads away in
disgust. Get Knotted!

"I used to be into *necrophilia* until some rotten
cunt split on me," he whimpered disagreably.

He struck a match on the side of the tinder
sandpaper to illustrate the illusion reached through
long drunken hours of cogitation.

With a simultaneous flick of his wrist the enigmatic
Bates impaled the burning stalk quickly into the soft
and tender crutch of his butchered palm, and gave a
fake little groan as he pressed the weapon home.

His smouldering flesh blistered afresh and his skin
quivered and cracked with a new scar gleaming among the
old.

"*Ragamuffin*!" he cackled with delight as he held his
arm politically in the air to demonstrate his foul
allegiance.

"Everybody look at me!" he bantered...as the
cemented matchstick stabilized in mid air without any
support at all. Was he going to call for a bucket?
Why weren't some of the leading Statesmen and women
Black magic Saucerers? Then!

The sore red palm griped with the blackened end of
the wood as Bates urgently screamed for another prong
to see how many could be stood on board. Sit on your
hands and keep buttoned-up.

Perlustrating this bizarre spectacle the Billiard-
Ball with the worn-out skirt of back mustered from the
distant *Cairn-group*. The *cider-makers* were obviously
perfect candidates for his recruitment drive.

His white dome glaring beneath the lamplight 'Wig'
propositioned them with one eye on the exceptional.

"I've just had a brain-wave!" he enthused.
"Some of us want to form a 'Fine Art' society in the
college to discuss points of mutual interest...do any
of you want to join?"

"And what do you propose to call this band of piss-
artists?" boomed the strummer. Said he was into
selling pharmaceuticals.

"Why not call your group *Fart*?" suggested
Bates...their rhetoric bucked like a rollercoaster!

They vacated the empty vaudeville after closing just as
the three Nags were starting away on the pavement, and
in a moment of rare spontaneity decided to shadow them
in the hope of breaking their duck. A natural calamity
had stunted his arrested development.

"Trust me!" Bates voice boomed from the bottom of a
well.

Like an *alternating current* the three Boggarts
dressed in buckskins tracked the girls as if their
whole future depended upon the outcome.

The cackling of broody hens made Nigel Bates feel
quite respectable as they footstepped over caravans in
the snow...

A marathon pool session that day had resulted in a
disorderly quarrel at the summit of their game. The
pool-shark had caleered the loser with disasterous
results. But it still wasn't worth breaking all his
fingers.

The cue had been suddenly hurled in his direction.
His spectacles had been trampled on the ground as he
scythed on his hands and knees.

Instead of retaliating against his opponent the
contestant had kicked the blockage at the exit with
such force that his foot had become rooted in the
timber panel...

As they trolled along the avenue Mathew could not
help noticing that Bates was not wearing any
buskins...the hole which blossomed at the pole of his
carpet slippers was now exposing his niggardly big-toe.

"I can hardly walk now!" he complained braggardly,
as the sickening pincer, like an enormous lump of jet,
set like serried ranks amid the sharp December fall,
spreading its poison from the base of his shaft.

"I always wanted to be a tramp when I grew up!" he
grinned.

"Where are we going?" It was hopeless, hopeful
situation...in time a limited conversation developed
between the drips.

"There's gonna be a *ripping*!" Bates tactfully
blurted...the girls began to get a sharp move on again!

"Why don't you ask them if they're married?" asked
Felix in his light fingered dialect. "I never try
anything with someone I really like..."

"Look, stop *projecting* your sentiments onto me!"
ranted Bates, and began his old ramble repeating
himself.

"Why do I keep on repeating myself?" he asked them,
seriously at first. "Why do I keep-on fucking
repeating myself?" he wrangled...on, and on forever.

An iron bar down the front of his forehead would
have met requirements...

From afar they carefully marked the number of the
terraced slum where the trio had imported.

After loitering outside their headquarters for an
hour they were miraculously invited in for a late night
cup of coffee after rapping on the knocker.

Explaining their wyrd antics was a piece-of-piss.
They arranged to meet them the following evening in a
more conventional setting. Apparently it wasn't even
their own accomodation. Another trick up his sleeves.

Bates raged that deodorants were enviromentally
repugnant.

After only twenty minutes the three stooges were
once more summarily ejected into the cold damp street
from where they came just as Bates was repeating the
joke about *convent practices*, with the seven mile
intercurrence to make home again.

"I'm sorry lads but some of us have to get up in the
morning," she glared and slammed the door. "Bog off!"

Bates was furious after this short respite, and
paralysis was edging up his bare calf towards his
thinking cap.

"I'm not going to be taken to the cleaners!" he
persisted in vile distress. "Don't give firewater to
the fucking Indians! Vogmeat!" He chastised the brass
plate of her cribble and screamed through the radiating
letterbox.

Then, giving his two fingered victory salute, Bates
viciously thrust the said two fingers down his
defecating throat... not so easy!

A spurt of vomit erupted out of his mouth and
obliterated the number plate. A treacle of gunge
trudged down to the embossed bleb of the door wart.
There was definitely something of the Grand-Bel in
Nigel Bates.

"Excellent!" he choked, and staggered off down the
lane....

Is there life on *Mars*? Pseudo-logique extraordinaire.
How are you celebrating your twenty-first?

Long after the kitchen clock had struck midnight the
vagrant lodger sneaked surreptitiously up the stairs
with the mechanism still clanking loudly in his
eardrums.

In the object red brick Victorian astragal the
vestibule pale was slightly open...a glimmer of
phosphor spangled from the sarkstone as he crept by
their four poster chamber.

'He hadn't touched her for years,' she moaned into
his taffeta phrases.

The Boarder ambled past the Snoopy door toward the
sink and scouted for the invitation card which she must
have forgotten to post.

"Oh! you have got a 'dirty' mind!" The doubtful
anguish had died away since their recent *diamond
jubilee* though. Thought he could hear a hoot.

With a backward glance he noted the bar of light
below their casement suddenly vanish.

The Post-Graduate Medical students living above had
enjoyed another brilliant copulation, so all was quiet
on the Western front...

Our *Boarder* set about arranging his gear, but no
matter how much he vexed, he simply could not decide on
a suitable attire...

Should he dress himself in the pair of pink
slippers, or slip into the nightie the gammer had
granted?

The knickers printed with 'Half-Way Inn!,' or simply
go in the all-together.

From pit to empyrean he fretted and held them both up
to the moonlight.

With no greater love than this he closed his closet
door, and approached the 'Snoopy' place cautiously at
first. What a stroke of luck it had been right next
door to his!

Carping his slobber to the paintwork his stethoscope
went on red alert. White noise!

"Come out little 'piggy,' where ever you are" he
sibilated. Whirling like a dervish he held one hand
over his eyes and pointed with his finger like a
Searcher.

His insatiable appetite homed in on her delicious
purring. Was it here the comical spectacle became
unending farce? He suppressed a sanguine howl with his
hands full of jockey.

Just when you weren't expecting such temerity
Grendel 'Nosferatil' had to make his presence felt.

The squeaking pivot slowly anchored, and he shuffled
his devious way inside with the kegs taut around his
scamping ankles.

With a rising flood of blood Grendel tossed the
scrap of garlic hanging above the portal in the
trashcan.

To a flourish of inner trumpets he danced a swift
lambada and examined her with his torchlight flush
against her maroon lips.

He frollicked confidently with her frock folded on
the buffet, snooping omniverously through her
underclothes and garments. With a queer contempt he
protested the impotent artifacts languishing round the
dingle and standing guard in the roundhouse of the
feeble atalaya.

His unmistakable imprint posed in the perspex of the
built-in wardrobe as the *fatted calf* snoozed on her
golden rug.

Cuddly toys and bric-a-brac, the aggravating Snoopy
clock, manuscripts, hieroglyphs, and even a Snoopy
duvet, failed to keep the ghoul in check, but simply
made him feel over the moon.

He knocked the largest Snoopy dog from his wicker
turret and declaimed at the crossroads that he should
ever be inhibited by such tame canine ikons.

Grendel trod deeply into the soft shag pile. He
skulked furtively by the leaded orifice until his
filthy habit could be satisfied with fresh blood.

Hug-and-mugging in cloak-and-dagger he prowled
through a veil of natural shroud. The floodlights of
the stadium had been dimmed...thank god!

In the *White room* Tiffany turned her darling head, and
rebuked the monster with her sighs for having been
delayed.

As if by common consent the pretty young petal
stared toward her fluctuating nocturne...the manic
beamed delightedly with aspirin looks of happiness.

With his rude awakening weighing into the eiderdown
he replaced the loose held diabolo which had fallen
insolently from her grasp to rest more securely
snuggled at her side.

With tender loving care the *unhallowed spirit* mocked
the presence of the flies and adroitly manoevered the
supple hand conveniently hanging over the edge of her
haven to wax-and-wane on his wavering snakehead...but
the nimble digits rapidly absolved and recoiled to hug
around her 'more' accustomed endearment.

In a fit of rage he cursed and spat.
How much longer till he got the damned thing straight?
He fiddled with the balance of her differing
shoulderblades.

Eventually Tiffany seemed to sense just what the
doctor ordered; she wriggled to rest dead centre with
her lucrative gallypot drooping dreamily ajar exactly
on the verge of the quilt...

Quivering with suspense his seething fangs clappered
like a night hawk. A black raven landed on the drain
to crow outside the falstaff.

Tossing back the superfluous material he removed the
grossly impeding plug from her desire-able griker and
laid it gently over her robot pillion.

The mist of his mien crawled over the bones like a
tarantula.

He manoevered his 'tower of Babel' to align with her
dread.

With *true dexterity*, and almost double-jointed, he
lowered the beast necessarily towards the gurgling
enterprise,...pressing tight against her soft wet gums
desiring the fragrance of her kiss.

At long last she recited the correct liturgy.

182

Shaded dark by moonlight with his misty vision cleared
he churned the unremitting labours of his love and
jarred against the rigid pearls of her sparkling
molars.

With his knee buttressing against her headboard the
tiny virgin semblance clenched and unclenched her
trapped and griping palm. With the tonne of his maw-
worm fagging his pounding heart he forced the hazard
stream to scale the heights of sophomore. He urged the
pouting mushroom to release the pressure building in
his toggle. Great balls of fire. A whitewash.

With his straining pick-a-back becoming numb *Grendel*
uttered the magic words; 'Open Sesame!'

But the incantation whispered so despairingly was
without its final charm, and this was no Arabian night.

Her free hand reached up to grip his stem
mechanically in her parchment.

Grubbling her taste-buds over their glittering grid,
where a glob of syrup wheedled its viscous path into
her swallow-hole, sweet Tiffany's eyes opened right on
schedule. She issued the penultimate command tickling
an eyelash on Old Lugger creamed in saliva.

Her eyebrows considerably narrowed as the tingling
sensation began to reach *boiling point*, and the pumping
began like an explosion down the *mineshaft*, filling her
gaping gap with the best of his life-kindling juices,
which splashed so abundantly over cheek and jowl.

Remnants of the guzzling flocked her feather pillow
as he quickly faded out of sight and lost himself among
the slobland.

From the nadir of her robes the prowling fiend
counted his blessings as sweet Tiffany sat bolt upright
in her shorties. She touched her creamy skin where the
ambrosia still dripped like molten sugar and began to
cough and splutter insults.

Grendel trembled beneath the cliff of the
escarpment.

Peering out of focus her hazy indignation snorted a
hum of exasperation towards the crouching bundle before
settling down once more to slumberland...

183

But the voyager had not yet reached his final port of
call; 'Nosferatil' wandered by the silken shards and
admired the portrait of her recent atavist. He
examined each intimate belonging before deciding with
which close encounter he would like to convene his
nuptuals.

The imminent pitch of dawn would still find him
tending lovingly to her crinal curtains with the
'Snoopy' comb....the troublesome Snoopy alarm would
still be waving its luminous limbs from the
mantelpiece.

Before she mounted the scaffolding he would be
chased away by the breaking of the 'making' spell.

The cat-burgular gave a disgruntled 'tut' 'tut' as
he envisaged how he would respectfully remit the white
door after his departure...

Mrs. Do-as-you-would-be-done-by, panting pathetically
at his valance, would gently knock on his latch in the
early morning streak.

If she was fortunate the old dutch might gain a peep
of his hard-on; but only if he forgot to put on the
bolt and pulled down his sheets like the best of all
people.

A shiver ran down the Sleep-walker's spine as he
wondered how long the debauched love affair could
continue nose to tail. He stalled like an alabaster
corpse...

Could no-one drive a merciful stake through his
heart, and convert this shame to sadness?...and say,
"Come on h-o-m-e, Mathew, all is forgiven!"

XXI

BALD EAGLE

The Golden Sunflowers brought tears of joy whenever
Mathew flashed across their vibratile seed of colour...

After visiting the 'Outsider's' exhibition at the
Hayward the Farters retired to the 'Elephant and
Castle' for pie and peas.

Otto Baldung had received a split lip after
attempting to ruffle his tattered plumage. The
corrugated steel shell of the tortoise was like a
motley bed of rags.

A senior lecturer languished in a nearby jail
charged with G.B.H. after attacking a bus conductor
with a bowl of jelly...

The *barley haired Germanic beauty* nudged her best
friend with her elbow.
'Who was the jerk with the rippling biceps?'
Mistook for 'Wings.'

His jerkin buttons seemed to disintegrate with ever
higher levels of intoxication....

Ulrike was the apple of every young blade's eye.
Even Nigel Bates laid claim that it was him who she
stared so longingly towards.

.Tented in her *perfect oscillations* the sensitive
Renaissance features added enchantment to her comely
Streepian smile.

How he longed to run his slippery fingers through
those gilded waves...

It was difficult to decide which were the more
beautiful. Should he gently brush her aureate curls.

She puzzled over small beer. He just resisted the
temptation to scorch his hand. The stray nipple
glimpsed in the exam.

When Gollum returned from the thunderbox he appeared
absolutely radiant. His most recent procurement was
still combing her straggly matted locks.

Earlier in the week he had been on show strutting his
wares in a male talent contest organized by *Calendar*.
But it had turned into a big flop.

If he opened his mouth he could shatter goblets.
"A right Jack-the-lad," Bates observed.

Spying the comb-collector surveying the 'Stocks and
shares' he immediately commented that 'Ram Elevators'
were on the 'up!'

Brandishing recent conquest so smugly on his face
Gollum tackled Mathew on surely his weakest point to
date. A perfect ten!

"You! *Bald Eagle*," he hollered across the
foyer..."When did you last have a wank you ugly-bald-
headed-*bastard?*"

His target postphoned publishing the highest
testosterone count in the city. Turned him into a
'smoothie' in the first place. The groupie turned her
chair away. Let some air get to it!

Spread-eagled in the middle of the company Gollum began
to discuss Mathew's ruling passion with the assembly of
carvers.

He stirred the group into another turbulent palaver.
'Rather snog the bell-ringer's hump?!'

Disguised in the darkened bar the kook frollicked to
some obscure reggae rhythms...

Bates reckoned he must have descended from the Red
Planet.

"Old Baldy must keep *Silvercream* in business!"
A few scarlet faces struggled desperately to channel
their energies into a more productive outlet.

Peculiar emissions erupted from the area of their
gullet, hands were rushed to cover up the
embarrassment, and tears prickled with dust in the
filament.

There was something of the 'Ryan Starbuck!' Fruity.
Gollum fanned the field of keeling wheat with another
tickling wind...put a screw on it.

Cram down the throat. Put a lid on your escapement.

He briefly acknowledged their thin end of the wedge
with a half puzzled smile, vaguely discerning perhaps
that he himself was the but of the knitting bee?

The music-master nonchalently persisted to strike
chords as beads of sweat glistened down the fine mousey
strands flying up his dinner jacket. Rachmaninov's
concerto in C minor. His glance flew round the walls
of the music-room.

Blotches of *mess-mother* appeared on Nigel Bates
corpulent curried neck as he capsized into a number of
odd contortions.

Cantillating like castrati he stumbled stupefied
through the recess, and threw himself into a *Van Dyke*
melancholia.

'Ghandi's revenge' he said. Couldn't make head nor
tail of it...

Felix had carried a haunted look ever since the first
blush of new term. He had spirited himself away to the
upper storey in an effort to muddle through the
anaglyph of plastic arts.

He pensively eschewed the wibble-wabble of the
rhythm method and gleamed skywards.

As he placed an X in the polling booth the Brummie
born and breed was approached by the first year.

The newcomer bellowed like a foghorn...his wrists
were still dangling in swab.

"Don't do it!" he grumbled blearily. "It's not high
enough!"

This unhinged minder-of-metal with the implacable
gesticulations of a fascist dictator had engineered a
tool-pattern of clods to be plied into operation,
carefully measured and announced, crammed with ever so
many mechanical devices, assembled in the gasification
plant of a distillery. Pinnochio had vanished once or
was it twice before..."Do you think he could be round
the twist?" wondered Bernice.

He demanded to know whether she swallowed or spat.
Palleted away on the stretcher he screamed *undying love*
for the girl he'd never met before, having already had
his wooden stems chopped across the kerbstone by a
lynching mob...

The oddball piece of blacklegging, uncannily resembling the reproductive images in his plans, pulled a sequence of harrowing expressions as he caught the 'life-class' in progress. He made several oblique references about his arms being roughly proportionate to the size of his penis. Needed a knee capping.

"Play the white man you thick black bastard!" he farted.

"The way I look, is because of the way I look!" he prattled. Bates instantly acclimatized with him. The blood-donor brimming with Prince Alberts looked about to land a blow. He was still wearing that liver-stained blue jersey set like iron over a month ago. Didn't give a monkeys. Only a harmless jape.

"Well, I've gone and done it at last!" sniffed Felix with a sense of doom and blithe despondency. He wiped the tears from his eyes.

"I just couldn't put it off any longer."
They both sympathized with his predicament, but even Bates had an eagle in his stomach.

Felix nodded sagely and dragged the skeleton clear from his wardrobe.

"You screwed her then!" gleamed the drawing-pin eater...

"Old fat *Bessie the black labrador bitch?*"
"Yes!" he confessed *'diis aliter visum.'* "And I enjoyed every minute of it!" He piped.

Duelled over pork scratchings.
"Who's been writing wisecracks all over my bedroom wall?"

'Still having those nightmares Gollum? When did you last smash up your shack in a frenzy of slumber?'

Bates swore blind he was a madman when he was pissed.While the craps away!

The exhibitionist in stars and stripes glared at Bates for letting the cat out of the bag.

"Bit of a touchy character yon, isn't he?" insinuated Gollum.

"What if he were a *latent homosexual and educationally subnormal?*"

"You will be!" interjected Bates icily...
"Will be what?"

"*Sorry!*" he drilled and grinned. "Have you got a cough?" asked Bates facetiously, and chaffed his itching testicles.

"No he couldn't be!" laughed Gollum shaking his head.

"Besides, he told me already that he was still a little virgin, and has never had a steady girlfriend!"

Linked to the phases of the Moon the invisible assailant carried his artful dodger piggy-back through the University campus towards the distant Zeppelin. It was All Souls.

Placing a pair of milk-bottle tops over his eyes he pretended to stumble around in the dark clutching a white cane. "I'm blind as a Blunkett tonight," he chortled. "How old are you anyway?" he asked.

"I was begotten on the banks of the *River Tigris* over five thousand years ago," he echoed. "There, or there abouts." The surly Bates proclaimed to the Big Dipper. "I challenge all the *bugbears* in creation to overwhelm this bird of prey," he blared.

'Similar invocations were not always consummated immediately,' he declared.

After a showdown at the *amusement arcade* Mathew landed at the digs for a special treat. He flicked through the family snapshots with Tiffany fidgeting nervously from the nearby escarpment. He yawned. His brain was fagged. Every hag needs her...

"And this is when we enjoyed a short spell in *Transylvania,*" she beamed.

"We were so happy in those days: I don't know why we ever left the forest."

"Can I ask you something in private?" she asked.
"Do you always believe in bloodsuckers?"

"Why do you wish to know?" he said studying her *grike.*

"One autumn festival I was in my room fast asleep when I woke up to find an enormous shape hovering above me..."

"My dad said, 'it'll be him!' What do you think it could have been?" She shuffled her feet and prepared to draw her own conclusions. Flagrant abuse of power and privilege.

Could have called for the batmobile. The lodger was polaxed for a second. His lips turned chalk white. Sitting on pins-and-needles.

"Perhaps it was the specter of your recently departed, dear old grandfather?" he answered.

Mathew belvedered for signs of open rebellion...he scrawled 'Vangled' across her maths homework.

On the jaded road below traffic flowed like a mysterious mutant army as he turned his head for what he vowed would have to be the penultimate injection of the radio-active wonder serum.

His bloodshot eyes rolled towards the roast insensible of all consequence on the banquetting cloth as he removed his bleeding biretta.

A flock of inquiring sycamore fell from the russet eaves above and floated by the window of the White room as the stealthy steganographer admired the X-ray photograph by the ebbing phosphor of Selene's silver lamp.

Like a repugnant gargoyle he flew in a flailing motion over to her bedevilled frame. The glitter of his discordant image appeared from the gray of his separate double life.

With a sickly grin spreading beneath the unturfed thatch from ear to ear he contemplated the tender excesses of his composition and began ringing the chimes of the 'Moonlight sonata Interfada.'

"You will!" he stated with expert venom. "You must!" he warned her vehemently with extra tocsin.

The single entity perching desolately on her naked reef prepared to meet the perspiring late night stalker shivering catastrophically.

190

His hand slid beneath the garb towards her unpledged hiney like a mole.

"Why did you?" he asked her..."Why did you?" he sibilated. "Who in heaven's name gave you permission to place a chair behind your virgin white ingress?"

But he would not be baulked, should not be baulked! The buffer had been gradually displaced to the doppelganger's delight.

'Nosferatum' gnashed his flints of calcite and snapped an eye from the crummy Snoopy boss...

With his bald dome bowed the silhouette placed two fingers over the twin small pikes, and pegged them together with a pinch of his lank fulvous nails.

Immediately Tiffany's mouth abruptly distended. He skreaked with elysium at having discovered how to settle old scores.

With his hook nose bent the journeyman explored the deepness of the tomb, where his brain-child's body supined in suspended animation.

To bay the moon he placed the ashdown thermometer in her hand...but the renegade quickly withdrew.

When he returned with greater force she gnawed the ridgelike waterway with her pins and her hand trickled down the rising stem... gummies!

In the amanuensis of the looking glass Grendel perlustrated his crowning glory, pressing the crooked spear into her quest of iron...illustrious crammer!

Suddenly Tiffany stirred, perhaps offended by his omnipotent position, and refused to take the sacred unction offered as a laxative.

Her contraceptive grip educated down the flinching tool to savour the flavour of his pubic region.

Nosferatum froze like acid marble as the pupil searched beneath his dripping testicles and held the hirsute bollocks stiffly in her cooler hands.

"Get stuffed, Bald Eagle!" she fathomed faintly, as if she were hailing from the bottom of some ancient Celtic ink-horn.

What a way to speak to her crammer. He mumbled the lord's prayer backwards and wailed 'Fool's mate!'

191

"For God's sake leave me in the Land of Nod," she
hissed with loathing.

"But...but I'm a doctor!" he stuttered. "You've
forgotten to take all your buttercup syrup."

The bungler flew like a bald bat out of hell back to
the secret recesses of his unhallowed pit and fell into
a melting mood. He shivered as if his useless
existence was finished, breaking out into a cold
unhealthy downpouring.

It looked as if he was floating in it. It was a dirty
bird indeed that fouled its own nest.

Was this to be the culmination of 'Nosferatil's'
cankered esse? He would surely be tried with a
sanctified stake through his palpitating core, and
final, unexpurgated *euthanasia*.

Head-hunters crunking in the *pantry*, entering their
chamber through the trap-door, she stormed, panic
stations, vain regret!

The irate *villagers* were gathering under the gloomy
shadows of the bell tower...shambling behind the
barrier reef..milkies!

Lanterns and shadows squiggled the dark-door as the
alert stockman pursued the passageway for the evil
manifestation.

A clarion call of yolks oscillated through the
entire house and into the dove-cote as he *copied a dead
man* with the iron bolt carefully drawn.

Anybody there? Thunders of the Vatican! Her father
examined the floor for a *poltergeist* disturbance but
still they omitted to vex his dampened bridge.

Crazy as a garbage collector. Six feet under. Sold
out of commission.

"Go back to bed!" the forces Chaplain pragmatically
recommended. "Ghosts can't hurt you, only the living
will!" Sleep safe my tortured love...

At the first cockcrow of dawn the morning blush of
sunlight found his webbed feet hopping rapidly over
pales.

XXII
THE CARROT MUNCHERS

The pale-face in the flag-room often seemed to be
suffering from *jet-lag* as the Soap floundered like a
dumb waiter on the screen.

From the lofty rear window passing shoppers could be
observed flitting through the streets like distant
ants.

Across the arcade the bimbo strained towards the
booby-hatch of kinetic mummy-cloth.

Sairy Gamp peered round the corner of the door to
check if he had swallowed all his pills.

She glanced in his *secret file* lying open on the
vestibule, complete with its dossier of sappy
snapshots.

'*Needs Heavy Sedation!*' was stapled to the front
cover.

The special nurse congratulated him on his
commitment to stay with the company at their never to
be repeated reduced rates.

In the proneos of the amphitheatre she craned over
his loss of condition with the flashbulb.

The distinguished quack had dodged in to the light
opera. His name and titles over the door were
practically obliterated with spiderwebs.

"From here?" she smiled, hesitating with the red
felt pen above his bald spot...Mathew trembled on the
edge of his swivel.

"Forward a bit more," he haggled. "I have a birth
scar on my bonce which used to be hidden, and I would
like it to do so again, if possible."

Before the *superficial* digging of his turf could
proceed...

"Replanted roots will not take on broken tissue, but
we'll do our very best, although I think the crown is
in a much worse state of repair than your receding
forehead!" Full marks for observation then. Boodle
and broke. She called a spade a spade.

Once the operator had marked out the *receiver site* they shaved a rectangle the size of a cassette, which would be used as the *donor area*, from the back of his memory device.

"We'll soon give you a 'head of hair' you can be proud of, cure you of this wretched illness and boost your flagging confidence. The holes in your scalp will shrink to the very tiniest dots on a cheese grater and become practically invisible to the naked eye."

He was helped to his feet and led swaying dizzily into the torture chamber. The Video was immediately plugged-in to divert his driving attention.

As they disregarded 'Rainbow' numerous injections from the steel spike were administered into both territories with local anisthetic. Cloud cuckoo land. Off 'his' bleeding rocker!

Before he could squeal the drill began to collect its hirsute cargo, sending circulation fluid spurting from the mincing blades cascading down his neck.

Each tiny disc bore between one and eight hair follicles it was alleged. A fact!

Prattling deliriously twenty to the dozen the macho man turned for them to calm his fevered grasp.

He postured in the armchair as if he was travelling backwards on the Corkscrew ride. Close your eyes.

Though it was directly against orders the girls offered him their *Lambert and Butler* which he chain-smoked throughout the entirely natural ordeal.

"I never liked Mr. Spore the dentist either," he trembled. "I would do anything to avoid his company on the way home from my lessons!"

Eventually the head case was in such a state that Mr. Marshall, the salesman with the pointed pencil moustache, and even the *concerned director*, were dragged in to stand warily by his side.

The only thing he had in common with E.T. was his lack of consistency.

That famous inventor of the *terrific-trefine* and all the rest of the management team were gathered in the pits calling out slap-happy encouragement.

His condensation interfered with their mechanical gadgets.

Over half a century of plugs were transported from one *bomb site* and stapled deliberately in another, while 'St. Joan' kept rabbiting on about her stay with the *Mad Brushman of Seville.*

The sharp fast teeth of the *carrot munching machine* gnawed into his flesh like a rat hungry rabbit.

Its mouth spat out the provisions like *buckshot* onto the *billiard ball* sweating profusely from all directions.

He turned slightly and caught the belligerent eyes of the director, who immediately warmed and passed this crumb of comfort...

"I hope you don't presume that this will make you good looking or alter your success with women," he advised, expiring to leave the room. "Some of our patients come here under the false impression that a hair transplant will suddenly make them attractive to the opposite sex...!" He laughed and rubbed both his hands together. All the way to the bank sir if you please!-a doctor. a medicine-man.

"All I want is a roof over my head!" sniffed the 'flying Dutchman' in his punishment chair, filled with preposterously high expectations.

The headcase continued to explain the hidden complexities of 'Mentalism' to his audience, discussing the "meaning of life' with the creasing bloodsuckers.

"But I believe our true purpose is simply pro-creation!" he suggested; the inventor seemed quite confident he knew what he was talking about.

Mathew paid a fast buck for this jump from the frying-pan. No six inch sutures at this juncture. No scrubbing away the scabs before time on this *six month cycle of a thousand cuts.*

Cold steel needles tunnelled under his stuff, as the fosser munched through the back of his wide open *water-melon.* With lymph glands juicing he stared fearfully into space like an automoton with paranoid eyes.

"Not long now!" she chortled merrily. "We're nearly done!"

"You'll soon be able to go home to your wife, but remember, *no sex for three whole days!* The grafts need a short period to re-settle. Do not wash your new hair for at least a fortnight."

She mopped the channel as his heartbeat pounded, and the red-hot lava trickled into his thought processes.

Suddenly there was a bright flash above the performance; the electric lightbulb had burst. The stuttering arc showered its glassy cartilage through the eclectic atmosphere, to explode on the giant base.

Both their lumpers looked stunned..."Oh! Golly," she gasped. "That's never happened before." She rushed to catch the salesman who was loitering in his newspaper.

But the proceedings were soon brought to a speedy conclusion.

Mathew was helped out of his drubbing for the *Great Dane* to swap places in the former *abbatoir*.

The surgical dressing wrapped tightly round his head added vertigo, and a sudden nausia welled up in his abdomen as he observed himself in the Gentleman's looking-glass carrying the flag.

The *numbskull* peered at his pale and ashen face and rubbed his mole-coloured sockets...he'd certainly aged five years during the four hour operating process, and yes, there was a white hair already avoiding his restricted circulation bodice.

"See you soon I hope!" she gleamed obligingly. "Reception has just advised me that your wife is here to collect you! If you encounter any problems please give our recorder a buzz..."

The lift plummeted to the ground floor where the woman waited on the thoroughfare beside the outer springboard.

Through the iron girders of the *locust* cage he glimpsed her etiolate spectre. Lump-shit...

He emerged into a grim and woeful daylight swaddled like the 'Phantom of the Pharaoh's Opera.'

The teacher cudgelled his arm as he tottered wearily over the cobbles. His swollen turnip-head throbbed like a football as he groped his way along the wall.

Familiar market dwellers stopped to pillory him as the gowk struggled to stretch the *tea-cosey* over his out-pouring clock...

"Oh! Mathew, well done!" she clapped. "At last you've had some decent 'common' sense. But it was all your own fault really. I always told you not to go on those awful sunbeds...You are a pain in the neck. If it hadn't been this it would have been something else," she warranted...Somebody left the door open, and the wrong dog came home.

The chump awoke from the recurring vision.which suborned him to return to that radioactive dungeon with a ringing in his ears. Dabs of dried fop still lingered to the stained night pillow, and he could hear his mother's call startling up the stairs.

"Come on down Mathew!" she moaned. "Look who's here to see you." Their pedal bikes were moored beneath the sunfilled foliage.

Withdrawing hastily under his tent Mathew flagged-down his wiry raddled nose-beard.

He tapped tentatively on the paintwork. His best friend paced up and down beside the grill.

"Don't you understand that you can't possibly emulate my honours of battle," he chuckled.

Ryan Starbuck rotated his round blue peeps and made them go all cross-eyed.

Mathew's solitary eyes peered out from the spunk-hole. He slowly emerged like a shy wrinkled hermit. Gone deaf as a.post. Nerves slashed. Couldn't fuck.

"The diving club all want to know where you have disappeared. I've brought Stephanie along to see you. We want you to be best man when we tie the knot in spring."

Mary led the *sun-tanned Aphrodite* to where the invalid immediately faded once more into his bundle of parchment. How now my fine feathered friend.

His hand wound like a thread-worm from the darkness. "My mother is so looking forward to meeting your acquaintance. She had an accident in the schoolyard on Wednesday while on dinner duty..."

"It was so windy that her hair-piece blew off and all
the children were in hysterics while she chased it
round the yard."

The *toxic warrior* materialized for a restorative
draught of skim. No cannibals or Milesian women.

"We think it's the best thing that you've ever
done," they agreed. He reared his ugly T-bag steak.

To his surprise Ryan Starbuck bent over and kissed
him on the head...."That does it!" laughed his fiance.

"I always thought there was something going on
between you two..."

His spire had been ravaged with fire and sword.
Head like a plastic dolls.

Mathew stubbornly rocked his bloater. Daft as a
brush. Mad as a fucking hatter.

"I'm definitely not going to put in the kitty until
this is all over," he pledged.

"That is going to be the last time anyone calls me
Bald Eagle!"

*   *   *

He tramped to the bottom of the trichonosis and glanced
sharply behind him.

All that the monstrous birth perlustrated were the
creepers entwined in the branches scaffolding the
flazen gable.

Crossing up the frozen stairs of concrete he emerged
into the plateau's baking summer heat wearing only his
blue jeans, except for that ridiculous batch of wool
the plasterers were always attempting to eviscerate.

In the mansion across the *boulevard* that *damned
loose-liver* lingered in her menagerie of felines.

At their garden gate the *innocents* were entering
with a *bag of rice.*

Dirty Harry stumbled like a Boston Strangler.
After karaoke night at the Beacon his artificial cogs
had been puked down the lavatory.

The hairy little gnome with the *garde-l-o-o-ed* glass
bauble fretted over his vagrant sleep-walking.

He was convinced that the tape-recording was a wild
goose chase.

The paralytic warbled his favourite rendition...
"No need to worry, no need to cry; I'm an undercover
agent working for the F.B.I..."

For the seventh occassion that transition Mathew
ascertained his aspect beneath the half-built window
arch and mounted the carefully laid firestep rostrum.

She had passed him earlier that morning sliding over
debris. The nubile nursing auxiliary had practically
blushed as they almost rubbed shoulders together.

He decided that when the 'jack was sprung' he would
certainly summon up the courage to say 'Good day!'

How many moves after hours when the quarriers had
returned to their nearest and dearest would the sun-
tanned torso of the litter lout have to fool around?
Cough, holler, and call; to loiter in his secret
seedbed to gain her fixed attention.

The spare plot of land was soft-hued as a muzzler.
His precarious platform quivered as he manoevered into
the correct position. The *dolls-house* with its many
exposed chambers lit the occupants of every single room
privately in their dwellings. Wasn't this a *red light
zone* though? Could have been almost anybody.

At last the mystified brunette arrived to mull-over
the box overlooking the juggler, casually champing a
green apple as she did so, and admiring the settlement
from her *rose-window.*

The dirty-Arab signalled from afar. She winced
uncomfortably but decided to outlast his creative urge
invoked for her eyes only. Disproportionately
represented! Little India.

The 'ganger' unzipped his denims and pulled out a
whopper, as the woman leaned forward to take down all
his details.

Thrashing away in the blistering hot sump she glued
her guns to the screen and hovered until he was
beginning to wobble. Cock-Crow!

Spurts of semen sprayed into a dry monsoon as the
punkah-wallah tottered on the pile of sunbaked slabs.

Her upper half seemed to leap clean through the nearby lattice-work shaking her point expressly up and down.

That's no way to treat a lover! There was a pounding in his brain and a scarlet river drizzled onto the waning lunarian's shoulders.

"Hey you! What the hell do you think you're doing down there *Bald Eagle*?" she clattered. He floundered like a Stormy Petrel.

"If you don't stop hawking me you filthy mugwump!" she sternly bellowed at the top of her timbre. "Then I'm going to get you put where you belong!"

It was a wonder that she had not disturbed *Dirty Harry* from his trance. With his Silver Key. Thus departed.

He tottered from his perverted pinnacle quaking like a moose.

A puddle of molten grampus bubbled on the red hot stoney ground.

When he arrived at the summit a *woman dressed in black* was once again consulting the dandiprat.

"Ere, Mathew love," he sniffed. "You're a big strapping lad, built like a *brick shithouse!*"

"What 'ave you been doing?" he drolled, in his drawling Lancashire accent.

XXIII
FALLEN IDOL

The prayer-meeting puffed along with 'Parochial' Pete, the pimply-faced creep, hamming his lines as confrere on the side-wagon. A spot-light of stale expressions.

His neutered voice echoed sadly throughout the establishment among the resplendent *speaking in tongues* and Yiddish utterances.

Another collaborator arose to announce its meaning, commended by 'simple' Simon, the ringleader of the college cult, and prime co-ordinator.

"Let out!" he stipulated. "Let out!" to the moron still holding out!

"Your human tears must flow in order for our Saviour to enter your heart and confirm you as a child of the creator."

The cast of the sect clasped their eyelids and clenched their teeth.

Mathew slyly undid his latches to focus on the member with the enormous brown plates also cheating the syndicate. She yawned so wide he could have built St. Pauls. Every atom owned by the lord.

The veneer's thick cherry lips motioned a slice of juice to roll joyfully over the *diabolical chant* giving him admirable spectacle to phanta-size.

Once more the evil hand reached out towards the achromatized church elders swooning in jim-jams.

With a shudder breaking from Felix the nebulous infection seemed to spread like a virus among the hosts from the grudging kingdom above.

"Welcome!" he cried..."The lord has been waiting for you, Mathew, to be solemnly *born again!*"

The sword swallower calmed the weird carnival with a *coded hymn of gobbledegook*, and right on cue Upstart sprang up to the ceiling, floating on his wish, to interpret the concatenation of circumstances, with

absolute certainty, that his altogether random
occurrance of flukes was without doubt a holy miracle.

The unco-ordinated interpreter deflated to his pew
and requisitioned at the ingress with the silver dish.

"The light of the world sends his *glad tidings*.
Blessed are the meek for they will inherit their
tenement of clay."

Polluting the oppressive atmosphere still further
with his carnal muse the watcher underpinned them with
a concentration of obtuse vibes.

"Some other time," they snarled. "The moment will
soon come when you will be ready to receive the holy
spirit."

'Not on your nelly!' he vowed...

A turncoat Jew daubed in PLO fabrics broke into a brisk
hosanna accompanied on acoustic guitar by the
pedagogue.

"I do hope that you can all come again," he effused.
The listless flock arose from the admirable sense of
well-being to plod sedately through the silent streets
guided only by the star-of-'David.'

There was a month of Sundays to reflect on the
afternoons proceedings...

When he reached the campus at mid-day the head of
department had asked him to explain the cartoon drawn
by *Gollum*, which had been found pinned to his tutor's
bivouac.

A very amusing portrait of the unmistakable power-
lifter climbing a ladder with a hod-full of bricks had
taken some explaining, especially when he had been
three days late in returning for the new term.

Heidi had called in the morning and unwittingly stopped
the whole carry-on..."Do they have harems in the
Universal Church?" he'd asked, but she didn't seem to
follow the essence of his diatribe.

The moon-faced maiden from Finland had spent many
hours trying to persuade him to attend one of their
kirks, but Mathew was only interested in what lay
beyond her skirt...

It appeared as if a nuclear warhead had hit the
cockroach cloister when he entered their shared
occupation. It was obvious at once that some sort of
disturbance had taken place while he was being press-
ganged.

Nigel Bates came charging down the stairs in his
coffee-coloured underpants with the pebbles of his
'Smartie' gravel *mantra* still sticking to his behind.

"Cholmondesly has just stuck his nut on me!" he
roared. "He thinks he knows my number!"

It was unnecessary for Bates to present the large
bump which had emerged on his forehead in such a
forthright manner.

Thank God he had recovered from the shakes when he
had not even been able to hold a glass of pagla pani.

His false bravado resulted from a row about whether
the moon was made of Cheese.

Following the skirmish in the studio Bates had been
swept along the corridoor helped by the size twelve
boot of an All Black.

The remains of that huge television set he'd
scrawned from the scrapyard had landed at the bottom of
the steps like a flying bedstead.

Bates began to spark. He was always very sensitive
to changes in room temperature. Said life was a gas.

He darted upstairs for what he could muster to take
the sting out of the artful dodger's draining
encounter.

Returning rapidly from the mess he pressed his faded
copy of *der Spunkenhousen* deftly into his grasp. There
was a splodge of green slime on the pigskin, from his
last supper we can only assume.

"Good and Evil are simply different sides of the
same wad of counterfeit," he advised.

"I think you ought to read the book of changes from
a totally unheard of perspective before making up your
mind. It's not what goes into the head, it's what you
utter out loud which comes from the heart!"

"If you're going to say orthodox things say them in
unorthodox clothes."

"You look as if you have been frightened half to death.
What you really need is a damn good quoff. If we hurry
we should be just in time for last orders. There's no
benefit to be had from scoffing rotten fruits. Send
your choppers into uncharted seas and all the rest.
Beware of wicked and corrupt influences."
   "Oh, Fuck the 'Holy Ghost,'" he cackled.
"That's excellent!"
   "I can't wait until I see Pete tomorrow to give him
'our' Glad Tidings. It's an absolute disgrace what
they have put you through. If I had my way they would
still be feeding them to *the Lions*...the only excuse
god has is that he doesn't exist! It would be far
easier for a camel to pass through the crotch of a
darning tool than for Captain Bob's knob to enter the
gates of Greyfriars."

It was four o'clock in the morning when Mathew suddenly
awoke to find the squatter standing half-naked over
him, munching a pork-pie, and waving an Axe between his
self-defacating fingers...he'd been meaning to put a
lock on that door for ages. Bates swore blind it could
be like a minefield. He wafted his strip of Parchment.
   The screaming thing had probably found the weapon
lying around in the *cellar* where he had recently
constructed a dark room.
   "What in blazes are you doing Nigel? We were only
pulling your leg."
   "I've been having some really spunky dreams!"
blurted Bates in a flurry. He gradually graduated into
delirium.
   "Now I'm sure of the worm that never dies; rulers
are meant to be knackered."
   "Well, I'll be damned."
There were three numbers smeared in tobacco-leaf across
his thorax. His voice sounded as if it stuttered from
the tip of a distant galaxy, and a shred of corn
projected from his arse-end. If Bates never smoked a
fag in his life, then how come his pincers were forever
covered in nicotine powder? Said he could perform his
own circumcisions. His ear was dripping with blood.

He boasted that he had sprayed graffiti all around the
town-hall time-piece.
   Spurting in fits and starts the sinister Bates began
to describe his bizarre voyage through the mysterious
rose-coloured Ark, and lifted up his arms to solicit
the horrid bite marks.
   "I've been taken for a ride by the bloody-bones of
the hobgoblins," he barnstormed.
   "They returned to whisk me away through the skylight
while declaiming loudly in high-pitched harmonies."
   "Don't be silly, but of course!" he barracked.
"We tossed through the canopy of an enchanted wheel of
oak, and landed in the dead-centre of an ancient stone
circle..."
   "A luminous green eye flickered from the devouring
element where we shagged."
   "My sire the toadman shelfed us down on tall fungi,
where we toasted his health in 'Theakston's Old
Peculiar.'"
   "It was truly out of this world," he blazed...
"They even drink their own piss," he vouched.
   "Three cheers for the headless-hunter...down in one!
A blasphemous affront to a great many of our polite
politicians."
   "But he's gone to meet his maker?"
Bates scowled and wiped his nose on the back of his
hand. ·
   "It was utterly marvellous! There's nothing at all
to be worried about on the other side. The hybrids
whispered the secrets of immortality in my lug·."
   "Then we climbed down a small rabbit warren to enter
Gae's topaz-coloured Eden."
   "I only cancelled my ticket because I accidentally
glared at my palms," confessed the deviant pilgrim.
   "I have the number now! I have it now!" he whipped.
As a result of his amazing encounter Bates was able to
move objects at will...

It sounded as if the night owl had been caught wrong-
footed when Mathew heard him bleating on the payphone
just outside his pigeon-hole.

"Yes mother, it's 'only' me," he heard him whimper. He
listened intently and attempted to prevent his mouth
from sniggering. "For Christ's sake!" yelled Bates.

A rare-boat of emotion rose and sank as Nigel Bates
blasphemed to high heaven.

"Oh, no!" he sobbed. "Not even that. It's
terrible, what?"

"How final...do you want me to shoot straight home
then?"

He threw the receiver down with such force that it
crackled like musketry.

Bates plunged up to his ramshackle dorp with the
whey of his vindaloo running down his left shank.

He came flying down the stairs again with the gnomes
fishing rod, and his sordes wrapped in a snotty polker-
dot, to trammel to the station, along with his
mescaline pipe.

"That's it now!" he bitterly rankled. "He's finally
got what he always wanted."

"Now he can go to visit the brothel whenever he
feels like the fuck-charge."

"My pretty young sister has been slugged by a lion
in the path," sniffed the Circumlocutor dismally.

Strange surreal noises plagued his rancorous gullet
as Bates set about smudging the puke from his upturned
collar.

Down below the oft stray laces of his sneakers had
been mischievously tied together. Said he could murder
a cereal...

He quickly reverted to rollicking laughter.
Mat bade farewell to his adversary at the station and
returned to the pile of dirty crockery *nine miles high.*

He persisted in piling a heap of junk between the
cooker and the chest of drawers until the queer
mountain had reached the desireable height for Farhat
the cat and all her grinning peoples.

The blunder of footsteps suddenly bumped down from
the thunderbox and the entrance burst asunder.

He winced at the awkwardness of the situation but
still received an invite while appearing to change the
light-bulb.

"By the way, someone rang for you..." cholered Pete.

"Coincidentally, I called to see if Nigel would be
attending our next function..."

"You don't know where he could have been?"
"His curtain was blowing in the draught and his bedding
was completely straight. And some kind of small wooden
'doll' was lying naked on the sheets."

XX1V

FORBIDDEN PLANET

She cleared her swanlike throat and brushed her
bleached blonde shards in the silver glass...smiled her
pretty smile, and at the calling of her mother's voice
charged down the staircase.

She tucked the sky-blue scarf around her neck inside
the orange kagoole, and jumped clean over the steps
onto the *pontoon bridge.*

Everyone's love skipped along the garden boulevards
to visit the *Beast of Hearts.*

Each glowing tulip trebled as she passed and
spreading pollen streamered.

She fixed the sweet red berry above her cerulean
buds and danced along the spangled arches with the cool
breeze bolstering those rosey cheeks...staring into the
light gale with her eyelids on the blink, and causing
tears to roll effusively down her angel face. It was a
rotten trick of hers.

"Summer loving had me some fun..." she warbled as
the 'Go-between' fell into line and finished at the
gate with a bump.

"Get a move on Scallywag!"
The summer snowdrop spun the green mowed lawn about the
congruent flowerbeds, and trotted beneath the splendid
Cherry tree refulgent with its blossom.

She paused to pull up her bobbysocks and received a
lick from the darting *throw-out.*

She giggled and hid inside her coat. Leaning
forward to rap on the knocker she tugged it over her
head.

"I've come to take *Patch* for a walk," she blushed.
"We live just around the corner at number thirteen
also. My name is Lin...what's yours? We were allowed
to play in your garden once before."

"Pardon?" he asked. "What did you say you're name
was?"

"My name is Lin..." she smiled immaculately.
Better ask her again.

"I'm sorry," said the young man. "I appear to be
going deaf in my old age. Did you say they called you
Linn..."

The girl flushed even deeper. "My name is Lin..."
she said and veered towards the drawbridge. Why was he
putting her through the hoop?

"Penny for them," he snapped.
"What?"

"Penny for your thoughts."
"Oh it's nothing," she flushed. "Only I've seen you
once before. You were passing nearby exactly two years
ago. I'd rather have a quid."

"Do you want to come in?" he asked.
"I shouldn't," she replied. "My mum has always warned
me not too since that time with *Mr. Ali.*"

She reminded him of someone but for the life of him
he just couldn't think who. He felt the air of another
planet waft by.

"How old are you?" she teased. "Your hair's
beginning to wave...wave goodbye!" she laughed. "Your
eyes remind me of flowers...cauliflowers! Your teeth
are like stars. They only come out at night."

Suddenly the girl reached into her pocket and pulled
out an enormous ripe tomato.

"Don't tell my mum will you," she whispered
earnestly. "She doesn't know that I've got one."

She handed him the fruit in her generous outspread
palm.

"A tomato. What on earth?" he complained. She sunk
at his ungrateful response.

"Oh, thankyou," he smiled. "I don't know what to
say."

Mathew galloped to the bay window where the girl
appeared once more.

Her eyes glittered like lapis lazuli as they waved
their magic spell and he pressed his face with
difficulty to the period ventanna until she disappeared
towards *Miles Rough...*

'You are my sunshine, my only sunshine,
You make me happy when skies are grey,
You'll never know dear, how much I love you,
Please don't take my sunshine away.'

Her luscious bare pink thighs spread around his narrow waist as he carried her across furlongs of the verdant fields.

Lindsey's soft repose rested gently on his arch when least expecting a warming ray of sunshine.

A troup of faithful followers tagged along in a band, and as he staggered round the corner her mother lambasted from the other side of the dewdrops.

"For god's sake put her down....she's bigger than you are! What are you? The *pied piper*?"

"I used to go out with a *black-man*," she bragged. "When we were up in the quiet house we practised Postman's knock."

"Why don't you go steady with Janet?" she asked. "Everyone knows that the farmer's daughter is keen on you. And even Anita likes you. I saw you chatting her up!" she teased. "That day you were on the telly! Hairy chests are sexy..."

They entered her toft and waited until Molly was in the kitchen placing her garments in the tub.

Mr. Barclay retired up to the lavatory to devote some time to his book of oaths. 'Doesn't he have a home to go to?' he enquired.

She flattered him with her ice-blue smile. Taking it in turns they each bent down and kissed the region of their navels, protected by the safe margin of the material. "I dare do it," she laughed. "But only once!"

Swinging her admirable legs up on the sofa she spread them wide and pulled down her navy knickers.

Like a 'sheela-na-gig' she exposed her pouting labia the same way she did on the back seat of the chemistry lab. Could even do the Can-Can.

Mathew stared in disbelief at the size of her giant canyon...she certainly knew how to do a strip-tease.

"Are you disappointed there are no hairs yet?" she asked. Her fingers fluttered over the surface of his zipper..."Now show me your thing!"

"You do it!" She blushed and would not believe he was still unhandselled. "A dirty old man like you," she joked. "You look about seventy five. Keep it inside," she sighed.

"My goodness!" she gasped. "You've got a hairy willy just like William...Quick, pull them up! Is that what it really looks like...long and fat, with the end like a plum?"

"As long as you don't spunk on me!" she said. "It's getting wet inside. Stop before you spunk on me and it runs all down my leg!"

Her gorgeous lamps lit up like burning fires and sparkled with a chilling blue deep in their heart.

Then the informer, Gretel, burst in on them and threatened to impeach her brother, invoking section E. She sneered that sooner or later he'd get copped!

"Look at this girl's face," she glared. "You can't tell me you weren't both up to something!" Lindsey began to cry and cover up her flaming cheeks...

"Do you know that she is a minor?" she fumed. "Leaving her alone with the likes of you. How dare you lead her on," she scorned. "Men like you ought to be castrated, and then it would be too good!"

Gretel hadn't seen anything for certain, but she definitely smelled a rat. Why should he be allowed to get away with it? Nobody else would.

"You can choose your friends but not your family," she disparaged, "just like 'chalk and cheese' they really are. I wouldn't put anything past him."

How many nights thereafter did Mathew supine by their fireside while the male fond girl cavorted in her shorties, flashing her silky stockings, lewdly lifting up her hem and pretending to place a penis into her vagina and St. Elsewhere?

"Will you be coming on Sunday papers in the morning?" She began to weep if he even appeared reluctant.

With the *Evening Star* chanting overhead he turned to
glance up at her bedroom window where he knew she would
be waving frantically.

As she blew kisses to the true-bad-door beneath the
street lamp her mother crooned towards the pretty
creature in their modest turret. This was not the
silent quintessence of seduction.

She opened her Valentine card while he loitered
strictly 'out of limits.'

"Oh, poor Mathew," she said. "Gone and cut his head
open. When did he trip over the stone? I must go
round to see if he's alright."

Each member of the tribe pulled on a woolly pom-pom
hat and arrived glimmering on the mat.

Her young man was still refusing to see visitors no
matter how earth-shaking, but for a few seconds they
persuaded him to acquiesce.

Mathew painfully exulted as they grinned up from the
bier...

Straddled to his back in symbiotic harmony he honked
the *Chevalier* tune.

To the mercy of Baal and the holy habit of religion.
I swear by almighty god that the evidence I give...

"My mum says it's okay for the time being," she
said. "We *can* go together."

"And you will make a good enough chum for our
Michael."

"Look at Nicholas!" she roared over the hedge.
"That's the pervert who's been *done* for stealing ladies
knickers from their washing lines. My mum told me
never to talk to him, or go for a ride in his car."

"Girls of that age will go with anyone!"
'You can only dispose of innocence once!'
"Whatever turns you on," she sneered.
She'd keep her mouth shut "for now!"
"You and your bald-headed boyfriend!"
"Why don't you go to hell!" she yelled.
"Do you have to keep saying you're sorry?"

Through every type of season Lindsey and Mathew
trammelled cheek by jowl over hill and dale.

'His' grant was spoken for with wine gums. 'She' was
born beneath the arrow of a bowman.

"Paul isn't my boyfriend anymore," she declared.
"It's you I li...It's you I love best from now on
Mathew...promise you'll never desert me?"

"Do you like Fiona? I hate her! She always thinks
she's better than us. Did you see how easily he went
off with her on the big dipper?"

"You're the only girl for me," he said. "I'm not
interested in her or anyone else!"

Lindsey was standing by the willow tree when they
knew they were alone...

"Why aren't you married yet?" she asked in fun. She
tried to tickle him as they chased around the skirt.

"Marry me then," he joked.
"But you look older than Mr. White."

"Can I meet you again in ten years time?" He simply
had to gather the harvest before returning to the
firing-range.

"In five years my dad says."
Leaving the grain and rain soaked pollen freeborn they
retired to the pumping-room tucked away safely in the
kush. One drop of semen to a hundred of Blood!

Although Scallywag barked for twenty minutes she was
not allowed to watch him train.

Before currenting the wind they wandered expectantly
in the shadow of a shade where the sign stood against
the far partition; *Pinewood Studios*. It earned him
some extra dosh while studying at the *Fart Academy*.

They stood admiring the craftmanship together.
Then he suddenly felt her hand sneaking lightly over
his bum. A hard task-mistress.

He discovered Infanta to be more than usually
coloured.

She began to pipe and purl...

"I must, I must, I must improve my bust!   I will, I
will, I'll make it bigger still! Hurrah! Hurrah! I
need a bigger bra!" She could even do the splits!

"*Nitimur in vetitum!*" he ventured.
Knuckling down on the bench she offered to demonstrate
a jape she had recently learnt at middle school. It
would only take a few seconds while he closed his eyes.

'Imagine there's a *cluri-chaune* standing in the
centre of my hand,' she propositioned.

"Now scratch her head! Point to her belly
button...she's wobbling because you tickled her. Touch
where you think the ends of her nipples are...she likes
that! Now put your finger towards her crack."

At this juncture Lindsey bent over to place her warm
wet mouth around Mathew's outstretched finger...The
surprised digit slipped sloppily out of her
accomodating oriel with a noisy slurp, and he jumped
back at the startled poking feel.

"I'd give anything to have a suck of your willy
Mathew," she said. Smiling happily she made out a case
with her wayward thumb. "You could get into trouble if
I ever told anyone," she squinted. "But don't worry.
I promise 'not' to kiss and tell."

Lindsey 'tuatha' lay down the length of the bench
and spontaneously dropped her frilly white knickers
adroitly to her ankles.

"Lick me out then," she exhorted. "I want to feel
what it's like inside my pussy."

"Pretend to be asleep," he suggested.
"No! You'll put your hairy willy straight in my
mouth," she insisted. "I've had that sticky lump in me
before...I don't have to!" She pouted disobediently and
exposed her expanse across the *Plimsoll mark.* "Cross
your heart and hope to..."

Kneeling down between the lush white virgin's legs
Mathew licked around the gleaming hole of the Infanta's
bald crutch.

It seemed to arouse the pungent odour of her sex.
His old Mahatma tongue pierced enticingly between the
young bay wedge.

Her weeping jib responded with a modicum of gum which
he gently lapped with trepidation. He masticated the
odd pickles of *double Gloucester*, until she panicked
and urged him to halt; "It makes me feel like jelly and
I want to go to the throne-room."

The Infanta's eyes sparkled with excitement and her
autocratic stars seemed to burst into rapture.

She pleaded with him to evince how human semen
manifested itself. He was apprehensive whether he
would be able to satisfy her want and did not wish to
disappoint the iron heel.

Greater Mogul slowly undid his peggies as requested
and she placed her curious hand inside the wrapper.
His penis blushed at the prospect of being guzzled by a
cherub.

"Why do you have to hold it in your hand?" she
complained. "Can't you simply let it go so I can see
your whole length?"

"Show me what spunk looks like," she demanded
intolerantly. "I know that you can! Make it shoot out
of the tag or I'm going home to watch *Blue-Peter.*"

Lord of the damned crouching in your secret lair was
this the tender maiden with whom to plight thy troth?

He cajoled her into helping with her firm young

grip...
"You toss it up and down?" she asked. Concentrating
all her attention on the bloated glans so that she did
not miss anything.

"That's to stop your hand from slipping off the
end," he nodded. "Trust me, I'm a medical man."

"No, just hold it still, that should be enough.
There's no need to pull it roughly about like that."
Should he insist she draw tight her flawless white
cornea in case he fluffed it?

Comfortably encircling the erect circumference of
his gentle penis she squeezed and relaxed alternately
as he had instructed.

Her vordant mouth strayed wider than Warrington gap
as she slipped unconsciously forward. A mizzle of dew
leaked from the ferret eye only centimetres from those
lovely baubles.

"Come on! Hurry up!" she scolded tartly from the desk.
"I haven't got all day and there's plenty more I could
be doing. Tell me when you're going to spunk so I can
be ready won't you? Why are you taking so long when
I've been holding it for nearly half a minute? It's
longer than you said, and now you're just being stupid!
I'm doing all the sodding work," she grunted.

The guru exorcised the lucrative limits of his
authority and could feel a tingling sensation beginning
to roll the clouds. He gave her effort full marks and
a bird's eye view.

She slowly pushed out her sipper, procuring a single
drop of his emission on the very tip of her tentative
probe, and tasted the fluid with a disagree-able mien,
as the straining fruit swelled ever further towards its
ripening.

With this singularily erotic act *Young Cyrano* in his
fleece began to spurt powerfully into the host of
heaven. With that he stole her fancy and flung it to
the firmament.

Her blazing stars were still mesmerized to the core
as she instinctively raced to cover her chomper. With
a gipping grunt of her gut her gripper reached
especially for her abdomenal area.

He eked-out the chockfull himself before he could
comfort her. The cascading continued endlessly before
her open gaze. She brayed desperately for her nunky.

Her senses swam and her lush young pins reeled
unsteadily. A sickly back-lash distinctly retched and
the snow-white face had surrendered its attractive
tinge of erubescence.

Between her outspread legs a pool of gippo
cloistered on the dry concrete base. Once more she
rose to leave as the footsteps of her mother trailed
across the yard.

"Oh, mamma, where's my mamma?" she cried through
pillars of beatified salt.

"Why didn't you tell me when you were going to drop
your load. You promised that you would before we
started."

Tears welled-up in those pretty blue buds as he tripped
over the dumbell.

"It smells like a pigsty in here!"
They both waved to 'Aunty' Mary drying the dishes
through the cabin window and 'sick of the sight.'

Mathew could not suppress the ecstatic smile which
spread over his gleaming aspect.

He wanted to hug her joyfully and to celebrate this
feeling of great deliverance.

"Is that what really happens inside a woman's body?
I didn't know it was going to be like that," she
gawped.

"I'm sorry," he said. "I'm really doing my
penance...but I never meant to cry wolf. Though that
which is done out of true love always has a certain
freedom of error beyond the pale of human endeavour."

"Well it's too late now," she gibed. "Oh, don't
keep going on about it. You already have, besides, it
never really happened!"

She soon tarried with the Piper's tribe as they
gathered the black fruit in twilight innocence. The
mut with cataracts wandered around the outskirts.

For a moment the indiginous felon strolled with his
head above steam. But when it came to push and
shove....

A silent dose of rain had bathed the ripened seed
with a succulent covering of moisture and within every
tiny mirrored globule appeared the distorted shapes of
Tuatha.

Like a decadent star the fallen hero sank into an
ever deeper morass but was still joyously happy.

He desired to pour holy water over her victorious
attributes now that *Grendel* had been put to death in
daylight hours.

The terra incognita had dared to mutter its moniker;
what a triumph to return to Gollum with!

Lead in her pencil. Ink in his pen. White men
can't get it up! Boloney.

Said she'd been screwed already by James the Crow-
bar. You big-bald-beautiful-bastard.

Suddenly she toppled broken-hearted from the step.
No amount of consoling seemed to prevail upon the heart
of the matter. Great balls of tears sprouted from her
pretty germs and plummetted over the water's edge.
'The darker the berry the sweeter the juice,' it is
said...
"Tell me what's the matter?" he pleaded. But she
was cast in a terrible scud of water-vapour. Seemed
like worlds apart.
Only after consultation with Mary would her mother's
visit to the surgeon become common knowledge.
He placed his arm lovingly around her shoulder when
she said that no-one in her family loved her and
squeezed her gently to his side. Mathew removed a barb
from her hair.
"But I think the world of you!" he insisted
despairingly.
"Well, *I hate you!*" she quickly retaliated.

XXV
HEART OF GOLD

When Mary and the 'lodger' evaporated over the cobbles
for another week the *little red riding hood* would sob
from her popcorn-bag in the back seat.
Why on earth was he stranded in *Antichton?*
Saucy Miss. Gibbon had been telling fortunes in the
gypsy tent at the festival, but no amount of fluttering
her eyelashes could persuade him to renege with her to
the hop.
He won the 'Welly throwing competition' with a throw
of over one hundred and ten feet...but the attractive
form inside the blonde's black bikini filled him with a
sense of trepidation. The Art Miss was learning Hindi.
Mary went bananas when she heard he was planning to
trudge on the stupid paper round after all her scheming
behind the scenes with *thunderthighs.* Lindsey said it
was like trying to get blood out of a stone sometimes.
Could learn anything by heart if he tried.
'There's nothing stopping you,' coaxed the Infanta.
"They've started. They've really started. No they
haven't, I'm only joking," she laughed.
Discharges of *white hot pus.* Gorgonzola? "Cross my
heart and hope to die," she said.
"Not with that little strumpet!" Back another inch.
"Noddy, look it's Noddy!" screeched the local kids.
"It's Noddy in his woolly hat. What's he hiding
underneath?"
Friends and neighbours boggled at their windows.
Butterscotch memories melted through the cornflake
blaze of festoons.
And what are little girls made of? Sugar and spice,
and all things nice...the sun danced in her eyes.
"I like men's willies," she giggled. "But I don't
like their hairy balls. I know it's wrong, but it's
right." And when they were up, they were up, and when
they were down, they were down, and when they were only
half-way up they were neither up, nor down...

A scarlet flicker of heat filtered through the charcoal
sunrise and he made her his own with the *band of gold.*

There was a twinkle in her eyes and her hair dazzled
him with its radiance as if love had repulsed the sands
of time. A long long time ago. The Happy Prince.

'Though this jewel fades, my love for you will never
burn in flames.'

"I'm dreaming of a white Christmas."
"Make a wish," he said, as if they were snapping bones.
A ray of light caught the solitary heart as she danced
around the totem with her eyes fixed on the rebound.

"Yippee, it fits," she cried, leaping into the air.
She splashed her sunshine like a merry bowl of rhymes.

The tiny fairy queen waved the plain motif
magnanimously at the spur and his breast soared like a
bird. There was a flighty look in her eye as he
attempted to share a knotty point. She tossed away her
daisy-chain. Whose heart was made of pure pure gold.

"Even if I fall out with you I still get to keep
it," she assumed. There were stars in her eyes.

"Kiss me a third time, and I might turn into a
woman," she conceded. Marooned in the marshes of the
Moon...

"Thirteen is going to be lucky for someone! If I
granted you three wishes what would they be?"

"I don't want to see you for a few days," he said.
"Have I done something wrong?"

But there was no mountain he would not climb, no
valley where he would not chase the magical blue
falcon, because, when Lindsey smiled at her Mathew, he
felt as if he had just been kissed by a beam of golden
sunshine. Was it not for you, the glacier, today,
exchanged its grey for roses?

Through harvest years they turned and changed,
navigating the vortexed land together, with an odd
hanger-on who disappeared after a period on the
Odyssey...her mother becoming unduly suspicious over
piggy-back riders in the white stuff.

Molly arrived to ask Mathew on holiday with the
family.

But she still appeared anxious when her daughter
flashed her new signet ring.

"It's harmless enough I suppose. I knew someone
like you at her age and he turned out okay....I think
Mathew is a very fine young man," she gleamed, and
smacked his bottom mischievously.

Molly placed her arm around his shoulder line.
"You don't know what you're missing! He's brave, hard
working and trustworthy. Not like some of the
layabouts you see in town. He's got a good future
ahead of him I'm sure."

"But take care with her," she warned. "Lindsey is
very immature for her age...you'd be surprised, even
though she is so self-assured and thrustful. As long
as you never touch her," she said. "Because you know
what will happen if you ever do!"

"Don't look so serious," she kidded. "I'm not as
green as I am cabbage looking! Don't squeeze the fruit
unless you're purchasing. The birds and the bees."

Mary scrutinized the rare metal article with
impatience.

"You are an idiot!" she scorned. "Buying a girl of
that age such an expensive overlay."

"You know what 'he' thinks about that sort of thing.
There better not have been any visitors while I have
been away."

"But what about 'his' behaviour with Felicity?"
Mary renewed her wide expanse and hissed just an inch
away from 'his pod. Just in case the broadcast was
being scrambled in his mixed-up befuddled brain.

"Don't give me any of your cheap tricks!" she
scoffed.

"Can't you see she's nothing but a wily *gold-digger.
Have you lost your sodding marbles?* She's man mad,"
she said.

Then she threatened him with the moral ogre of
common-sense and human decency.

"Go and live with the Barclays if they'll have you,"
she repeated.

"Let them find out what you are really like inside."
"But get out of my hair once and for all and leave us

in frigging peace. And don't you start talking like
'that,'" she warned. "Gretel's new boyfriend has a
theory about men like you. Just you try talking to him
like you do to me."

At this moment the pygmy in rat's wings began
sparring like a flyweight.

"Love her," she barracked. "How can anyone in their
right mind say that about a twelve year old child?"

She shattered the back of his skull with a flat
crack from her palm. Said she'd reached the bitter
end. Held a diploma in how to re-write history.

With the charms of an all conquering *Amazon Mary*
swept into command. Takes not a blind bit of notice!

"Monstrosity, when are you going back to college
instead of tramping the streets with her?" she
bellowed. "You don't want to be around when she starts
experimenting with men!" Of course.

"No son of mine is going to be known as a reprobate.
Who ever heard of a grown man paying so much attention
to an insignificant whelp. The lawn wants mowing, the
roses clipping, and the soil needs tilling." she
fermented. "You're only half as good as Esmerelda's
son. Muscle always turns to fat."

"Then you won't be surprised if I only act half as
good! Have you got a cough?" he asked.

"Don't you even care about her reputation as soon as
this is over?" bolted Gretel. "Don't you realize you
are fighting a losing battle? In years to come she'll
look on you with loathing. Box his ears for him
someone." Whatever happened to her little boy?

"Just look at his eyes!" implored Fiona. "Do you
love her? No, of course that's *impossible*. Are you
fond of her then? Is she your friend? Well, that's
alright then. That's quite 'normal.' As long as there
isn't anything else going on which you haven't told us
about."

The *Milesian* woman made a lunge at him with the
rolling pin and connected on his *calcium bonnet*.

The milkjug standing conveniently on the tray nearby
was emptied over his bald spot.

"Get the message!" she cried. "Go to the other side
of the room!"

Lindsey appeared rather taciturn about the invitation
but he tried to accept her word that she was only going
at his sister's request. The vernacular granted as
part of the *round to buy her friendship* had been used
to purchase an expensive gold fountain pen. She said
that it was none of his business who it was for and
that his constant questioning was infuriating.

When he left her at the gate as if butter wouldn't
melt she turned and hurried up the drive without a
single wave, looking more captivating than ever in her
high heels and mauve paint.

As promised he returned at ten o'clock with
Jonathan, who stood with Mathew at the bottom of the
stairs waiting for the missing guest to materialize.

'He' was the only lad in the house it transpired.
Once more his sister *Cheryl* charged up the steps and
clattered on his bedroom door next to the bathroom.

"Quick, hurry up in there you two. Your dad's here,
and he's looking rather sore."

After a pause of several minutes the key eventually
turned in the lock and the couple emerged reluctantly
to face the music. As she led the procession her
Prussian eyes glittered like watered gems. She was
flushed like the days on which she was truly tickled
pink. A chorus of 'Ooh, what have you two been doing?'
met them as they slowly descended from above. "As if
we don't know!"

"We didn't do anything, honest," he occulated. "So
it's you who coughs up the loot."

"I don't think that Mathew is my friend anymore,"
she intonated...

The Rainmaker brought the house down.

The blizzard was veering westward as he assured the
young woman that all was *hunky-dory*.

He would only be a few minutes more before returning
into the house to help her crack a bottle.

He hurried through the freezing downpour.

Through the furnace of the *French Windows* he could
harbour his strange obsession while the honoured guest
tinkered with her irons on the grate.

From the pumping-house purdah he shuffled furtively
in his Mackintosh.

Deep in the *Marish* cold Mathew pedantically peered
round the edge of the frame.

A narrow chink of light crossed his gules from the
warm interior of the lounge.

She floated round the uncertain circle of the kiln
like a vixen chastised with sting-rays.

He jumped back suddenly as she passed, not wishing
to be exposed at such short notice.

Her cloak-and-dagger eyes searched the miserable
void for sparks and settled on the walls covered with
seasonal greetings. Her recent betrothal had allowed
her partner a permanent refuge.

One by one she worked her way around the jewelled
interior, turning the covers.

From time to time she paused to ponder through the
barrier of the velvet water line.

As she neared the *'Place of Sob'* his lungs burst
like a pair of clapped-out bellows, and she knelt down
on the oriental rug with the occasional glance towards
the rustic. Weird scenes inside the gold mine!

Who was the crooked demon glaring in the glass?
Which devouring spirit shuddered in the pouring hail.
She stared in disbelief at the mantel.

Uncannily obscured by the dim light from the orb the
fly-blown canker-worm, puissant with pent-up need,
pressed his sordid glans against the dreary lens which
masked his faint reflection.

If cruel fate should not permit our angelet to
return...the sky seeks you out, and the wind and clouds
press higher in the blue, longingly they crowd aloft in
search of you.

Her mouth hung open and gasped for oxygen. Was it a
slummy or just some foul thing in high dudgeon?

Caught in a shadowland outside the winter's door the
daring fiend lurched precisely into the aperture of his
dangerous liaison. She seemed as if her mind was cut

by winsome cares, and became overtly interested in the
magic of the cards.

At last a great slurry and an even greater
outpouring of slime issued from the tunnel of his penis
end and splattered against the pane. He quickly melted
into the dilating fog from where he had lugubriously
emerged. Was it the chilling return of a 'has-been?'
Nor heaven peep through the blanket of the dark?

His buck-basket had been rifled and the perishable
goods vanished like spit in the rain.

XXVI
THUNDERBOLT

Awakening from recurring nightmares of filthy vermin
thriving beneath rotting floorboards in the basement.
he called out for his mother in the sweat stained
environment...

Clarissa had calmly continued typing her 'curriculum
vitae.' It had been seven long months of pins and
needles since the 'dies nefastus' of the rogue Carol
Singers, the day before Yule-tide.

The attractive archivist had turned to scrutinize
his eccentric behaviour at the edge of the living room
floor where he dropped a clanger. Had the growler been
worrying sheep again?

"Ooops!" she cried, and reached for her tippex.
He rejected her cordial invitation even when she
complained she was lacking a suitable escort.

'*Sater venter non studet libenter*,' he remarked.
Knock! knock! "Who's there? Lindsey who...?"
"Can I come in?"

They peeped through the letterbox, they peeped in
the hall, and any other place which had peep-holes...

From tiny seedlings mighty Oaks do crash through car
window-screens! Love her to death. Shoot the apple
from her head.

At the fuel-pump station an Irish *tinker* had asked
the manager if the *Buckfast* 'Flasher' ever exposed
himself while on active duty.

Then the rough and ready hoydens had actually
appeared at the house and been invited inside.

It was a malign attempt to gain a bird's eye view of
the pervert who had defiled their lovely Catholic
daughters.

Mary immediately began proselytizing as if her mouth
was on fire. Step into line there!

Mr. Mullins had pointed to the *wicker chair* standing
behind the kitchen door.

He declared its awful presence triumphantly.

His terse young son casually nodded as if the case was
proved beyond all reasonable doubt.

"Was he pissed out of his mind?" quoffed the
Tinkerman bloated with moral indignation.

Otherwise it would be unthinkable to withdraw the
charge since the matter was so indisputably serious.

"Oh! my god, he'll never get another job now!" she
fretted. "We do our level best you know, but there's
something the matter with him."

"He was going to go into teaching," she blubbed.
"He's much too shy to do such an objectionable thing.
Not another sound out of you! It certainly isn't
natural. One would like to say."

"I'll never be able to hold up my head at the
'Women's Institute' again. What a *terrible scandal*!
Gretel will go mad."

It was an absolute charm to see her expression as
the *party snoopers* departed in a much happier frame of
mind. They'd even refused his gift of the stereo.

When he had returned that evening from a rare
reconnaissance mission with Jonathan they had
questioned him on the earlier encounter. Was he a
copper in plain clothes asked the customer?

"An Inspector called but wouldn't tell us what it
was all about," glared the lodger. "Only that a very
grave incident had arisen which involved a *missing
person*. ·He'll be calling again later to see about your
alibi."

"Perhaps it was a burglar?" they said. "Are all our
doors safely bolted and secured?"

Even the lodger had been under suspicion, until they
had matched him with the perfect description; *Bald,
bandage, approximately fifety.*

The part-time *balloon dancer* and *bouncer arrived
with the woman dressed in black* grinning like a
Cheshire cat. In view of the gravity of this offence.

Felt as if he had received a hefty blow in the
midrift. Two wrongs do not make a right. He was
asking for it! ; that...

The constable stepped lucratively into the kitchen
armed with the concepts of even-handed what ought to
be.

Inspector Drip-white ticked-off all his details
while he listened to the accused indicting himself with
every crazy sentence.

He stated that he was certain of the culprit.
The woman from Sunhill stared blankly forward as her
chief collaborator read him his rights.

"Anything you say will be taken down and used in
evidence." Why on earth was he wearing the three-
cornered stetson?

The lodger suddenly went haywire and stormed up the
stairs to pack his bags at once. She accused him of
totally ruining their remunerative affiliation.

"The dirty bastard. Anything but that!" he
shrieked. "We'll have to leave the area."

Mathew's attempts to explain were met by stoney
silence. What a way to celebrate one's 'coming of
age.' Though I waltz through the valley of death.

"Tell them you had nothing to do with it," insisted
Mary. "Stand up for yourself and convince them you are
innocent."

"Ask them what part of your anatomy you are meant to
have exposed. Launch a petition to find out why they
only called at our house."

"Your penis!" he coyly noted. "You exposed your
penis before the choir showed a clean pair of heels."

To everyones surprise Mathew quoted the occassion of
their fellow officer in the 'Dog and Gun.'

"Please make sure you notify us if you intend to
leave the country. A hairdressing appointment? How
much?" No right to rob the unadulterated?

"The shite of the earth," he muttered, as they
manoevered towards the exit.

The constable insisted that the final outcome was
dependent upon whether his Pace-maker had enough data
to bring about a successful prosecution.

Despite the growing ship of spies he faithfully

complied to increase his decreasing chances.

"Am I a Prostitute?" she'd asked.
"Don't be silly," said Mathew. What on earth was the
world coming to?

"Are you dying?" she smirked. "Is that all it is
then?"

When he told her the filler she nearly hit the roof.
"You stupid idiot!" she said. 'How could you have
acted without due care and attention. I don't believe
it either,' she said..."You were on your way down from
the bathroom? Were you born in a field?"

He had anticipated his name appearing in glorious
print, and a colour coded snap.

"A 'Flasher!'" Mollydod cooed. "I didn't think that
you were that capable."

"Make the most of your semester"...then a fuitine
was totally out of the question?

As he stood nude in the shower she turned on the hot
water tap over the Father-of-Steps.

"Get one together! Look at that!" she quivered.
"It's standing to attention. Let me see you piss or
are you going to fuck me?"

Infanta led him into the cabin where she first let
down her intimate particulars.

She was careful that he didn't touch her with his
light companion or kiss her when he was filled with
fondness.

"You ought to see our Jonathans'!" she gasped. "I
wish he'd let me sleep for once."

She attempted to force his sensitive glans between
her flaps.

"Avast!" he yelled. His 'Plummy' had been skinned
alive.

Then she complained again. Nothing was mentioned
about going on the pill. Or the scud marks on her
frillies.

"Shove harder and get into rhythm, I'm doing all the
work"....had she already been through the motions?

The door suddenly moved but she slammed it quickly
shut again.

"Just sign a full confession and we will send the
results as soon as possible"

Mathew quickly donned his signature in order to
return from this rough coinage. Who needs a solicitor
when you're *right up Queer Street!* 'Bent as a nine
bob note,' as Bobby used to say.

She led him into the staff car park where he
automatically climbed in the front of the *Panda* beside
his host. He continued in conversation until they
approached the Chemical plant.

"You should know better," she nodded
sympathetically...then he noticed that she too had
broken into a hot flush.

He turned and watched her beaming face as they
travelled along the now deserted streets still bathed
in evening sunshine.

"Just don't do it again!" she warned. "Find
yourself a nice girlfriend. It shouldn't be too
difficult. But I can't promise she'll withdraw her
allegation. Apparently you were making a nuisance of
yourself since the start, although I'll convey your
deepest remorse. No, I don't think it will be a good
idea if you told her so yourself."

The short skirt had lifted well up the lithesome
blonde's admirable young thighs, which beckoned his
lazy hand with a covering of creamy silk...

Should he break the habit of a lifetime and make a
pass? Whether to leave it another minute or move his
hand idly across while he still festered unfulfilled.

Good sense seemed to have prevailed for the moment
but the *young woman dressed in black* seemed to sense
the strong vibes he was despatching by male.

When they arrived at the row of cottages beside the
loading bay the yard was empty of the jeering crowds.

How cliche-ridden it had been continually patrolling
the building's circumference, until the hobnobbers had
strolled onto the terrace, on this, his last day 'on
the job.'

As he closed the door behind him he peered toward
Belinda's Moon and smiled.

232

Mathew apologized once more for making such a spectacle
of himself. She simply shrugged her shoulders and
pushed her foot firmly on the pedal.

Mathew stepped away from the kerb, careful that he
did not disturb the flat cap now resting on his bonce.
He swayed along the rusty pavement like unoiled
clockwork as people hurried from their doors and
slammed them shut.

He had a final gander towards the Riding Stables
where the spectator's lusty eyes had studied him for
hours. Her sister had only been a-watching for half
that time.

Like Beckett's 'Catastrophe' in his 'Flasher's Mac'
he loitered with new nostalgia in the region of his
favourite perch.

It seemed only minutes before he had spent all his
lunch time trying to attract the secretary clearing the
files, sitting on the thunderbox sucking his thumb with
the door open-mouthed.

Like a hammer from the sky the horserider had
jockeyed like a thunderball.

He had tottered from the pile of pallets stacked
man-high and sprained his ankle.

The tygress in her mid thirties had obviously never
seen a semi-erect penis in her life before so she ran
screaming through the rows of workmen like a siren.

"Take a good look at his repulsive clock!" she
bawled pacing up and down the den with her forked
tongue lashing vehemently.

"How can we sleep safe in our beds with a *dangerous
monster* on the loose!"

When he walked calmly into the house suffering from
catatonic shock only Gretel noticed the bright cherry
on his cheek...but then he was always sun-bathing.
Serves him right the so-and-so.

The *herald on set* was reporting a television
newsflash...and sexy Miss. *you-know-who* had escaped on
a majority verdict for wielding a whetted blade on the
march.

233

"You're gonna get done!" shouted William.
He'd said that Mathew was too good for her from the very beginning. "I'm telling my ma...na, na, na na na!"
"Mathew's only showing me his etchings." She pressed some caramel under the drop and stared with awe at the colour of his scotch. Peek-a-boo!
One wet finger did it very well...two were even better; she reached down to grip his wrist and guide the hand in closer.
The *bald* crutch-head lock-jawed as her eyes sunk into a 'Wonderful land.'
Poking progressively towards the stars she moaned and deepened, fixing his hand even more firmly than before as he concentrated wisely on the task.
Her gorgeous buds began to flutter between hawk and buzzard.Afraid of being struck-off?
She seemed oblivious to the customer and groaned like a bomber as she rapidly reached climax...tiny spots of grume stained her knicker-lining.
"If that's what an orgasm is like, I want to do it some more!" she murmured. "I can't wait until I get to bed tonight when I can pull down my blanket!"
Lindsey pushed the *trinket* into his raincoat pocket for a mangled summer evening.
"Are you taking us all down to the woods to eat our pic-nic at dinnertime?" she asked.
"And remember, no mis-behaving yourself! I hope Reverend Brown doesn't see us together in the bushes. I'm tired of saying that you're just my brother's friend.
"If you go down to the woods today, you're sure of a big surprise," she trilled.
"If my man knew about this she might think you were really naughty!" she teased.

    *   *   *

"Done this sort of vile thing before?" asked the Peeler as they checked the station records..."He's *clean!*" the factotum comfirmed (computers never lie!).

230

"There's no-one on our patch who looks remotely like the suspect."
"Did you hope to turn her on? Her husband's in the force and he's twice the size of you! It was all I could do to persuade him not to give you a bloody good drubbing!"
Like putty in their hands the student agreed to every single term. Frontal lobotomy. Chip on his shoulder a mile wide.
Guilt ridden. Bogged down with guilt. Blood on his fingers. Consumed with guilt. Guilty as fuck. Guilty as charged.
"I hate these left wing commi bastards," stormed the sergeant..."You're not one of those are you?"
"Of course not!" he snapped.
The virgin's prickly heat spread over his entire coin-face and down his back.
It felt as if his whole body was becoming a *red hot giant*, and he didn't know where to look in the frame to do himself justice.
"I believe that this is truly a *flash in the pan*. You won't do it again after this shock to the system. Best make a sincere apology and get yourself sorted out."
"Do you have a steady girlfriend? How long is it since you had a really good bang?"
Did he confess?...'I'm a virgin, and I have been all my life'..."It's been three whole weeks since I last had *an intimate coupling*," he paltered.
"Three weeks you say?"
"She swears that you had an *erection*. Would you deny or dispute this fact? Were you masturbating, come on admit it, we haven't got all day to mess about! I have several other *good eye witnesses* who are willing to come forward."
The hare-lipped *head of vice* supined coolly on his swivel and scrutinized his transfixed guest.
"Okay, we've finished for the time being," he gesticulated (had he passed the interview?). "Belinda will chaperone you back to the scene of your crime to pick-up your Post Office van."

231

Blackbeard had been safely captured after wearing false
number plates...they interviewed Ryan Starbuck as a
close neighbour, and asked him his impression of the
mad pandemic necromancer. Frigid, or Sandra, or both?

'Just an ordinary sort of chap, never really spoke
much out of turn,'...on his way to the ritual abattoir.

"You're home rather late tonight?"
Gretel instructed him to read one of the passages in
her manual.

"Neurotics always hurt the people who are most
trying to help them! Although you certainly haven't
much to offer even that vindictive little hussy."

"But it's only the 'myth of mental illness'," he
stressed. "I've always compared myself to the
matchless of this world!"

Mathew wasn't in the mood for her hortative. He
bolted up to his dorp and began playing with his pipe.

In the garden below Juliette was folding up her deck
chair. Bad weather on the way?

She was a delicate blushful of curls with the
complexion of peaches and cream.

Through the green leaves and the apple blossom he
admired her natural tendencies as he did so often when
they were in tryst.

He approached from the edge of his seat to the
windowledge, revealing his titanic erection and
smacking away as expeditiously as possible. Consistent
with his strawberry mark.

Juliette turned as she pulled the wooden clothes
pegs from the line and glanced in his direction right
on cue... Bashing the bishop!

How many secret gardens had he sojourned below the
arc of the covenant, or in the privacy of their
boudoirs, where a note-book on his bedside cabinet
contained the results of his challenge?

His huge shiner spurted the mounting proceeds of his
edification through the yawning hiatus.

A downpour of hotstuff glaired over the cradle of
branches and ended their life on the low tide. Q. C. -
Quality counts!

Mary insisted he borrow the lodger's finest three
piece; it was badly fitting, but it was important to
create a good impression. Was he attending an exchange
of nuptial vows? Pawn to king four.

Before you could say 'John Robinson,' '*Bald Eagle*'
was sitting bolt upright in the dock beside the burly
Big Blue Whale...Fatso had met him with a grin in the
foyer. In court number 6 the pale pukey face of the
white dwarf gaped from the backseat while the merry
Tinkers pawned around their confident barrister.

A mixed party of teenage truants crammed into the
public gallery to view the debacle, and listened
intently to the 'victims' giving evidence. Strength in
numbers. They tittered melodically when the officer
read out the wicked deed.

When the clothes were off his dickie-bird didn't
even come out of the cuckoo clock to sing.

It was the incorrect address, but the defendant's
representative from '*Goose, Gander & Gosling*' said it
didn't matter one jot. He was only 'splitting hairs.'

Hated and reviled by all who cocked their eyes the
dirty flasher trembled as the sport of wind and
waves...like a 'bookful of gossips.'

Gretchen described how he had offered them fifety-p
to sing 'Away in a Manger,' and how he wedged the chair
against the door while he went into the living room to
flaunt his ugly penis. Not allowed to wolf-whistle!

At this point there was a thunderous fanfaronade of
plaudits and a storm of jubilant flag waving, but it
was only a militant tendency I expect.

"Did he do anything while he held it in his hand?"
she billetted her second witness. Her voice was filled
with melancholy for their potash.In check.

Mathew couldn't help waving across to their kraal,
which was duly noted by the Justice of the Peace. He
flashed them his Eddie Murphy smirk.

"I didn't see, it was too dark," she said. "I only
looked because my sister said that I should do."

"Did the accused have an erection?" she asked. Then
they had to go and explain what all that meant.

The precise details of his adamant penis were discussed
before the teeming oceans.

"Why should you concoct a story like this?" she
tendered. The congregation turned to scrutinize his
alien presence.

Then it was Mathew's turn to take the stand. He
read out the chips in his best public speaking voice
and swore feign allegiance to the captive.

Before the hearing he described how he came to be
serving up his broth that evening. Under cross
examination there was a burning in his breast when the
lady asked him if he was using his organ to obtain
unacceptable gratification: but did not...

He stammered when he came to the prose where the
girls had kicked open the turnstile. And he paled when
Mary Moonighan blew in her hanky.

The highly experienced aid rushed to his side. "We
must have the name involved" he vexed. "Why do you
think those girls were conducting a vendetta against
you." Can't castle!

"And just who is this...this Lindsey?" asked the
leading Magistrate huffly. "What has she to do with
all this coming and going, mainly going?"

"How old is she...thirteen? Is she your girlfriend?
Do you seriously expect the court to believe that you
are having a relationship with a thirteen year old
minor?" Queen takes pawn!

Mathew was on tender hooks as the three pillars of
the establishment retired to deliberate.

Postman Pat had already passed on his recorded
telegram that same morning for a return appointment in
three weeks time. Another feather in his cap!

Rumours circulated in the public gallery that there
would be further complications.

A spectator called out "Baldy!"
"It's fifety-fifety," sibilated the postulant. "Let's
pray that they will be lenient."

The hydra returned with the verdict; *guilty*...a
hundred pound fine! The depraved person must have been
the only onlooker who wasn't smiling. His ego grinded
to a halt.

Once more Mary was vindicated in her views about his
true character though she offered to stay on his side.

As he walked from the court building in the centre
of town a flurry of mocking taunts echoed behind him.

The tinker woman leapt on his back with her running
commentary. Check-mate.

"Do you see my poor girls!" she screamed, pulling
their hair. 'Look how chaste and vulnerable they are!'

"You're a very wicked and evil man. All I want is
that you apologize for your disgusting behaviour and
swear it will never happen again," insisted Mary.

She stated that if he continued pumping iron he
would surely shrink in height.

Mathew turned to stare at the two gleaming wretches
in their neatly pressed jungle-green. Expect she
already had a bun in the oven. But when push came to
shove. Cortes burnt all his ships...

He recognized them both instantly as 'Southern'
Milesian Women, with the medal of carnal knowledge
already etched in the corners of their crooked leering
mouths. Three rings for the elven kings...

Two enormous *brillo pads* were no doubt growing like
hell over the *black holes* between their opprobious
hips! Mudslinger!

Lindsey hardly batted an eyelid when he said that he
had been found responsible. She simply asked for a
rise in her pocket money. Filthy animal!

"I'll let you fuck me if you wear a *black johnny*,"
she whispered. "Okay, Dr. Fox, show me what ya got!"

All afternoon the man in the woolly festoon
whimpered paranoically whenever the pair locked eyes on
a handsome young stud. Wet her knickers as soon as
look at him. Now Prancer, now Dancer, now Vixen...

After all the fun of the fair she demanded another
ice-cream. Knight takes rook!

Mathew handed her the cone careful not to drop
it....Lindsey tipped it carelessly in the gutter and
carried on up the lane.

His hopes were hanging on a heartbeat as he rapidly
approached crisis point.

But it was no use shutting the stable door after the horse had bolted.

When they arrived home in the kitchen the 'lodger' was urinating in the basin.

Lindsey edged closer to the bottom of the stairs with a lustful ardour on her fresh young face.

"Cor!" she said. "Get a load of him. He's a nice bit of stuff and right. Try running your fingers through 'his' hair."

The 'lodger' returned doing up his trousers as she feasted her eyes on his cock bulge...he sneaked out towards his clandestine appointment with Mary safely absent.

His Sicillian charm bore down on them like a cart of shite and onion. But his 'but' was higher from the ground than normal men.

"Now that's what I call fit!" she motioned, and pretended to pat where her eyes concentrated most. Tit for tat killings. Hah!

Then the music was finally over...he prepared to raise a storm and fight them tooth and nail.

Mathew flew into a rage and accused her of taking him for a ride...Superfluous to requirements. She had set her sights on greener pastures.

The words so sincerely sneered had a ring of truth in them. Like peas in a pod.

"'Your' girlfriend!" she mocked. "Don't be such a broody hen. Alright," she sneered. "Always said you were a meanie." Pull the other one, it's got bells on.

"Keep your hair on! Wouldn't fancy you if you were the last man on earth. Shouldn't mock the afflicted."

The rainmaker glanced at her friend as if he'd fallen off a flitting as he fluttered like a duck in thunder and his complex sonnets didn't rhyme. Said she was 'shagged out.' Always showing her up.

"Your not going to cry again?" she sniggered. "Why can't you leave me bloody well alone. I'm never touching you again. Didn't think I was going steady!"

"And he's bigger than you are puffta."

"Why don't you get a girlfriend your own age," she assailed..."if you can that is!"

Said she'd blown him totally out.

Though he promised them a milky way Phoebe slammed the shaft behind her and she promptly *fell from grace*, like a barrel of tear gas to the bottom of the ocean.

When the music's over baby, turn out the light, turn out the light. The spirit left him...

Molly's bloated face crushed exigently against the porthole attempting to catch a look in the place.

The bouquet of forget-me-nots had been tossed in the trash-can, and on the blower the misfit had been too distraught to speak. You've got to run before you can walk. His batonic hands quavered like a burst conductor's Brahm.

Always with a ciggy in her cake-hole. Wasn't the sort of woman who took 'no' for an answer. Watch your language! This is the last straw.

The tapster put her arms around him, and said that though they were still friends, it was better for all concerned that he no longer attended the reception.

She was wearing the 'Heart of Gold' on her finger because her daughter said the metal was too irritating.

"It's just for now," she added softly, "I'm sorry, but in time you'll both get over it!"

"You can't expect to hold a girl to promises she made so young."

"The path of true love never runs smoothly. That's a fact of life! Give it a while and then just say hello when ever you meet. Completely ignore her for a change. Anyway, you'd need a buffet to kiss her."

"I can't force her to take you on board. For now it's over and done with. It gave her the hump when you called her a *tart*. She needs her own freedom to skim off the cream."

"If you found a more suitable companion you'd need no reminding. We can't always get the one we desire...but don't start making up stories."

She was certainly startled when he told her that he had indeed been struck by a charge of electricity...but all her family were a cut above the rest.

Someone had even whipped the time-piece.

"Personally I don't care what they do in private, as
long as they don't scare the horses."

She showed him the door.   Tiny bit camera shy.   Set
off like a six year old looking for his sock.

He pulled the camera strap over the shoulder of his
leather bomber jacket and wanted to hug her so much
that he thought of nothing else...knocked the stuffing
right out of him.

When he sat down in the queue the licence dodger
eventually gave breath.   It was like watching the
formation of a snow crystal through a microscope.   His
pulse seemed to quicken.

"Press Photographer?" he asked, nodding at the
Pentax.

"Only for the 'News of the World!'" soft-pedalled
Mathew.

Just before dinner time the snapshotting dude was
summoned into number 6 court as the final entrant in
their group.

With his dome flapping like a ragged patchwork quilt
the ugly monstrosity loped like a squiffy mechanism.
His heart in a silvery cage.   Rood-loft.

He entered the wooden pulpit beside the pews to
strut and fret his hour upon the planks.   Blushing to
be encountered with a cloud.   She howled like a bitch
bringing herself off.

Once again he was staggered by the extravagant
luxury of the proscenium arch which paled all other
dressings into insignificance.

This grossly obnoxious farce unwound with
unmitigated opulence.   Step into line!   She showed him
the door!   Choose who she bloody well wants.

The usher who had been making such pleasant
conversation quickly averted her eyes.

"That you did openly, lewdly, and indecently, with
intent to harrow the anvil, expose your erect *penis*
outside her Riding Stables....." contrary to the
vagrancy act of 18...something or other.

Thank the lucky stars.   Once again the chamber was
free of blasted reporters.   Retracting his Sigma.

And they said that 'lightning couldn't strike twice' as
he teetered in the dock place.   Burst through the
stratosphere.   Drop the dead donkey.

"And this is his first offence!" stated the
prosecuting attorney.   Stand to attention!   Looking for
a showdown?   Never drunk on duty.

But as fortune would have it the same burly *Big Blue
Whale* occupied the stand next to him and walked calmly
forward after a few seconds hesitation.   Why do all the
Plods have size twelves?

He whispered something odd inside the old man's ear.
Only doing the decent thing.   Another bloody prodigy.

"It doesn't count!" he heard him say, shaking his
head, as they settled the matter under duress.

Like a *Gordian knot* scud under bare poles Mathew
tottered in the kiosk with no lack of courage.

Calling occupants of inter-planetary craft.   Fish-
faced enemy of the people!   Dirty-Den the role model.

The prosecutor indicated that the defendant would
like to offer a few token words in his own defence to
explain his gross abandonment of privilege.

The law required that he be punished by small fire
through a deckful of tropical runes.

Greatest dispensation since the days of Manu.
Perhaps a stiffer sentence would teach him the error of
his ways?   Just ignore him and he might go away.

One of the great unwashed.   At any moment he
expected to be swept under the carpet.

Out streamed a pack of lies.   The *magistrate* leaned
over with a superlative gleam and coyly flashed her
pendulous bosom.

Without reference to a pin or a speared clay effigy.
He squeezed the soft brown owl and held the diplomatic
baggage in his other pad entitled 'Catching
snowflakes.'

A sexual albatross around his neck...stick a pipe in
its gob, nail its foot to the flipping deck.   What a
carry on!   A fly on the wall.   She was dying for it!
"The dirty old git!"

Victim's 'support.'
My dearest Linnet, it ran;

Here is the letter I've been meaning to send you,
meaning to send you for such a long time now.
I know when you read it, I may be dead...
I may be dead for such a long time now.
But read it, I know that you will one day!

Do you remember when I carried you quite far?
I was loaded with scales but did not think twice,
Oh, what a pretty girl always to me!
I felt very tender, I only felt tender,
and penned the way some porters do...

If ever I hurt you, which I know was not seldom,
then you'd climb and come round with the tide.
From *Whitecastles* I swung you, and sweetly embraced
you, forever I hoped this would be!
But then I grew serious, and you frowned with sad
Autumns, though I should, I never quite understood
why...

But there's something quite often, I meant to beseech
you, which tossed like a leaf in my mind.
Will you quite often, or just for a moment...
will you please *be my bride*,
will you please *be my bride?*

Though I once left you, to shelter your secrets,
and for once march on alone with your cares,
You never quite left me, you never deserted me,
if I could, I'd just like to explain;
I loved you, I love you, I always adored you,
and think of you where ever I glide.

Justice has been done.

"Only jealous!" hissed the Infanta.

XXVII
WICKER MAN

"White man speak with forked tongue!" squirmed the
unsentimental Nigel Bates, who appeared about to
eviscerate another of his smouldering *Cobra* skins.
"I suppose you've been indulging in some more of
your cardio-vascular exercises by the look of you."
A *Blackhole* had materialized in the septic armpit of
his decrepit Afghan coat, and he boasted about not
having his hair cut professionally since he was a *page
boy*. Now he called himself the 'last of the Mohicans.'
He had pawned his fine collection of discs for a
mingy sum in order to pay for his slops.
"There's so many conflicting conflagrations in the
pipeline," he complained; "I simply don't know who to
take on trust." Thinking of entering the church.
Bates immediately paid over his loss after disputing
which was the closest star to our duce.
"It's all a matter of suggestion," he announced.
"I've erected your chart, and my interpretation is that
you are like a *Phoenix* eternally rising up from the
bones. Toss it over the shoulder. There's no point
crying over spilt knacker-milk," he decreed.
"If you set the great unwashed a bad example," he
suggested, "then 'you' pretend that it's they who are
totally 'out of order.' The dregs of society are so
fucking docile. I wouldn't be surprised if one day
even a leading man was elected to become leader of the
free world. I've even heard a rumour that there's
already a bluffer in the Whitehouse."
"You've hit the nail right on my nut."
"Don't give it a moment's thought," nodded Bates.
"I've been called all the names under the sun in my
time. Look how adeptly I always avoided giving my
seminar. There's nowt sa queer as folk," he tittered.
"You should always attempt to hide a portion in the
dark. Are you still moonlighting?" he quipped.
"See all, hear all, say nowt!"

He paused for breath and adjusted his quare nippers.
"I've been talking to a chick from the homeground who
used to have the low-down with you," he sniggered.

"Her boyfriend chains her bare arse to the
blistering red hot radiator and screws the hell out of
her! She swears that you were a scruffy little eel at
kindergarten." All shook up!

"She couldn't believe me when I informed her how
much you had burst at the seams. It's a pity she's no
babe." Vassal miscreant! Edge of the known galaxy.

"I've had that recurring dream again!"
He giggled just like 'Willie Carson' riding a flea.

"I dreamt that I was just a shiftless, spineless
Jellyman without any real backbone at all in me... and
that without my complete works of prestidigitation I
wouldn't even appear capable of far-sighted folly, or
voluntary euthanasia. World's so full of shit man."

But it was always difficult to discern if Bates was
just manoevering one of his many sides, and he had
already rebuked the *hoi polloi* more than once for being
too afraid to fib. Mental detecting. *Boings* were
unemployable! Givers or Takers. Which one are you?

The Cock-or-two repeated his story several times and
offered his 'screwed-up' sketch of 'Lucretia Borgia'
with a penis lodged in its cochlea. Once had a brush
with the law. What's hot on the catwalk Tophat?

They discussed the gouache water colour which
someone had presented as part of their final
exhibition; a gnostic metaphor containing an *Oran Utan*
being fellated by a member of the 'Tuatha' as it hung
on the cross at Calvary. Only the good die young!

Underneath its horrid caption, 'Suffer me to come
onto little children;' obviously a biblical allusion
regarding the sacrificial crucifixion and entering into
heaven. *Shunga*...no black without white.

Its effect on the evangelical movement at the
college had been diabolical. Sins of the flesh! Below
the salt. Must have gone through a fortune in tracing-
paper conscientiously objecting. Defended his
intellectual property throughout.

244

When he ascribed the nature of the thunderbolt the
rabble-rouser immediately placed the incident in the
realm of holy curse. Well weird! He whistled the
incredible demon.

"Hell's broth, I need to make myself scarce!" he
jinked in a hotch-potch of alternating pastels.

"But I did warn you not to issue challenges you
couldn't hope to cope with many moons later. Only the
day after tomorrow belongs to the scumbag."

"That's awful!" he seethed, supining awkwardly in
the quiet room and lessening his thud. "He who
hesitates is gone forever."

Scales were beginning to spread over his blistering
skin. "It's just a normal bodily function like
crapping or stuffing your gut with oysters." That
orgasm was to the benefit of organisms.

"I do wish you wouldn't burden me with the knowledge
of your worsening crises. But now that you have
confided in me I promise not to pin it to the door.
Never judge a book by its newspaper write-ups. There
are times when a man's gotta do what a man's gotta do."

"One must always be aware of the feelings of
beatniks," quibbled the side-kick gloomily.

"Money is honey! What a load of baloney"
Said his whole existence was in tatters.

"Do you realize?" he gasped. "This could affect the
rest of your adult life!" "I don't believe you
would..." Safer after the water-shed?

Then he began yapping about the latest advances in
technology. The only tool he didn't possess must have
been an arse-trimmer. "Hair today gone tomorrow," he
cackled. "If you fall from the saddle then quickly
remount." Spare me the clod-kicker wisdom.
Mathew divested the *X-certificate* insurrection.

"They're holding a prayer meeting in the chapel at
lunchtime today," he grinned. "The *Chaplain* thinks you
have an abnormal 'manifestation' which will take some
getting rid of...and that you have a peculiar
disfiguration on your right side which can only be
healed by their devout determination."

245

"What are you giving up for Lent? Fight fire with a
prick up the bum. That Mr. Wroe had some serious
wickedness in him! There was a time when women were
but two-thirds the size of mortal men. We keep on
getting pegged back," he hammered. "If you can't score
in your twenties. Great hurricanes announce themselves
with but a single breeze."

The idea occurred to ask Bates if he really was
still a creeping encratite, but the thought of
broaching such a sensitive subject with the prickly
Jellyman could easily have rebounded.

He continued with the ongoing charades...
"Mr. and Mrs. Bates were taking their young son along
for his first day at public school to meet his new
headmaster. The young lad was ushered forward by Mr.
Bates and introduced to the harsh disciplinarian in his
capital study..."And this here is young Master Bates,"
said the father to the schoolmaster.

"Don't worry old chum..."
"We'll soon put a stop to that!" chirped the master
sternly, with a wry twirl of his moustache.

"The two-faced back-stabbing bastard!" he hissed.
Had a cynic's eye for logic.

There were questions about Bates that never seemed
to be answered. For instance; did he always wash his
hands after every visit to the lavatory, or before?
Peel slowly and sink your teeth in.

He finally elected to visit the Ferryman.
Apparently *carrot juice only turned his urine orange,*
but the mescaline was increasing his powers of
observation.

J.B. said that he knew of a power plant which could
make him split his britches, but he was better at
keeping things up his sleeve. He suddenly came to his
senses. Treat 'em cruel, make 'em drool!

He always seemed to be on the run.
Said he was more screwed-up than a pen-pusher's reject
slip and it was impossible to turn the clock back.

It was like picking fleas from a dead donkey.
Call him a free-mason, sometimes a green-man, call him
a fool...

Said he'd made a new year's resolution never to make
any more new year's resolutions.

"There, but for the grace of the undying entity go
I," quivered the undeniable Jellyman...

Being of sound mind and body Mathew knew at once that
he couldn't follow where angels feared to tread, so he
disappeared up to the ninth floor, wearing his straight
jacket. Whatever tickles your fancy does you good!

There was bound to be a wraith alone in the changing
room with its large peephole in the broken portal.

A foreign distrust followed his every step from
colleagues who had once been so boot licking. He
needed to put on a face-mask.

Chang gradually approached the mature brunette
chatting on the admin blower until she perlustrated his
rum residence. Snapper of keys in their locks!

She glared at him then smiled. He enquired if there
was a way onto the roof to take some snapshots.

"You'll have to get permission!" snapped the head of
department. "But I'm sure that you will be able to
obtain some good views from the *Rear window* of
Furniture design."

He placed the workchair against the door and began
stripping as she covertly watched him...he panned the
subject with his lens. Cheap thrills. Bodies
throughout the world. Ball-breaker.

Occasionally taking a sip of her Capacino and
doodling on her sketchpad she scrutinized the stunt-
merchant while giving a running commentary. Another
bloody generalization...!

Before occultation eventually elapsed another staff
member appeared from the nearby liftshaft.

Blue Jeans gandered quickly towards him as she
zipped past and tore into the empty L-shaped room to
his left. She floundered at cock level as he moved
more riskily into the open savanna. Place a little
acid in the water supply... bloody great general!

In the twinkling of an eye he was standing
motionless in the corridoor outside the Georgian wiring
of the door glass.

She accidentally nudged the scissure wider and sang her macaronic verse...exposing himself to further serious risk.

Quickly away he returned to his private studio where *Chia Swee* would be bearing fruit next to his own miserable space.

He darted like a whippet between the boardwalks to mount his position behind the huge canvas of Gollum's; a leaning chimney stack breathing smoke across the *Chersonese.*

He opened the filthy rag, the remainder of which had been used as someone's crude exhibit, and reckoned on he was doing some colouring before slowly rotating to see if she was current.

Chia Swee was putting the finishing touches to her admirable desiderata, while the cult of 'Born again' christians chanted away in some long forgotten corner forever banished, gradually rising to a crushing crescendo of *caterwauling.*

Then he stole over to arrange the man-high polythene structure, which was framed with bamboo, to just the right angle. It was a damned nuisance how it was always moved whenever the bird had flown.

He began to expose his skyscraper, peering intensely through the hive, as the *Chink* prepared herself for what was coming.

Her solid eyes grew dark as he edged indecently closer to the webbing, the seedy fabric of which, was the only device separating her untrammelled view from his routine extravaganza.

With his *glistening lens* he snapped her hazy sockets through the transparent screen of kite.

Suddenly Geraldine appeared at her side and began integrating her *pastiche.*

Both students studied hard while Geraldine repeatedly stroked her eyebrow. From tiny ejaculations mighty pontiff's do appear!

She bit her desirable scarlet lip in a southerly direction, to extend his *temporary bliss.*

Pain in the arse of the cantankerous old git!

Her chaperon glazed over as the blonde peered over to obtain a better compass, his geyser spurted into the upper chamber...and the eye of the voyeur quickly scarpered from the vantage point, on hearing the group of students perambulating closer.

He coolly rubbed the sticky moisture into the sawdust and ground his cowboy booted heel.

The overtrick of his emission he touched up on the back of the brushwork, which was the only article separating him from *complete notoriety.*

Too late cracking the whip after the horse had bolted! He wore the purple.

"It's a septic tank of loathsome poison!" sneered a voice only centimetres away and blocking his flight path.

As he arrived down the driveway he met *Griselda* taking her poodle, Mitzy, for a walk towards the Blackheath.

The old retired 'factories inspector' stopped to reminisce for a while before submitting her treatise on the sterility of public office.

Some git had rung college to say that he had been found gagged to a chair with his throat slashed.

"How many times did I see her slouching at my gate," she said. "Holding her head in her hands and not wishing to go home just yet." Must have had a real ding-donger. Something Mathew had said.

On *tulip court* Lindsey was swaggering in the middle of the road with her fresh band of onlookers.

As his *lambswool* bobble flopped from side to side the jeering would begin in earnest as he crossed to the sunny side of the street. Eat more spinach!

She called for a French-Letter, but beauty was said to be only skin deep. His purple-pronged-penis!

His heart beat like a miner's recant to the sound of tearing straw but he still wasn't climbing in the car with a treacherous crimp. Plead for a clean break.

"Flash, Flasher!" hollered the new recruits from the fence. "Why don't you get a hair transplant?" they imparted. A pedestrian with wheels on his toes.

"She's got more hair underneath her armpits than you
have on your baldy head."

But he still possessed her last Valentine's card of
a 'Partridge in a pear tree.' Called him a Big Puff!

"There's plenty more fishes in the sea...Julie's a
nice respectable girl," said his mother calmly.

"You're like a blackbird striving to be a peacock."
"She would like to arrange a date for tomorrow evening.
Why don't you take her to the flicks when she comes
around for brunch? She puts that other girl in the
shade."

"She's too plain and dull!" he said. "Far too
conventional for my outlandish tastes. I'd prefer
someone more provocative, rather than a frustrated
window dresser afraid of being left on the shelf..."

Conveniently, her mother emerged to hang the dirty
linen, when the pin-pricks had left the neighbourhood.

Just as Mollydod was passing the entrance Mathew
lightly entered the old pumping-house in his swimming
trunks and nothing else.

Conducting a pleasant conversation over the ha-ha he
stood on tip-toe to see if it really was a hair-
piece...loyal to the past was one thing.

Working her way tirelessly around the ledges the
older woman eventually kneeled to water the greenhouse
plants of her potting shed, exactly opposite the
plotting magenta faced pumper frozen in the door hole.

Through the wicker fence the *Vickerman* focused on
her browless buds to be sure that they were observing
him...they frequently gagged, but seemed on the whole
to be rather like whirlpools.

A purple glow-worm shining incandescently above
reflected on the window glass to highlight his star
attraction, as he peeled away his splendid foam-flecked
nakedness and his bell-end glittered magnificently from
the plat. The smeared ambrosia of his cloth.

She loitered supererrogatively round the base of the
shaft tending and nurturing the stalks, as his erect
penis phosphored in her medium brown eyes growing dim.

At regular intervals she tipped her eager spout to
moisten her prospering sprigs with her cloudy eyes
occasionally watering.

As his penis proudly prodded the late afternoon
weather-wise and began to spurt fresh semen on the wind
Griselda commenced her croon of *Gilbert and Sullivan* at
the top of her lungs, and made up her mind never to
flinch from the organ of vision. Kojak's revenge!

He fried to a frizzle under the boiling acid.
By the time he was due to retire his body was like a
blackened bonfire twig...

In the kitchen her *Shout* magazine lay open in its usual
place on the sideboard...

Unfaltering in her bond she climbed the stairs to
freedom when no concrete answer came.

Below him in the pot was one of Mary's soiled
tampons which she had scrupulously omitted to flush.

Every other step she trod Caroline called out
anxiously to discern if he was really in the house or
just a pussy obnoxious twat.

"Mathew are you there?" she tremoured, as her hand
crept over the squeaky bannister rail, mixed with
increased suspense and mouth-watering anticipation.

"Hello?" she asked again...standing white faced
before the full length mirror.

"Is anybody there? What are you doing now?"
Not a word in reply did the deviant utter, as she
paused good manneredly before turning the brow...

Her long golden threads began to edge around the
wooden surface, above her sultry smile.

Should he let her into his cranny? He was seriously
winded.

One more step and she would have a blockbuster to
particularize to her peerage.

"Are you there?" she brayed in a weak and yearning
tone, awaiting a reply, but none arrived.

Mathew quickly slammed the door shut and began doing
up his flies. Too much flare makes a desert.

Appearing from the restricted cubicle minutes later he
still found her face an absolute disgrace.

"Don't you ever creep up on me like that again!" he
angrily rebuked her.

"Never come upstairs unless you have a permit," he
nervously chastised...She looked like the morning sun,
but he could not remember.

She was as cold as December, F. could not forget
what she had done...

But if broad daylight scoured his eyes then welcome
night was his happy home!

For hours he waited at the side of the kerb and
managed to follow the blue saloon into the brushwood.

The motor cruised along the road and then turned
into the wooded grove below the plague of houses.

Parked at the top of the spinney he maundered while
the goose was dressed.

He carefully unfolded his *Gannex raincoat* from the
duffel-bag and closed his door quietly on the catch,
before quaking to the 'hawking grounds' of the heath,
like a killer on the loose.

It was during a particularily dense spica of gloom
that he paced up and down the wicket, where he could
stand in their grotto to watch them through the awning
envelope...the *Night hunter!*

In the summerhouse a frequent visitor trotted to
discharge a solitary muezzin's cry, unaware that a
disturbed person was loitering in her vicinity
exorcising his compulsory tendency.

The eldest boy seemed to be completely'under her
thumb...' His earth fell through the skies.

Venturing over to the living room of *the house with
yellow brick* the stumbling Tom drooped through to the
narrow chink of light, which seeped past the window
blind near to his 'Argus.'

He perlustrated her in close proximity for the first
time in light years, contemplating how clearly she had
bloomed in the intervening period.

"*You will* do it!" she screamed at the older child.

"You will do as you are told at once and switch it
off to come and play with me."

Her wide pink lips were prettily covered with fresh
make-up as she kneeled between his straddled legs and
ordered him to snog the entrance to Paradise.

Suddenly she gobbed in the ashtray.
There was a growl and her eyes sky-dived towards the
fracture. She leapt to her feet intending to
investigate further. The sun fell in his shoes.

"Who is it?" she called to the terrier. "See if
you can find the dirty rotten scoundrel."

I only knew what hunted thought quickened his step
and why, he looked upon the garish sky with such a
wistful eye. My sunshine, my sweetheart, my rain...

Is there anything you'd like me to do?
"Stand a little out of my Sun!"
Smiled the *Wickerman.*

"I could have been great with someone, and someone
could have been great with me."

All-the-World

From the brunette of my pit
I swerved my bevelled spine,
to face the curtain of the falls,
tugged with a dulcet tone.

With radiant colours on my eyes
walking hand in hand,
I reached to touch the tinted gauze,
abstraction in my palms.

From my cave of night I flew,
and stepped upon the ground,
the valley trembled in my path,
the world turned round and round.

Across the torrent in one stride,
the tulips far and wide,
I reached to touch the clear blue sky,
with words to dry my eyes.

Around the sun I chased the moon,
the earth beneath my wings,
my sunbeams on the grass I laid,
with gentleness and pride.

But when I scuffed upon the earth,
ungainly and half blind,
my golden scales and lizard's tail,
were all that you could find.

Beyond the field of thorn I rose,
near captured in their net,
and sneezed upon the land of Chill,
synged with my loving breath.

With yearning eyes I pressed the flowers,
a fire within the clouds,
with tears I turned, with haste I burned,
a brand upon your hand.

With nurtured wind upon my land,
I want the world to know,
why you are my All-the-World,
and all the world must know.

I stumbled to the stairway cliff,
and why I love you so,
the parted contours of your waves,
and vanished far below.

A LITTLE BIT OF GLOSSARY

Aabboo	>	the children's neighbour
Archamara	>	An Insect
Albion	>	Britain
Aliunde	>	Another place
amanuensis	>	copier
Anticthon	>	planet on opposite side of sun
Augean stable	>	dirty place
Austrian Emmental	>	cheese
Bighouseonthehill	>	psychiatric hospital
black swan	>	valuable stamp
Brobdingnagian	>	Another giant
burin	>	metal engraving tool
clypeus	>	insect head
Cthonia	>	The Underworld
Daanite	>	A Jew
Dagda	>	Spirit of the 'tuatha'
decajaar	>	ten year old
Diaeneces	>	Leonidas's General
diddi meo	>	a corruption meaning 'get out!'
diis aliter...	>	of higher life
fanfaronnade	>	underage hunter
fuitine	>	elopement
Ge	>	The Earth
gegenschein	>	effect of light
Giant Copenhagen	>	large horse
Great Obscurity	>	The Moon
Grendel	>	the night stalker
Guardhouse	>	local council estate
Horrida Bella	>	Terrible War
houdinize	>	to escape
Hy Brasil	>	heaven of the 'tuatha'
Hyleg	>	Ruling planet of one's birth
Hyperion	>	The Air and Sky
in medias res	>	there's the proof!
Koyanisqaatsi	>	troubled world
layette	>	birth cloth
lazzarone	>	an Italian beggar or crook
luddites	>	Mill-smashers
Milesian	>	The Invaders
Moggie	>	the headmaster
nitimur in...	>	no chance!
Ogger	>	his grandad
Organ of Corti	>	sensitive mechanism of the ear
Perseids	>	shooting stars
planan et con...	>	to bring together
pöngye	>	despot
Predella	>	A window
purlieus	>	equal land
ramekin	>	a piece of cake
Roxanne	>	the dawn
Red Dan	>	Father of Danny
reparatrice	>	of the 'reparation'
Rombald	>	Giant of the Pennine moors
sater venter...	>	watch what you eat!
Setanta	>	cuchulain!
sighle na gcioch	>	female flasher
Slack Alice	>	granny
Scylla	>	A whirlpool
Sunbeam	>	a sixties motorcar
torque	>	a ring or crown
trichonosis	>	baldness caused by pulling
Tuatha de Danaan	>	The Children of Danu
turlough	>	a lake
Ulsterman	>	also a coat
velutiinspeculum	>	just as you see
Vulsella	>	instrument of birth
Xala	>	incompetent youth